PATENT LAW

By

CRAIG ALLEN NARD
Tom J.E. and Bette Lou Walker Professor of Law
Case Western Reserve University School of Law

R. POLK WAGNER
Professor of Law
University of Pennsylvania Law School

CONCEPTS AND INSIGHTS SERIES

FOUNDATION PRESS
75TH ANNIVERSARY

THOMSON
WEST

395 Hudson Street
New York, NY 10014
Phone Toll Free 1–877–888–1330
Fax (212) 367–6799
foundation–press.com

Printed in the United States of America

ISBN 978–1–58778–902–1

TEXT IS PRINTED ON 10% POST CONSUMER RECYCLED PAPER

For Victor, Gabriel, and Elsa

CAN

For Sunny, Ellie and Trip

RPW

*

TABLE OF CONTENTS

PATENT LAW

*

Part I: An Overview of the Modern Patent System

Chapter One

What is a Patent and Why Do We Have a Patent System?

I. What is a Patent?

As a formal matter, a "patent" is a document—an official paper, published by the U.S. Government (specifically, the United States Patent and Trademark Office (USPTO)). What a patent does is describe (in written text and diagrams or drawings) an invention that, according to the USPTO, meets the standards for patentability established under U.S. Patent Law (specifically, Title 35 of the United States Code). The holder of a patent is thus entitled under law to exclude others from making, using, offering to sell or selling, goods or services that fall within the scope of the subject matter of the patent grant.[1]

Patents, then, occupy multiple roles. First, they provide a standardized, public, authoritative source for the evaluation of the rights granted by the patent system. That is, the patent document is designed to be written so as to both inform the public of the context of the invention, as well as provide fair notice to competitors concerning the scope of the subject matter protected.[2] Like a deed to a plot of land, a patent document establishes the boundaries of the patentee's rights. Unlike most real estate deeds, the patent document also provides important contextual and background information concerning the invention. (The many and complex rules regarding how, and how well, a patent document achieves this goal is, of course, a major subject of this book.) As one would expect, patent documents are publicly accessible and searchable.[3]

Second, patent documents provide the framework through which prospective patentees seek to have rights to their inventions recognized and protected. That is, patents are written by the patentees themselves, and are reviewed by the USPTO for compliance with relevant rules and regulations. This compliance regime—

1. See 35 U.S.C. § 271 (2006).
2. See 35 U.S.C. § 112 (2006).
3. See http://www.uspto.gov/patents/ and http://www.google.com/patents/.

patent prosecution—forms the procedure by which (in theory at least) only those inventions that are "novel," "non-obvious," within the approved subject matter, and fully described are deemed eligible for patenting.[4]

Third, patent documents are a fundamental component of the social bargain that the overall patent system represents. In exchange for the legal right to exclude others from the subject matter of the claimed invention, a patentee must fully disclose the invention to the public, including her best known way of using it—in the patent document itself. Thus, by policing the adherence to the legal requirements for disclosure, we can enforce the social compact at the heart of the patent system.

Fourth, patent documents provide important information concerning the state of the technological arts, and encourage further disclosure. A formal, standardized disclosure of information about inventions has a number of important social purposes, including the ability to evaluate the status of later-developed inventions, and providing incentives for patentees and others to disclose information about current inventions. Even if the actual documents themselves don't provide information in the same way that, for example, an academic paper would, the existence of the patent document, and the requirements concerning its substance, are likely to be enough to significantly reduce (if not eliminate) any incentive to hide information about an invention. Further, the ability to enforce rights over ideas notwithstanding disclosure is important in facilitating transactions related to innovations, which might otherwise be subject to a fundamental paradox—wherein the buyer of an idea cannot be told of the details of the idea by its creator without destroying the prospects for returns.[5]

II. Parts of a Patent

Patent documents are, as noted above, carefully designed and structured so as to provide information in a fairly standardized way. In this regard, each patent document typically contains the following sections:

4. See 35 U.S.C. §§ 101, 102, 103, 112 (2006).

5. See Kenneth J. Arrow, *Economic Welfare and the Allocation of Resources for Invention*, in THE RATE AND DIRECTION OF INVENTIVE ACTIVITY 609–25 (1962).

US006302230B1

(12) **United States Patent**
Kamen et al.

(10) **Patent No.:** **US 6,302,230 B1**
(45) **Date of Patent:** **Oct. 16, 2001**

(54) **PERSONAL MOBILITY VEHICLES AND METHODS**

(75) Inventors: **Dean L. Kamen**, Bedford; **Robert R. Ambrogi**, Manchester; **Robert J. Duggan**, Northwood; **J. Douglas Field**, Bedford; **Richard Kurt Heinzmann**, Francetown, all of NH (US); **Burl Amesbury**, Cambridge, MA (US); **Christopher C. Langenfeld**, Nashua, NH (US)

(73) Assignee: **DEKA Products Limited Partnership**, Manchester, NH (US)

(*) Notice: Subject to any disclaimer, the term of this patent is extended or adjusted under 35 U.S.C. 154(b) by 0 days.

(21) Appl. No.: **09/325,978**

(22) Filed: **Jun. 4, 1999**

(51) **Int. Cl.**[7] **B60K 31/00**; B60K 28/00; B62D 63/00; B60Q 1/00

(52) **U.S. Cl.** **180/171**; 180/213; 180/271; 180/21; 340/441

(58) **Field of Search** .... 180/218, 271, 180/274, 170, 171, 21, 41, 440; 340/438, 441, 440, 439, 905, 936; 313/465, 461, 798; 188/181 C; 280/455.1; 298/175, 5, 20 R

(56) **References Cited**

U.S. PATENT DOCUMENTS

849,270	4/1907	Schafer et al. .
2,742,973	4/1956	Johannesen .
3,145,797	8/1964	Taylor .
3,260,324	7/1966	Suarez .
3,283,398	11/1966	Andren .
3,288,234	11/1966	Feliz .
3,306,626	2/1967	Kawada .
3,348,518	10/1967	Forsyth et al. .

(List continued on next page.)

FOREIGN PATENT DOCUMENTS

2 048 593	5/1971	(DE) .
31 28 112 A1	2/1983	(DE) .
3411489 A1	10/1984	(DE) .
32 42 880 A1	6/1989	(DE) .
298 08 091 U1	10/1998	(DE) .
298 08 095 U1	10/1998	(DE) .
584127	6/1897	(EP) .

(List continued on next page.)

OTHER PUBLICATIONS

Teruaki Self Supported Carrier Machine and Automatic Carrier Device Using the Same in Patent Abstracts of Japan, Dec. 21, 1989, #63149523, Japanese Patent Office, Japan.

Kawaji, S., Stabilization of Unicycle Using Spinning Motion, *Denki Gakkai Ronbushi, D*, vol. 107, Issue 1, Japan (1987), pp. 21–28.

Schoonwinkel, A., *Design and Test of a Computer–Stabilized Unicycle*, Stanford University (1988), UMI Dissertation Services.

Vos, D., *Dynamics and Nonlinear Adaptive Control of an Autonomous Unicycle*, Massachusetts Institute of Technology, 1989.

(List continued on next page.)

Primary Examiner—Brian L. Johnson
Assistant Examiner—Matthew Luby
(74) *Attorney, Agent, or Firm*—Bromberg & Sunstein LLP

(57) **ABSTRACT**

An automatically balancing vehicle having a headroom monitor. The headroom monitor determines the difference between the maximum velocity of the vehicle and the present velocity of the vehicle. An alarm receives a signal from the headroom monitor and produces a warning when the headroom falls below a specified limit.

7 Claims, 16 Drawing Sheets

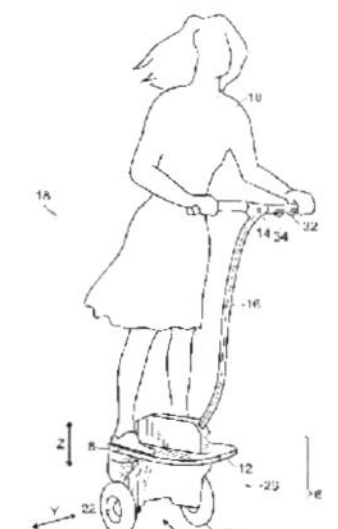

Figure 1–1. U.S. Patent No. 6,302,230

Front/cover page. The front page of the patent is designed to impart the most critical pieces of information, including the title of the invention, the relevant dates of the patent (the issue date, filing date, and priority date), information about the inventors and assignees, references to related applications, a list of citations to other documents found relevant to the examination, a brief abstract describing the invention, and, in some cases, a representative drawing or diagram. The idea of the front page is to allow for rapid searching—searchers can, at a glance, observe most of the pertinent aspects of the patent from the front page.

Drawings. Patents must include drawings or diagrams if they assist in understanding the invention. Depending on the particular technology involved, these range from detailed manufacturing-style depictions of the invention, logical flowcharts, chemical structure diagrams, and so forth. Though they formally constitute a separate section of the patent document (ordered just after the front page and before the textual part of the document), analytically, drawings are part of the disclosure of the patent document, and are thus subject to the same considerations as the specification, noted below.

Specification. The specification is the written portion of the patent, which in most cases comprises the bulk of the disclosure. Within the specification, there are two key components: the written description, and the claims. The written description, as one might expect from the name, is the textual description of the invention, and usually includes sections relating the background of the invention, the advantages of the current invention, and specific details of "embodiments" (examples) of the invention. It is very common for patent professionals to refer to the written description as the specification; thus, henceforth, the book will refer to the specification and claims as distinct features of the patent document. Specifications are not, however, intended to be exhaustive treatments or akin to textbooks about a particular field. Under the patent law, the specification must "enable" a "person of ordinary skill in the art" to make and use the invention.[6] As a practical matter, the specification thus must contain enough detail so as to allow those in the relevant field (or fields) to grasp the invention and how it differs from already-existing technology, but it needn't describe widely known principles or the already-existing technology itself. For example, an invention relating to a new method of purifying water would not describe how to boil water (this can be assumed to be widely known in the field), but would explain any new techniques used to accomplish the result.

Another important feature of the specification is that while it is *not* supposed to define the scope of the invention (that task is left to the claims, described below), the specification is often used by the courts as a key (and often the only) interpretive tool, providing key

6. See 35 U.S.C. § 112 (2006).

guidance concerning the meaning of the claim language. Thus, although the specification is conceptually distinct from the claims—providing a "disclosure" of the invention rather than "delineating" it—in reality (and increasingly in recent years), this distinction has become rather blurred, increasing the strategically important aspects of the specification.

Chapter 5 below discusses the various disclosure requirements and their effects in detail.

Claims. After the written description (at the end of the specification) are the "claims" of the patent, which express the specific subject matter which the patentee "claims" as her invention. Claims are typically written in numbered sentences, and are signaled by introductory phrasing, such as "I claim," or "What is claimed is." Claims are the operative part of the patent document—the words that define the scope of the patent grant. That is, "infringement" of a patent occurs when unauthorized activities (making, using, selling, etc.) occur within the scope of the patent claims. Therefore, as one might expect, the language used in claims is at once broad (so as to maximize subject matter coverage) and yet precise (so as to avoid prior art or disclosure problems). Given the importance of claim language, a variety of rules and conventions have developed surrounding claim language—which means that, in general, claims are not written using ordinary syntax, and they can be difficult to parse without a good understanding of the patent law. As a quick example, consider the following claim to an everyday item:

> 1. *A writing implement comprising:*
>
> *A wooden cylinder with a hollow core,*
>
> *A cylinder of graphite in said hollow core,*
>
> *A small cylinder of eraser material attached to one end of the wooden cylinder.*

While this might appear to be little more than a profoundly inefficient way to describe a pencil, there is a method behind the complexity. In defining the scope of inventions, claims must be *both* broad and precise: broad so as to maximize the scope of protection, and precise so as to carefully position the invention within the provided disclosure and distinct from prior technology. Thus, in our pencil example above, the invention is described in terms of the key functional elements (a hollow wooden cylinder, some graphite, and an eraser), and each of these elements are included in the claim, as well as their relationship to each other.

Shown below is claim 1 for U.S. Patent No. 6302230 (the "Segway" patent shown in Figure 1–1, above):

1. A vehicle for carrying a payload including a user, the vehicle comprising:

> *a. a platform which supports the user;*
>
> *b. a ground-contacting module, to which the platform is mounted, which propels the user in desired motion over an underlying surface;*
>
> *c. a motorized drive arrangement, coupled to the ground-contacting module; the drive arrangement, ground-contacting module and payload comprising a system being unstable with respect to tipping when the motorized drive is not powered; the motorized drive arrangement causing, when powered, automatically balanced operation of the system wherein the vehicle has a present velocity and a maximum operating velocity, determined by a requirement of acceleration to maintain balance and, in operation, has a balancing margin determined by the difference between the maximum operating velocity and the present velocity of the vehicle;*
>
> *d. a balancing margin monitor, coupled to the ground-contacting module, for generating a signal characterizing the balancing margin; and*
>
> *e. an alarm, coupled to the balancing margin monitor, for receiving the signal characterizing the balancing margin and for warning when the balancing margin falls below a specified limit.*

Comparing the two examples, one will note that patent claims have a structure and language all their own, complete with specialty words ("comprising," "said") a somewhat precise-yet-vague style, and a formal, careful structure. Also, as noted above, claims need not describe their elements in any detail whatsoever; that task is for the patent's disclosure, especially the specification. Claims, then, are both the heart of the patent document—the crucial language that defines the invention—and unable to stand alone. Chapter 9 deals extensively with claim language and the rules of interpretation.

III. The Philosophy of Patent Law

On the surface, patent law might appear to be a simple reward system: a benefit for inventors who create patentable inventions. And while on one level this is certainly true (inventors do reap benefits as a result of patenting), the operating philosophy of patent law considers inventors not simply as deserving recipients of governmental grants for their own sake, but as instrumental to the larger utilitarian purpose of the patent law. The basic philosophy of the patent law, then, is that expressed in the U.S. Constitution: "to promote the progress of science and the useful arts." Patent law is thus straightforwardly utilitarian in outlook: we grant patent rights not to reward inventors for their achievements, but to stimulate others to seek the same reward—and thereby contribute new innovations for the good of society. The reward function of patents, then is not based on a sense that inventors have a natural right to the fruits of their inventions, but because it is the mechanism by which we have chosen to implement our utilitarian system.

Note of course that a utilitarian approach is not the only possible way to conceptualize the basis of the patent system. For example, a view that inventors, by expending their labor, might have a *natural right* in their intellectual creations would fit with at least some of the reward aspects of the current patent system.[7] Under this view, which roughly follows the philosophy of John Locke, an inventor who has mixed his labor with the common pool of knowledge, and created something new and different (i.e., something that can be appropriated and yet leave as "enough and as good" for others) has an inherent right to that creation—the invention.[8] Thus the patent system's right to exclude would be based on the inherent ('natural') rights of inventors rather than the more consequentialist or utilitarian ideas noted above. Although the natural rights approach has some appeal, the general view in the United States is that the patent system, at least, operates on a fairly strict utilitarian basis, as noted above.[9]

Importantly, basing the patent law on a utilitarian model has some important consequences for thinking about the way the system should operate. Note, for example, the following:

The Importance of the Incentives–Innovation Link. The philosophical basis of patent law assumes that incentives (the prospect of a marketplace reward) will spur more and greater innovation of the sort that will benefit society. While most would agree that this

7. See, e.g., Adam Mossoff, *Rethinking the Development of Patents: An Intellectual History, 1550–1800*, 52 HASTINGS L.J. 1255, 1266–66 (2001) (asserting natural rights theory played prominent role in intellectual property development).

8. See John Locke, *Second Treatise on Civil Government, in Two Treatises of Government* (Prometheus Books 1986). See also Justin Hughes, *The Philosophy of Intellectual Property*, 77 GEO. L. J. 287, 296–330 (1988).

9. Arguably, natural rights and other deontological theories have had an effect on intellectual property law, especially copyright, in other countries. See Neil Netanel, *Copyright Alienability Restrictions and the Enhancement of Author Autonomy: A Normative Evaluation*, 24 RUTGERS L.J. 347, 365 (1993).

is a reasonable assumption, it is not incontestable. Much invention would occur without the prospect of a financial reward; the quest for knowledge and/or the search for truth are themselves powerful motivators, as are non-monetary rewards such as reputation or recognition. Indeed, many academics operate within this reward structure, though this may be changing in modern university environments.[10] The second important aspect of the incentives-innovation link is that even if one determines that incentives will stimulate innovation, there is little known about how much incentive is required to stimulate an optimal level of innovation. It cannot be true that greater incentives will always yield more social benefit in the form of innovation; there will certainly be some form of diminishing returns as incentives increase, or the incentives themselves might distort innovation in favor of certain types of inventions over others. So while the patent law represents a judgment that incentives are necessary to generate a socially-desirable level of innovation, one must understand that the details of that relationship are very much subject to uncertainty.

A Compact Between Inventors and Society. The utilitarian model of the patent law, as noted above, treats inventors as instrumental to the overall policy objective. Thus, the object of the patent law is to strike a balance between rewarding the activities of the past (successful inventors) just enough to stimulate activities in the future (future inventors). From this viewpoint, inventors have no inherent claim to good treatment under the patent law, except to the extent that treating them well will yield more and better inventions in the future. Indeed, society is clearly best off if patentees are unable to capture the full social value of their inventions—but we must allow inventors to capture enough of the value to stimulate future growth. The patent law, then, must enforce a compact between inventor-patentees and society: wherein patentees receive a specified reward (a term-limited right to exclude), but must provide significant benefits to society (full disclosure of the invention, among others).

The Use of the Market as a Reward System. As noted above, the theory of the patent law is that the right to exclude others from the scope of the patented invention will yield enough of a prospect of a financial reward as to encourage further innovation. The quantum of the reward (and indeed, its existence) is set not by government

10. For an argument about whether patents conflict with or perhaps enhance the norms and practices of the scientific community, see Arti K. Rai and Rebecca Eisenberg, *Bayh–Dole Reform and the Progress of Biomedicine*, 66 LAW & CONTEMP. PROBS. 289 (Winter/Spring 2003) and F. Scott Kieff, *Facilitating Scientific Research: Intellectual Property Rights and the Norms of Science—A Response to Rai and Eisenberg*, 95 NW. U. L. REV. 691 (2001).

fiat, but by the marketplace: the patentee can reap what she can sow from the marketplace, whether by being the sole source of the good or service during the patent term, by licensing the right to provide the good or service to others, or even by simply selling the patent grant outright.[11] Utilizing the market to set the reward has a number of critical consequences. First, it makes the existence and amount of the reward probabilistic rather than known. Indeed, most estimates suggest that about 95 percent of all patents have no marketplace value (and thus provide no financial reward for their owners).[12] Second, it means that patented inventions are assessed on the basis of their private value to participants in the marketplace, which might—or might not—represent the true social value. Consider, for example, a pharmaceutical drug that treats a very rare disease. Its marketplace value may be substantially less than its actual social value. Third, basing rewards on the marketplace will inevitably bias innovative activity in favor of those inventions that have some expectation of commercial success. And while this may be good—marketplace success may well be a reasonable proxy for social value—there will be classes of very useful innovative activity that will be systematically underrepresented. For example, basic scientific research, much of which is very attenuated from commercialization, and yet is socially valuable in the long term. Fourth, by privatizing the reward system, the government has minimal day-to-day control over the patent system, other than to set the general ground rules for patentability. This seems likely to be good on balance—one would want to avoid allowing politics to determine the reward for innovation—but it does mean that there is one fewer policy lever at society's disposal.[13]

IV. The Economics of Patent Law

Economic principles are at the heart of the U.S. patent system, both because the system is critically important to the economy, and

11. See B. Zorina Khan, *The Democratization of Invention: Patents and Copyrights in American Economic Development*, 1790–1920, 66 (2005) (stating that in the United States, patent "statutes from the earliest years ensured that the 'progress of science and useful arts' was to be achieved through a complementary relationship between law and the market in the form of a patent system").

12. See Gideon Parchomovsky and R. Polk Wagner, *Patent Portfolios*, 154 U. Pa L. Rev. 1, 12–19 (2005).

13. See Peter Menell and Suzanne Scotchmer, *Intellectual Property Law*, in *Handbook of Law & Economics* 1477 (2006) (referring to decentralization in intellectual property systems as a "virtue" and stating "[p]robably the most important obstacle to effective public procurement is in finding ideas for invention that are widely distributed among firms and inventors. The lure of intellectual property protection does that automatically.").

because its utilitarian basis demands a positive return on the cost-benefit analysis.

We start here with first principles. Most goods follow the laws of supply and demand, which suggest that additional quantities of a good will be demanded (purchased) as the price drops (and vice versa). In a competitive market, the price for goods will stabilize (e.g., reach an "equilibrium price") where a firm's marginal revenue equals its marginal cost.[14] Marginal revenue refers to the additional revenue gained from selling one additional unit; marginal cost is the additional cost of producing an additional unit. Put another way, as long as firms can price goods above their marginal costs, they will make profits. In a perfectly competitive market, the equilibrium price is driven down towards marginal cost; firms participating in this market cannot price above the equilibrium price, because consumers would not buy.

A non-competitive market—for example, a market where a patent provides the patentee with the ability to exclude competitors—will look quite different. In this case, firms will maximize their profits by reducing the quantity of goods sold, and charging more for them.[15] But while this result will increase the producer's total profits, it will reduce what is known as "consumer surplus"—the value that consumers attach to the good, minus the cost of the good. Absent special circumstances, however, the producer will not be able to capture all of the lost consumer surplus, which means that the total social value of the exchange—the producers' profits plus the consumer surplus—will be lower in the non-competitive market. This difference in total surplus is known as "deadweight loss," and is the basic economic rationale against monopolies.[16]

If the existence of patents shifts the market away from the competitive equilibrium, causing deadweight loss, then how are patents economically defensible? The answer is that we think that patents provide benefits to society that overcome the imposition of deadweight loss. Understanding these benefits requires the introduction of one additional economic concept, that of a "public good." A public good is one that is non-rival and non-exclusive in nature.[17] Non-rival means that it cannot be consumed by multiple users, and

14. Robert S. Pindyck and Daniel L. Rubenfeld, *Microeconomics,* 333–352 (1989).

15. Firms with such market positions will still price where marginal cost = marginal revenue, but the lack of competition alters the slope of the marginal revenue curve. See id.

16. See id.

17. See, e.g., Robert Cooter and Thomas Ulen, *Law & Economics* (4th ed. 2004), at 46–49, 108–119 (1988); Pindyck and Rubenfeld, *Microeconomics, supra* note 14, at 617–641.

non-exclusive means that consumers cannot be effectively excluded from the good. These features mean that such goods—information and national defense, are classic examples—will be systematically under-produced in a free market. Without the ability to exclude, there will be little means for firms to profitably produce such goods, and consumers will have large incentives to "free ride" on the investments of others. Thus, governments typically intervene in the market to ensure that public goods are produced. In some cases this takes the form of direct taxing and spending; in others—such as the patent system—the government alters the structure of the market so as to better encourage the production of such goods.[18]

We come, then, to the basic equation of the patent system. The production of information, especially that related to innovation, has public good characteristics, which suggests that it will be systematically underproduced in a free market. Therefore, the patent system has been established as an intervention into the free market, providing patentees the ability to charge higher prices than would be possible in a competitive environment. We know that this approach has substantial costs: deadweight loss, the costs of administration, etc. But the patent system represents a judgment that these costs are outweighed by the societal benefits of encouraging more and better innovation.

At least in theory. While understanding the overall economic basis of the patent system is relatively straightforward, any student of the patent law needs to recognize the limitations of the economic theory. The first and most important is that we don't have good empirical evidence about the actual benefits of the patent system: that is, whether the benefits outweigh the costs, and by how much.[19] To the extent we do have such information, it is often contradictory and contextual. For example, it is widely believed that the development of pharmaceutical drugs would not occur at anywhere near the current pace without the patent system. At the same time, the effects of patents on technologies such as software or semiconductors are less clear. On balance it seems that the patent system is probably a net benefit to society, but again, the specific quantity of the benefit (and, as importantly, how it distributed) is far from clear.[20]

18. See id.

19. *See* William M. Landes and Richard A. Posner, *The Economic Structure of Intellectual Property Law* 310 (2003) ("Although there are powerful economic reasons in favor of creating property rights in inventions, there are also considerable social costs and whether the benefits exceed the costs is impossible to answer with confidence on the basis of present knowledge.").

20. See Robert Mazzoleni and Richard R. Nelson, *The Benefits and Costs of Strong Patent Protection: A Contribution to the Current Debate*, 27 Research Poli-

Second, hand-in-hand with the uncertainty about the net benefits of the patent system is a deep uncertainty about whether the current state of the patent law—the balance between inventors and society—is anywhere near optimal. That is, even if one understands the patent system to be broadly beneficial, one could still be deeply uncertain about whether the current parameters are justifiable. Relatedly, it is difficult in the patent context to know what the effects of a policy change might be—even if the change alters the inventor/society balance in a straightforward way (such as a reduction in patent term length from 20 to 10 years, for example), whether the change would benefit society is not at all clear.[21] In the example here, the reduction in term will reduce the costs of the patent system, but it will also reduce the incentives to invent—thus also reducing the benefits. Of necessity, much of patent policy is based on limited knowledge and assumptions; indeed, this is one of the reasons that many scholars of the patent law find it so interesting and dynamic.

CY 273, 281 (1998) (Noting "[i]n some areas, patent rights certainly are economically and socially productive in generating invention, spreading technological knowledge, inducing innovation and commercialization," but in other "areas of technology ... strong broad patent rights entail major economic costs while generating insufficient additional social benefits").

21. See Richard Brunell, *Appropriability in Antitrust: How Much is Enough*, 69 ANTITRUST L.J. 1, 4 (2001) ("[I]f the vast economics literature on intellectual property conveys one message, it is that the relationship between intellectual property protection and economic welfare is unclear.").

Chapter Two

Trends and Challenges to the Modern Patent System

I. Trends of the Modern Patent System

The American patent system is over 200 years old, but at no point in its long history has the system been more important and controversial than today. The growing importance and controversial nature of the patent system is reflected in the significant rise in patent filings and issuances over the past thirty years, the increasingly complex character of patent applications, and the escalating rate and cost of litigation. This section explores these three trends.

The patent system has also been the subject of several reform initiatives, most notably two major reform studies sponsored by the Federal Trade Commission and the National Research Council of the National Academies.[22]

A. Increasing Patenting Activity

One major trend in the modern patent law is a dramatic rise in patenting activity over the last two decades; since 1986, the number of U.S. patents granted per year has increased by 140%, while the number of applications received by the PTO has risen by 240%.[23] Figure 2–1 shows this trend. This rise in patenting activity has been largely mirrored among major patent offices worldwide. The European Patent Office (EPO) received 208,502 applications in 2006 (up 60% from 1995), and issued 62,780 patents (up 22% from 1995).[24] The Japanese Patent Office (JPO) received 408,674 applications in 2006 (up 13.5% from 1995), and issued 141,399 (up 11.3% from 1995).[25] In addition to raw filing numbers, ownership of

22. For the publication of the National Academies, see A Patent System for the 21st Century (The National Academies Press 2004) and for the Federal Trade Commission's, see To Promote Innovation: The Proper Balance of Competition Patent Law and Policy (FTC 2003) http://www.ftc.gov/os/2003/10/innovationrpt.pdf.

23. See U.S. Patent and Trademark Office Annual Reports, 1986–2006.

24. See EPO Annual Report (1995, 2005). According to the World Intellectual Property Organization (WIPO) there were nearly 1.6 million patent applications filed worldwide in 2004 compared to 884,000 in 1985. See WIPO Patent Report at http://www.wipo.int/ipstats/en/statistics/patents/patent_report_2006.html#P93_7755.

25. See Japanese Patent Office Statistics at http://www.jpo.go.jp/shiryou_e/index.htm.

patent rights worldwide is highly concentrated, with American and Japanese residents owning 29 and 22 percent, respectively.[26] The number of "busy" patent offices is also highly concentrated. The largest recipient patent offices in 2004 were, in descending order, the JPO, USPTO, EPO, South Korea, and China.[27]

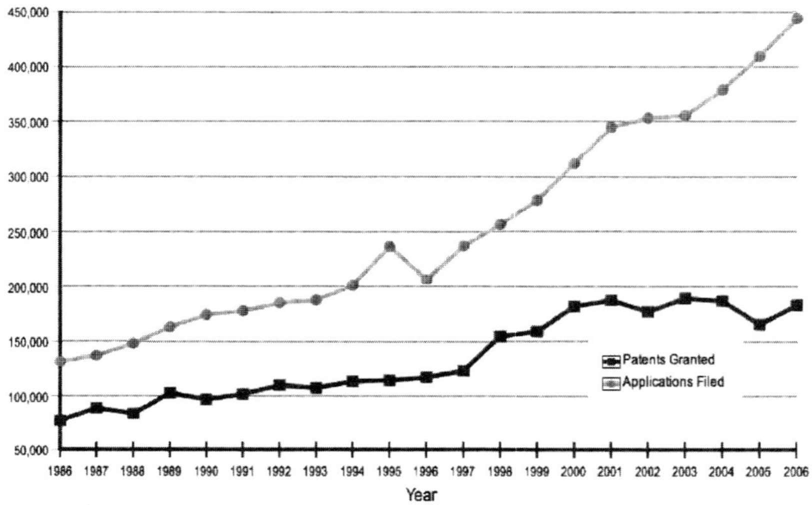

Figure 2–1. Patenting Activity, 1986–2006[28]

Perhaps even more striking than the raw numbers is that this rise in activity surpasses the (also large) rise in research and development spending over the past two decades. That is, one obvious possible cause for the rise in activity is the rise in economic activity, especially related to innovation and high technology. Yet even when one normalizes patenting activity by the amount of private investment into research and development (thus measuring "patent intensity"), you see similarly dramatic trends, as shown in Figure 2–2, below.

The legal fees for obtaining patent protection, in addition to the PTO filing fees, have also increased over time. A recent survey of patent attorneys shows that the median costs for preparing and filing a patent application in the biotech/chemical arts is $12,393,

26. See World Intellectual Property Organization Patent Report (2006).

27. Id.

28. U.S. Patent and Trademark Office, Annual Report (annual series 2006).

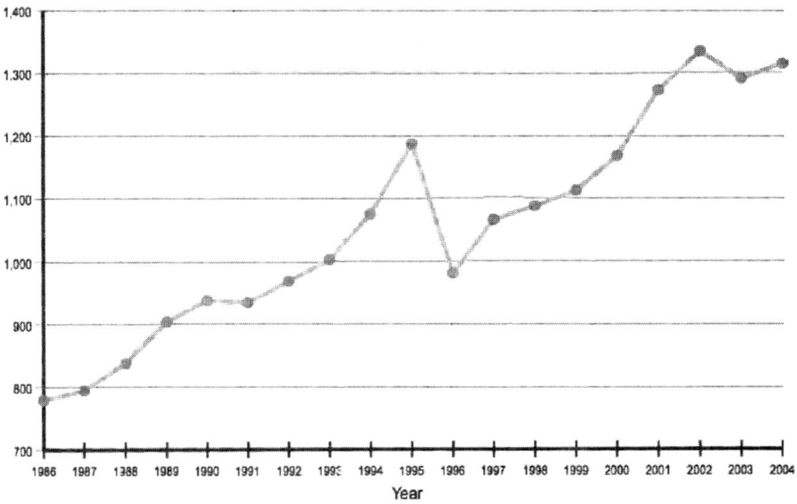

Figure 2–2. Patent Intensity, 1986–2004[29]
[Patent applications per $B of non-government R&D investment]

for electrical/computer arts $10,993, and for mechanical, $9,412.[30] As these are median costs, some applications, depending on the complexity of the technology and geographic location of the law firm, can be considerably more. And there are, typically, after-filing costs that have a median range $2,000–4,000.[31] The high cost of drafting patent applications relates to the difficulty of claim drafting—an art at which years of experience are need to become proficient. See Chapter 4 for a discussion of claim drafting.

B. Increasing Enforcement Activity

The amount of litigation, in absolute terms, has roughly paralleled the rise in patent application filings. And while enforcement has clearly increased substantially, whether the rate of patent enforcement has risen depends to some degree upon how one measures. For example, one recent study found a tenfold increase in patent litigation over the past two decades,[32] but noted that after

29. National Science Foundation/Division of Science Resources Statistics National Patterns of R&D Resources (annual series), USPTO Annual Reports (annual series).

30. See *American Intellectual Property Law Association, Report of the Economic Survey* I, 72–3 (2007). These numbers reflect attorney fees, not the PTO filing fee, which are relatively modest in comparison.

31. Id. at I, 73–4.

32. See Jean O. Lanjouw and Mark Schankerman, *Protecting Intellectual Property Rights: Are Small Firms Handicapped?* 47 J.L. & Econ. 45 (2004). See also Josh Lerner *Patenting in the Shadow of Competitors*, 38 J.L. & Econ. 463, 465 (1995) (noting "the U.S. patent sys-

controlling for the significant rise in patent grants, litigation has in fact not increased, and is concentrated in companies and patents with particular characteristics.[33] On the other hand, when one considers the number of lawsuits filed per in-force-patent (patents granted but not expired), this measure of litigation intensity has increased significantly—albeit not as dramatically as patent applications (about 45% during the period 1988–2005). Figure 2–3 shows this relationship.

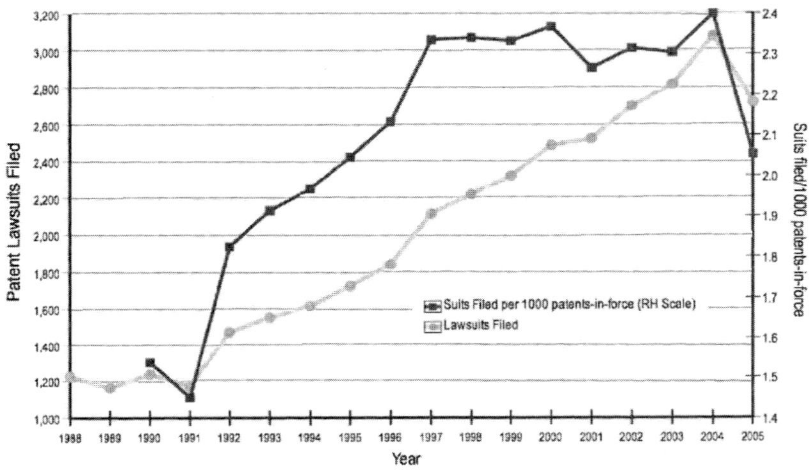

Figure 2–3. Patent Litigation Activity, 1988–2005[34]

Though whether the rate of litigation has increased is subject to some debate, it is clear that patent litigation has become much more costly. One survey showed that for litigation with fewer than $1 million at risk, litigation fees, inclusive of all costs, were $767,000; with $1–25 million at risk, the fees rose to $2,645,000

tem has seen a dramatic increase in both litigation and administrative proceedings over the past decade.'').

33. Id. See also John R. Allison, Mark A. Lemley, Kimberly A. Moore, and R. Derek Trunkey, *Valuable Patents*, 92 GEO. L.J. 435, 471–75 (2004) (finding ''patents on medical devices, computer-related inventions, software, electronics, and mechanics are significantly more likely to be litigated than the average of all patents. By contrast, chemistry, automotive, and semiconductor patents are significantly less likely to be litigated.''); Lerner, *Shadow of Competitors*, *supra* note 32 (finding biotechnology patents more likely to be litigated).

34. Administrative Office of the United States Courts, Annual Statistical Reports, U.S. Patent and Trademark Office, Annual Reports. The number of in-force patents was estimated by using lagged data on patent grants to calculate a maximum of potential in-force patents, and then correcting (reducing) that number using the patent renewal rate data shown in Table 1 of Parchomovosky and Wagner, *supra* note 12, at 15.

million; and when more than $25 million is at stake, litigation expenses approached $5.5 million.[35] While patent litigation is costly and rising, it is important to note that only on the order of 1.5% of patents are litigated, with a mere 0.1% making it to trial.[36] Of course, these statistics reflect the fact that many more patents are issuing today than 10 years ago and that only a small percentage of patents are commercially significant.[37]

C. A Changing Role for Patents?

What explains such a steep increase in patent-related activity?

It seems obvious that an important driver of the two trends noted above—increasing patenting activity and increasing enforcement of patents—must be that patents themselves are becoming increasingly valuable to commercial entities. And yet this fact is not at all clear. Estimates of patent value are difficult, but those that do exist suggest that, in most industries, the value of a patent is less than $2,500—or probably less than its acquisition cost.[38] Why, then, is patent activity increasing—and quite dramatically?

There are several potential answers. First, it can be quite difficult to gauge commercial potential during the application phase;[39] indeed, commercial potential may not manifest itself until several years after issuance, thus increasing the incentives for filing a patent at the first possible instance. Second, the perception in the business and legal world may be that patents are increasingly

35. *American Intellectual Property Law Association, Report of the Economic Survey* I, 90–1 (2007).

36. See Mark A. Lemley and Carl Shapiro, *Probabilistic Patents*, 19 J. ECON. PERSP. 75, 79 (Spring 2005).

37. See Allison et al., *Valuable Patents, supra* note 33. And there is significant skewing with respect to distribution of value. See *id.* at 80 (stating top 1 percent of patents are "more than a thousand times as valuable as the median patent"). See also Lemley and Shapiro, *Probabilistic Patents*, *supra* note 36, at 80–1; Mark Schankerman and Ariel Pakes, *Estimates of the Value of Patents Rights in European Countries During the Post–1950 Period*, 96 ECON. JOURNAL 1052 (1986); Allison et al., *Valuable Patents*.

38. See Parchomovosky and Wagner, *supra* note 12, at 16–18 (discussing and reporting various studies). See also Mark Schankerman, *How Valuable Is Patent Protection? Estimates by Technology Field*, 29 RAND J. ECON. 77 (1998) (presenting evidence on the value of patent rights in France); F.M. Scherer, *The Innovation Lottery*, in *Expanding the Boundaries of Intellectual Property: Innovation Policy for the Knowledge Society* 3 (Rochelle Cooper Dreyfuss et al. eds., 2001) (showing wide disparities in the relative growth of investments in technology companies); Wesley M. Cohen, *Protecting Their Intellectual Assets: Appropriability Conditions* and *Why U.S. Manufacturing Firms Patent (or Not)* 3 (Nat'l Bureau of Econ. Research, Working Paper No. 7552, 2000), http://www.nber.org/ papers/w7552 (indicating that firms often patent for reasons beyond profiting from a patented innovation).

39. See F.M. Scherer, *The Innovation Lottery*, in *Expanding the Boundaries of Intellectual Property* 3–21 (OUP 2001 Dreyfuss et al., eds.)

important, irrespective of the data. For example, the creation of the United States Court of Appeals for the Federal Circuit,[40] from its beginning in 1982, altered the legal landscape of patents, resulting in a significant strengthening of the patent grant.[41] Indeed, "the Federal Circuit has taken its role as defender of the patent system seriously."[42] The altered landscape was not lost on the corporate world. After witnessing significant damage awards, the power of preliminary injunctions, and the generous interpretation of the subject matter eligible for patent protection, corporate players viewed their extant patent portfolios in a new light, as so-called "Rembrandts in the Attic."[43] And these same corporations, to the extent they were dubious about the value of patent protection for any given invention, erred on the side of filing for patent protection. As two commentators noted, the Federal Circuit "has had a significant positive effect on both the number of patent applications and the number of patent grants."[44] Third, Congress has enacted patent and other forms of legislation that has spurred certain economic segments of society (e.g., research universities) to pursue patent protection for their innovations.[45] Fourth, a patent is often an important tool to attract venture capital and financing.[46] Fifth, a patent can be used to reduce information costs by acting as a vehicle to publicize information, in addition to being used for privatizing information.[47] Patentees may also want to block competitors from patenting similar technology,[48] enhance their bargaining position during licensing negotiations,[49] or deter law suits.

One important possibility may be that the value of patents is not in their individual worth, but instead lies in their aggregation

40. See Chapter 3 for a detailed discussion of the Federal Circuit.

41. See John R. Allison and Mark A. Lemley, *Empirical Evidence on the Validity of Litigated Patents*, 26 AIPLA Q.J. 185, 241 (1998) (noting increase in patent validity rate after creation of Federal Circuit); Glynn Lunney, *Patent Law, the Federal Circuit, and the Supreme Court: A Quiet Revolution*, 11 Sup. Ct. Econ. Rev. 1 (2004) (finding percentage of cases where the Federal Circuit held patents invalid dropped considerably).

42. See Lunney, *A Quiet Revolution*, *supra* note 41, at 2.

43. See Kevin G. Rivette and David Kline, *Rembrandts in the Attic: Unlocking the Hidden Value of Patents* (2000) (discussing the value of patents).

44. Landes and Posner, Economic Structure, *supra* note 19, at 340.

45. See, e.g., Bayh–Dole Act, 35 U.S.C. §§ 200–205.

46. See Bronwyn H. Hall, Adam B. Jaffe, and Manuel Trajtenberg, *Market Value and Patent Citations*, 36 Rand J. of Econ. 1 (2005); Paul A. Gompers and Josh Lerner, *The Money of Invention: How Venture Capital Creates New Wealth* (2001); Mark A. Lemley, *Reconceiving Patents in the Age of Venture Capital*, 4 J. Sm. and Emerg. Bus. L. 137 (2000).

47. See Clarisa Long, *Patent Signals*, 69 U. Chi. L. Rev. 625 (2002).

48. See Wesley M. Cohen et al., *Protecting Their Intellectual Assets, supra* note 38.

49. Id.

into a collection of related patents (a "patent portfolio") that effectively increases their power well beyond the sum of the individual patents themselves.[50]

Regardless of what theory explains the current trends, the pattern that follows from these examples is this: modern patenting behavior cannot be adequately explained by the traditional "appropriability" story, i.e., that patents are obtained because they provide marketplace protection to the patentee. Instead, the modern patent has a range of uses for its owner, and it is perhaps this trend—the broadening role of patents in the 21st century marketplace—that is the most important to understand.

II. The Policy Challenges of the Modern Patent System

The modern patent system faces several policy challenges that have become increasingly more conspicuous as patent law has grown in importance. This section discusses three challenges. First, it is important that judges, policymakers, scholars, and students have an understanding of patent law's effect on society, including those it seeks to incentivize and benefit. To this end, we take a look at the empirical and social science evidence relating to patent law, particularly with an eye towards patent law's relationship to social welfare. Second, we will highlight some of the challenges facing the PTO, and lastly, briefly touch on a few of the challenges confronting the Federal Circuit. The PTO, Federal Circuit, and the challenges facing both institutions are explored in greater detail in Chapter 3.

A. Patent Law and Social Welfare: An Evolving Relationship

The American patent system, as you read in Chapter 1, is grounded in utilitarianism, which means that patent law is designed to enhance social welfare through the production of and access to innovations. Thus, it is important that we have an understanding of the relationship between patent law and social welfare. Unfortunately, while the private value of patents has increased,[51] our understanding of patent law's relationship to social

50. See Parchomovsky and Wagner, *Patent Portfolios, supra* note 12.

51. See Robert P. Merges, *As Many As Six Impossible Patents Before Breakfast: Property Rights for Business Concepts and Patent System Reform*, 14 Berkeley Tech. L.J. 577, 603 (1999) (noting the "increase in the private value of patents since the early 1980s"). See also Allison, et al., *Valuable Patents, supra* note 33 (exploring what makes a patent

welfare, although more sophisticated today than it was 50 years ago, is incomplete and difficult to measure.[52] Therefore, one of patent law's most pressing challenges, particularly for those who toil in its field, is to continue adding pieces to the social welfare puzzle. A related concern that exacerbates this problem is that there is rarely a monolithic or universal viewpoint in the realm of patent law and innovation policy. But that is not to say there are no answers.

Indeed, scholars have begun to add resolution to this puzzle as reflected in the increasing amount of empirical and social science scholarship. Much of the scholarship that forms the empirical current has examined the relationship between patent law and innovation practices of firms in various industries, including research and development decision making and the extent to which divergent industries rely on the patent system or other appropriability mechanisms.[53] For instance, the patent system's role in inducing technological innovation is more important to some industries (e.g., drugs and medical equipment) than to others, which may rely more on trade secrecy (e.g., petroleum) or lead time into the market (e.g., software).[54] And some industries seek patent protection with

have private value and how to identify those valuable patents).

52. See George L. Priest, *What Economists Can Tell Lawyers About Intellectual Property: Comment on Cheung, in Research in Law and Economics: The Economics of Patents and Copyrights* 21 (John Palmer and Richard O. Zerbe, Jr. eds., 1986) ("[I]n the current state of knowledge, economists know almost nothing about the effect on social welfare of the patent system or of other systems of intellectual property."); Landes and Posner, *Economic Structure, supra* note 44, at 310 ("Although there are powerful economic reasons in favor of creating property rights in inventions, there are also considerable social costs and whether the benefits exceed the costs is impossible to answer with confidence on the basis of present knowledge"); Richard Brunell, *Appropriability in Antitrust: How Much is Enough*, 69 ANTITRUST L.J. 1, 4 (2001) ("[I]f the vast economics literature on intellectual property conveys one message, it is that the relationship between intellectual property protection and economic welfare is unclear").

53. See Cohen et al., *Protecting Their Intellectual Assets, supra* note 38, at 24; Richard C. Levin et al., *Appropriating the Returns from Industrial Research and Development*, 3 Brookings Papers on Econ. Activity 783, 793–95 (Martin Neil Baily and Clifford Winston eds., 1987) (analyzing 650 responses to a questionnaire using a seven-point scale to rate the effectiveness of alternative means of protecting new or improved products or processes); Edwin Mansfield, *Unauthorized Use of Intellectual Property: Effects on Investment, Technology Transfer, and Innovation, in Global Dimensions of Intellectual Property Rights in Science and Technology*, 107 (Mitchel B. Wallerstein et al. eds., 1993).

54. See Cohen et al., *Protecting Their Intellectual Assets, supra* note 38 ("We find that the key appropriability mechanism in most industries are secrecy, lead time and complementary capabilities"); Landes and Posner, *Economic Structure of Intellectual Property Law, supra* note 19, at 312 ("Many highly progressive, research-intensive industries, notably including the computer software industry, do not rely heavily on patents as a method of preventing free riding on inventive activity").

an eye towards commercialization and generating revenue, while others obtain patents to block competitors from developing competing products or to enhance their bargaining position during cross-licensing negotiations, particularly when a "complex" technology (i.e., a product or process that comprises several patented components) is involved.[55] Some scholars have suggested firms may patent for reasons related to reputation and informational signaling, rather than privatizing knowledge.[56] Indeed, patent law is not a one-size-fits-all regime. As two commentators recently noted:

> In some areas, patent rights certainly are economically and socially productive in generating invention, spreading technological knowledge, inducing innovation and commercialization, and providing some degree of order in the development of broad technological prospects. However, in many areas of technology this is not the case. In a number of these, strong broad patent rights entail major economic costs while generating insufficient additional social benefits. And in some strong broad patents are simply counterproductive. One needs to be discriminating and cautious on this front.[57]

Other lines of empirical work have focused on the role of juries in patent cases;[58] Federal Circuit voting patterns;[59] patent filing,[60] litigation trends,[61] and patent law's effect on innovation in specific technologies.[62] A good deal of the social science work is law- and economics-oriented, focusing on the important normative issues of proprietary claim scope and patentability standards in the context

55. See Cohen et al., *Protecting Their Intellectual Assets*, *supra* note 38.

56. See Long, *Patent Signals*, *supra* note 47.

57. Mazzoleni and Nelson, *Benefits and Costs of Strong Patent Protection*, *supra* note 20, at 281.

58. See, e.g., Kimberly A. Moore, *Judges, Juries, and Patent Cases: An Empirical Peek Inside the Black Box*, 99 Mich. L. Rev. 365 (2000) (illustrating patent holders' success rates in jury and bench trials).

59. See, e.g., John R. Allison and Mark A. Lemley, *How Federal Circuit Judges Vote in Patent Validity Cases*, 27 Fla. St. U. L. Rev. 745 (2000) (chronicling patent validity decisions).

60. See, e.g., John R. Allison and Mark A. Lemley, *The Growing Complexity of the Patent System*, 82 B.U. L. Rev. 77 (2002)

61. See, e.g., Jean O. Lanjouw and Mark Schankerman, *Protecting Intellectual Property Rights: Are Small Firms Handicapped?* 47 J.L. & Econ. 45 (2004) (studying patent litigation and settlements and concluding firms with small patent portfolios are at higher litigation risk); Josh Lerner, *Patenting in the Shadow of Competitors*, 38 J.L. & Econ. 463 (1995) (analyzing patenting patterns of firms with differing litigation costs).

62. See, e.g., John P. Walsh, Ashish Arora, and Wesley Cohen, *Effects of Research Tool Patents and Licensing on Biomedical Innovation*, in *Patents in the Knowledge-Based Economy* 285–340 (The National Academies Press 2003); Julie E. Cohen and Mark A. Lemley, *Patent Scope and Innovation in the Software Industry*, 89 Cal. L. Rev. 1 (2001).

of innovation policy;[63] and patent law's relationship to research and development (R&D)[64] and innovation.[65] This scholarship adds resolution at the feature level of patent law. And to the extent answers remain unclear, scholars are continuing their work, lest we remain mired in economist Fritz Machlup's famous quip in 1958 about the patent system: "If we did not have a patent system, it would be irresponsible, on the basis of our present knowledge of its economic consequences, to recommend instituting one. But since we have had a patent system for a long time, it would be irresponsible ... to recommend abolishing it."[66]

B. Operational Challenges: Administrative and Judicial

There are also several operational challenges facing the modern patent system. For instance, some commentators have argued that the PTO is issuing too many low-quality patents and should employ a more rigorous examination of patent applications,[67] particularly in certain subject matter areas such as software and business methods.[68] This unease about the examination system has prompted some commentators to call for the creation of a registration sys-

63. See, e.g., Robert P. Merges and Richard R. Nelson, *On the Complex Economics of Patent Scope,* 90 Colum. L. Rev. 839 (1990) (concluding that law should favor a competitive environment for improvements rather than one dominated by the pioneer firm); Suzanne Scotchmer, *Standing on the Shoulders of Giants: Cumulative Research and the Patent Law*, 5 J. Econ. Persp. 29 (1991) (investigating the use of patent protection and cooperative agreements to protect incentives for cumulative research); Arti Kaur Rai, *Regulating Scientific Research: Intellectual Property Rights and the Norms of Science*, 94 Nw. L. Rev. 77 (1999).

64. See, e.g., Ashish Arora, Marco Ceccagnoli and Wesley M. Cohen, *R&D and the Patent Premium* (National Bureau of Econ. Research Working Paper No. 9431, 2003).

65. For a nice overview of the empirical literature, see Bronwyn H. Hall, *Business Method Patents, Innovation, and Policy* (Competition Policy Center, Univ. of California, Berkeley, May 4, 2003) (Working Paper No. CPC03–39).

66. *An Economic Review of the Patent System: Study of the Subcomm. on Patents, Trademarks, & Copyrights of the Comm. on the Judiciary*, 85th Cong. 18 (1958) (prepared by Fritz Machlup, Department of Political Economy, Johns Hopkins University).

67. See, e.g., Robert P. Merges, *As Many as Six Impossible Patents Before Breakfast: Property Rights for Business Concepts and Patent System Reform*, 14 Berkeley Tech. L.J. 577 (1999); Jay Kesan, *Carrots and Sticks to Create a Better Patent System*, 17 Berkeley Tech. L.J. 763 (2002).

68. See, e.g., Jay P. Kesan and Thomas S. Ulen, *Forward: Intellectual Property Challenges in the Next Century*, 2001 Ill. L. Rev. 57, 65 (noting that in "the area of business methods, the Patent Office is often understandably unaware of patent-defeating prior art"); John R. Thomas, *Collusion and Collective Action in the Patent System: A Proposal for Patent Bounties*, 2001 U. Ill. L. Rev. 305, 319 (stating "the Patent Office has yet to develop a comprehensive library of prior art business materials"); Merges, *Six Impossible Patents*, *supra* note 67, at 591 ("There are persistent reports that patents in the software area, and perhaps especially, patents for 'business methods' implemented in software, are of extremely poor quality.").

tem.[69] And recent patent reform initiatives by the National Academy of Sciences and the Federal Trade Commission have resulted in the recommendation to implement a post-grant opposition proceeding, whereby a third party can challenge the issuance of a patent.[70]

Lastly, the United States Court of Appeals for the Federal Circuit, patent law's exclusive appellate judicial body, faces challenges. Certainly, the court has accomplished a great deal in its short history, but it has not escaped criticism in recent years. For example, Federal Circuit watchers have questioned the court's lack of deference to district court judges on certain issues[71] and seeming reluctance to engage economic and empirical patent law scholarship in their decision making.[72] Moreover, some commentators have argued that the court can do a better job at employing the common law of patents with respect to certain industries such as software and biotechnology.[73] The Federal Circuit and its place in the patent system are discussed in greater detail in Chapter 3.

III. The Boundaries of the Patent System

Patent law, while a significant form of intellectual property (IP) in terms of its relationship to innovation and commercial value of a firm, is only one form of IP. Other forms include trademarks, copyrights, and trade secrets, each of which can be distinguished from patent law and from each other in terms of what they seek to

69. See, e.g., Mark A. Lemley, *Rational Ignorance at the Patent Office*, 95 Nw. U. L. Rev. 1495, 1496 (2001).

70. For the publication of the National Academies, see *A Patent System for the 21st Century* (The National Academies Press 2004) and for the Federal Trade Commission's, see *To Promote Innovation: The Proper Balance of Competition, Patent Law and Policy* (FTC 2003). http://www.ftc.gov/os/2003/10/innovationrpt.pdf. See also, Bronwyn H. Hall, Stuart J.H. Graham, Dietmar Harhoff, and David Mowery, *Prospects for Improving U.S. Patent Quality via Post-Grant Opposition*, in *Patents in the Knowledge-Based Economy* 74 (Wesley M. Cohen and Stephen A. Merrill eds., 2003) (asserting that post-grant opposition can lead to substantial welfare gains).

71. See, e.g., Craig Allen Nard, *A Theory of Claim Interpretation*, 14 Harv. J.L. & Tech. 1 (2002); Arti K. Rai, *Addressing the Patent Gold Rush: The Role of Deference to PTO Patent Denials*, 2 Wash. U. J.L. & Pol'y 199 (2000); Craig Allen Nard, *Deference, Defiance & the Useful Arts*, 56 Ohio St. L.J. 1415 (1995).

72. See, e.g., *A Patent System for the 21st Century* 86 (The National Academies Press 2004); Rochelle Cooper Dreyfuss, *The Federal Circuit: A Continuing Experiment in Specialization*, 54 Case W. Res. L. Rev. 769, 780–81 (2004); Craig Allen Nard, *Toward a Cautious Approach to Obeisance: The Role of Scholarship in Federal Circuit Patent Law Jurisprudence*, 39 Houston L. Rev. 667 (2002).

73. See Dan L. Burk and Mark A. Lemley, *Biotechnology's Uncertainty Principle* 54 Case W. Res. L. Rev. 691, 733 (2004); Dan L. Burk and Mark A. Lemley, *Policy Levers in Patent Law*, 80 Va. L. Rev. 1575 (2003); John R. Thomas, *Formalism at the Federal Circuit*, 52 Am. U. L. Rev. 771, 773 (2003); Arti K. Rai, *Specialized Trial Courts: Concentrating Expertise on Fact*, 17 Berkeley Tech. L.J. 877, 887–88 (2002).

protect and the form of protection. But they also share conceptual and operative similarities, such as the creation of incentive structures aimed at inducing the production of different types of subject matter. Thus, it becomes important to understand the similarities and differences among these four IP regimes.

A. Trade Secret Law

Trade secret law provides an important form of protection for valuable commercial information. Information eligible for trade secret protection may or may not be eligible for patent protection. (The issue of preemption was addressed by the Supreme Court in 1974, discussed *infra.*) If information is eligible for both, recent empirical studies have shown that many industries prefer trade secrecy as an appropriation mechanism, particularly for process-related inventions.[74] Trade secret protection is particularly attractive when the invention is not easy for others to discover once the owner makes use of it (i.e., not easily reverse engineered). Some secrets, such as the invention of the paper clip, disclose themselves when the product is put on the market. Other secrets, such as the process for manufacturing a particular type of crystal, are not revealed by selling the product.

Types of information eligible for trade secret protection are much broader than that which is patentable. Trade secrets include not only technologic information, but also formulae, customer lists, business plans, and marketing strategies. The Coca–Cola Company's formula for Coke is often cited as a famous example of the best kept trade secret. Trade secret law considers the forms of information that are subject to trade secret protection to be socially valuable and encourages their production. Trade secret protection can last in perpetuity as long as the information remains secret and maintains its value, whereas a patent expires 20 years from its filing date.

Trade secret law is grounded in both property and tort law. Under the property theory, trade secret law has a utilitarian justification, encouraging the production of valuable commercial information—much like patent law. The tort theory of trade secrets, first expressed in the 1939 Restatement of Torts, is more concerned with deterring unethical commercial behavior (e.g., theft). Thus, while trade secret law is considered a form of intellectual property, creating a protectable interest in valuable information, it is also concerned with ethical duties and behavior among commercial entities. As such, a cause of action for trade secret

74. See Cohen, et al., *Protecting Their Intellectual Assets*, *supra* note 38.

misappropriation will arise only if the trade secret is acquired by "improper means" or through a breach of a confidential relationship, which is usually in the form of an express or implied contract. Indeed, independent creation and reverse engineering are defenses to a trade secret misappropriation claim because they are not unethical. Those defenses are unavailable to an alleged patent infringer. Note that, like patent law and copyright law, trade secret law also has social costs. Trade secret law has the social advantage of not giving a legal monopoly over secrets other firms discover independently or through reverse engineering. This avoids the social costs associated with patents. On the other hand, trade secret law does not encourage disclosure to the extent patent law and copyright law do, and it fails to provide some of the social benefits of those systems.

Trade secret law is also concerned with protecting employers' secrets from being disclosed to competitors by departing employees. If the secret were disclosed, the employer's competitive advantage would diminish, along with the incentives necessary to encourage research on improved methods of doing business. On the other hand, restraining employees' economic mobility and personal freedom to pursue alternative employment is also undesirable. An employee would become shackled to his or her present employment if unable to use the increased expertise that came with experience in the industry. Should an employer be able to prevent a former employee from disclosing the employer's trade secrets? Prevent an erstwhile employee from working for a competitor?

With the exception of the Economic Espionage Act, trade secret protection is a creature of state law and is recognized in one form or another by every jurisdiction. While trade secrets have their origin in state common law, over 40 states have adopted the Uniform Trade Secrets Act (UTSA) in its original form or a version thereof.

The issue of preemption, natural to arise given that trade secret law and patent law potentially offer protection for the same subject matter, was addressed by the Supreme Court in *Kewanee Oil Co. v. Bicron Corp.*[75] In *Kewanee*, the trade secret related to a process for making synthetic crystals used for detecting radiation. It took nearly 20 years to develop a 17–inch crystal using the secret process. A former employee of the trade secret owner started his own company and developed a 17–inch crystal in one year. The district court found the former employee violated his employment agreement, issued an injunction, and awarded the trade secret

75. 416 U.S. 470 (1974).

owner damages for trade secret misappropriation. The appellate court held that Ohio trade secret law is preempted by federal patent law. The issue of preemption went before the Supreme Court. The Court held that trade secret law is not preempted by patent law.

The Court stated "whether the trade secret law of Ohio is void under the Supremacy Clause involves a consideration of whether that law 'stands as an obstacle to the accomplishment and execution of the full purposes and objectives of Congress.' "[76] While patent law does not expressly forbid or endorse trade secret law, if "the scheme of protection developed by Ohio respecting trade secrets 'clashes with the objectives of the federal patent laws,' then the state law must fall."[77] The Court then looked at three types of trade secret information in the light of patent law's policy of disclosure. First, there are inventions that clearly are not subject to patent protection, but would nonetheless serve to benefit society if produced and commercially exploited. Here, in the absence of patent law, trade secret law steps in to "encourage invention" and "prompt the independent innovator to proceed with the discovery and exploitation of his invention."[78] The Court stated there is no conflict between trade secret and patent law under this scenario. Second are inventions where patentability is dubious. While the power of a patent may prompt some "fence sitters" to apply for a patent on these types of inventions, the expense and lingering doubt as to whether a patent will issue will most likely force owners to look to trade secret law. For some of those who decide to file for patent protection, a patent may never issue. And while some patents that do issue may be valid, there are likely to be many patents invalidated or that result in unwarranted royalty payments. As the Court stated, "[t]he point is that those who might be encouraged to file for patents by the absence of trade secret law will include inventors possessing the chaff as well as the wheat."[79] Thus, without the availability of trade secret protection there will likely be greater inefficiencies and more invalid patents issued. The Court, therefore, held there is no preemption here because "[e]liminating trade secret law for the doubtfully patentable invention is . . . likely to have deleterious effects on society and patent policy which we cannot say are balanced out by the speculative gain which might result from the encouragement of some inventors with

76. Id. at 479.

77. Id. at 480 (quoting *Sears, Roebuck & Co. v. Stiffel Co.*, 376 U.S. 225, 231 (1964)).

78. Id. at 486.

79. Id. at 488.

doubtfully patentable inventions which deserve patent protection to come forward and apply for patents."[80]

Lastly, there are inventions that are clearly subject to patent protection. This category is the most controversial. The Court noted that patent law's interest in disclosure is paramount, and it is the production of these types of inventions that patent law was designed to incentivize. If trade secret protection posed a "substantial risk" that an inventor would opt for trade secret protection under this scenario, the Court noted that it would be "compelled" to strike the state regime down. But the Court held that such a risk was "remote indeed" because inventors will opt for patent protection due to the relative strength of a patent vis-à-vis trade secret protection; indeed, wrote the Court, "[w]here patent law acts as a barrier, trade secret law functions relatively as a sieve."[81]

Given the recent empirical evidence on firms' preference for trade secret protection over patents in many industries,[82] *Kewanee's* rationale appears less convincing.[83] But this evidence also highlights the importance of trade secret law to innovation. Without the prospect of a trade secret, would the pace of innovation diminish in certain industries? Or would patent protection be the appropriability mechanism of choice?

B. Copyright Law

Copyright law and patent law have the same broad goals, but they achieve these goals through different legal means and focus on different subject matter and creative segments of society. The two regimes have much in common at the conceptual and historical level. For instance, both are expressly grounded in Article I, Section 8, Clause 8 of the Constitution, which reads:

> To promote the progress of the Science and useful Arts, by securing for limited Times to Authors and Inventors the exclusive Right to their respective Writings and Discoveries.

80. Id. at 489.

81. Id. at 490.

82. See Cohen et al., *supra* note 58.

83. Justice Marshall, in a concurring opinion, did not believe the risk was "remote." Rather, he noted that trade secret protection is substantial, particularly for inventors who do not intend to license their trade secret. *Id.* at 493–94. Justice Douglas filed a dissent, arguing that the majority opinion cannot be reconciled with *Sears, Roebuck & Co. v. Stiffel Co.*, 376 U.S. 225, 231 (1964). In *Sears*, wrote Justice Douglas, the Court held that "when an article is unprotected by a patent, state law may not forbid others to copy it, because every article not covered by a valid patent is in the public domain. Congress in the patent laws decided that where no patent existed, free competition should prevail." Id. at 496.

Copyright law protects authors' creative, non-functional expressions of their ideas (not the ideas themselves) in whatever tangible form the expression might take, such as sculpture, drawing, writing, or music. Thus, like trademark law, one does not need to register to acquire protection, but there are important advantages to registration. An owner of a copyright enjoys several exclusive rights, including the right to make copies of the copyrighted work, to prepare derivative works, to distribute copies of the copyrighted work, to perform and display the copyrighted work publicly. The term of copyright is life of the author plus 70 years, or 95 years if the copyright is owned by a corporate entity or the like. There are also important limitations to these exclusive rights. For instance, others may make a "fair use" of the copyrighted material (e.g., uses related to parody or scholarship). And unlike patent law, independent creation is a defense to copyright infringement. There is no "fair use" or independent creation defense in patent law. Copyright law is exclusively federal and is set forth in Title 17 of the United States Code.

C. Trademark Law

Trademark law protects the symbols firms use to indicate the source, quality, and characteristics of their products and services. These symbols can include words, logos, pictures, slogans, colors, smells, symbols, and product packaging and designs. For example, the name of a restaurant can be protected as well as the trade dress or "look and feel" of the restaurant design. There are three principle policies underlying trademark law. First, exclusive rights to trademarks prevent consumer confusion and reduce consumer search costs. Trademarks serve as signals to consumers, allowing them to make certain qualitative judgments about a product and identify otherwise unobservable characteristics. Second, these consumer expectations encourage trademark owners to invest in and maintain a consistent level of quality. Thus, it is important that trademark law protects the good will a trademark owner has in a given mark, which may be worth millions of dollars. Lastly, because would-be competitors cannot free ride on the good will of the trademark owner (e.g., a soft drink upstart cannot use Coca–Cola as its own mark), parallel state and federal trademark laws force competitors to produce a quality product and develop a trademark of their own.

Trademark law has also been extended into areas where confusion is absent or irrelevant. The dilution doctrine, which finds expression in both state and federal law, seeks to protect trademark owners from use in a disparaging way ("tarnishment") and from overuse by others ("blurring"). An example of a use that puts the Kodak mark in a bad light is "Kodak XXX Adult Movie Theatre." Examples of uses that diminish the firmness of the connection between Kodak and the original seller of camera film would be another's use of Kodak in connection with the sale of watches, tires, or shoes. The idea is that through these types of uses, the power and signaling effect of the Kodak mark as used for photographic-related products would be weakened or diluted. Dilution treats a trademark as property, not as a source identifier, giving its owner the right to exclude others from using the mark in ways that do not cause confusion.

Trademark rights protect against confusing and dilutive uses of the mark, and last in perpetuity as long as the mark is continuously being used in a source-identifying manner. Trademark protection does not extend either to functional aspects of the product or to generic words that are the customary name of the product or service being sold. Functional features are the domain of patent law and generic words should be free for all to use in customary language.

Unlike copyright and patent law, which will be discussed below, Congress derives its power to enact trademark legislation from the Commerce Clause of the Constitution. Trademark law is a mix of federal and state statutory and common law. The federal statutory scheme is set forth in Title 15 of the United States Code and is frequently referred to as the Lanham Act after its long-time sponsor, Representative Ernest "Fritz" Lanham of Texas. The Lanham Act was enacted in 1947 and has been amended several times. Because federal trademark law is based on the Commerce Clause, federal rights in a mark exist only when the mark is used in interstate commerce. (State trademark law, which is nearly identical to federal law, applies to intrastate commerce.) One does not have to federally register a mark with the Patent and Trademark Office (PTO) to obtain federal trademark protection, although there are several advantages to registration.

D. Channeling Towards Patent Law

Built into copyright and trademark law are various doctrines that channel or shift the creation at issue away from copyright or trademark law and toward patent law. For instance, the doctrine of functionality in copyright law expressly prohibits copyright protection for "any process, system, method of operation, concept, principle, or discovery."[84] The classic case of *Baker v. Selden*[85] is represen-

84. 17 U.S.C. § 102(b).

85. 101 U.S. 99 (1880).

tative of this point. In *Baker*, Charles Seldon sought copyright protection on a "peculiar system of bookkeeping" that was set forth in a series of books. The books contained an introductory essay explaining the system of bookkeeping and several blank forms illustrating the system. The Supreme Court stated that, "the question is, whether the exclusive property in a system of bookkeeping can be claimed, under the law of copyright, by means of a book in which that system is explained?"[86]

The Court answered in the negative, stating that while copyright protection is available for a book on the subject of bookkeeping, "there is a clear distinction between the book, as such, and the art which it is intended to illustrate." The Court continued:

> The copyright of the book ... would be valid without regard to the novelty, or want of novelty, of its subject matter. The novelty of the art or thing described or explained has nothing to do with the validity of the copyright. To give to the author of the book an exclusive property in the art described therein, when no examination of its novelty has ever been officially made, would be a surprise and a fraud upon the public. That is the province of letters-patent, not of copyright.[87]

Similarly, trademark law's functionality doctrine precludes certain items from trademark protection.[88] *In TrafFix Devices, Inc. v. Marketing Displays, Inc.*,[89] MDI obtained utility patents on a spring mechanism associated with road signs. Upon expiration of the patents, MDI sought trade dress protection for its dual-spring design, arguing that the design was visible to buyers and users of the road signs. The Court held that trade dress protection was not available because the spring mechanism was functional. Strong evidence of the design's functionality was the existence of utility patents; therefore, whether the spring design acquired secondary meaning "need not be considered." According to the Court, the "Lanham Act does not exist to reward manufacturers for their innovation in creating a particular device; that is the purpose of the patent law."[90]

86. Id. at 101.

87. Id. at 102. See also *Publications Intern., Ltd. v. Meredith Corp.*, 88 F.3d 473, 481 (7th Cir.1996) (holding recipes not subject to copyright protection based on § 102(b) because they merely set forth functional considerations).

88. See *Qualitex Co. v. Jacobson Products Co., Inc.*, 514 U.S. 159, 165 (1995) (stating "a product feature is functional, and cannot serve as a trademark, if it is essential to the use or purpose of the article or if its affects the cost or quality of the article").

89. 532 U.S. 23 (2001).

90. Id. at 34.

Chapter Three

The Federal Circuit and the Patent System

I. Introduction

The emergence of the United States Court of Appeals for the Federal Circuit as the most powerful and influential institutional actor in the U.S. patent system is foremost among the trends that have shaped the modern patent law environment. Indeed, the significance of this development is impossible to overstate: even as the patent system has grown tremendously in economic importance, technological complexity, and public awareness, the management of the entire enterprise depends increasingly upon the twelve active judges of the Federal Circuit.

Even aside from its special role in the patent law, the Federal Circuit represents a unique experiment in the federal appellate system: the demarcation of jurisdictional power by subject matter, rather than by geography; the conveyance of nationwide appellate authority, albeit within specified fields. At present, the Federal Circuit has exclusive appellate jurisdiction in at least sixteen areas, ranging from the high profile (patents, government contracts, and federal takings cases) to the more mundane (such as employment disputes within federal agencies, the allocation of veterans' benefits, and the administration of the national vaccine compensation program).[91]

II. Federal Circuit: Facts and Figures

A. Caseload

In total, the Federal Circuit hears about 1500 appeals per year across all areas of its jurisdiction. Over the seventeen years from 1988 to 2004, the court's overall caseload increased, on average, 1.9 percent per year. Note that this is about one-third less than the rate of increase for all other federal appellate courts, in which filings rose about 3.2 percent. The overall workload of the Federal Circuit is below that of the regional circuit courts of appeals.

During the 1988 to 2004 period, the court's patent jurisdiction (combined appeals from district courts and the PTO) represented about one-third of the total caseload. Cases originating at the Merit Systems Protection Board, concerning federal civil service employ-

91. See 28 U.S.C. § 1338 (2004).

ment issues, make up slightly more than one-third; the rest of the court's jurisdiction combined comprises the balance.

1. Judges

At present, the U.S. Court of Appeals for the Federal Circuit is authorized for twelve judgeships. The currently active judges are set forth in the table below.

Judge	Appointment Date	Prior Positions	Patent Background
Michel [Chief Judge]	March 8, 1988	Prosecutor, Senate staff	Limited; legislative
Newman	May 7, 1984	Scientist, in-house counsel	Extensive; in-house counsel
Mayer	June 11, 1987	Private legal practice, government	None
Lourie	April 11, 1990	Scientist, in-house counsel	Extensive; in-house counsel
Rader	August 9, 1990	Judge, Ct. of Claims, House staff	Some; legislative
Schall	August 19, 1992	Private legal practice, government	None
Bryson	October, 7, 1994	Government	None
Gajarsa	September 12, 1997	Private legal practice	Some; private practice
Linn	January 1, 2000	Private legal practice	Extensive; private practice
Dyk	June 9, 2000	Private legal practice	None
Prost	September 21, 2001	Senate staff	Limited; legislative
Moore	September 5, 2006	Law professor	Academic, with a focus on patents

Table 3–1. Current Federal Circuit Judges

2. Judicial "Camps"

Broadly speaking, Federal Circuit judges come from traditional Washington, D.C., legal backgrounds, either from government positions or local private firms. About one-half of the current active judges have at least some patent experience prior to ascending the bench. As of 2006, eight of the twelve active judges were appointed by Republican presidents, and four by Democrats—though given that patent law issues rarely separate neatly along political party lines, this statistic is of only limited relevance.

Although there are differences among the judges, identifying any stable "camps" or "factions" on the Federal Circuit is difficult. One possible split could be between the set of judges with prior patent backgrounds, versus those without prior patent backgrounds. There is little evidence that this is true, however. More important, perhaps, is the distinction between those judges with (1) primarily private law firm backgrounds; and (2) those judges with public (government) or in-house counsel backgrounds. (The most-recent appointment of Judge Moore, with a primarily academic background, does not fit well in either category, of course.) A recent study of claim construction methodological approaches among judges found statistically significant differences among the judges roughly along this dimension, with group (1) noted above being in favor of rule-like approaches, and group (2) being in favor of more open-ended standards.[92] But even this is an issue which may be in some flux, see Chapter 9 on Claim Construction. Generally speaking, the Federal Circuit, on patent law questions, is unburdened by distinct and stable factions or persistent infighting.

B. The Theory of the Federal Circuit

The story of the rise of the Federal Circuit to preeminence in the patent field is not one of accident or oversight. There is little doubt about what Congress believed it was doing when it passed the Federal Courts Improvement Act (FCIA) in 1982, establishing the Federal Circuit and designating that court as the exclusive venue for patent appeals, whether from decisions of the U.S. district courts or the United States Patent and Trademark Office (PTO).[93] Unifying appellate jurisdiction under a single court was seen as an effective (albeit largely untested as of 1982) response to the widespread perception that the legal infrastructure of the patent law was not being effectively managed. And there is some reason to believe that the situation in the late 1970s and early 1980s called for action: Congress was presented with reports suggesting that the PTO was largely "freelancing" with respect to the standards of patentability, resulting in an increasing divergence in the legal framework applied by the judiciary and the PTO, as well

92. See R. Polk Wagner and Lee Petherbridge, *Is the Federal Circuit Succeeding?* 152 U. Pa. L. Rev. 1105, 1156–70 (2004).

93. See Federal Courts Improvement Act of 1982, Pub. L. 97-164, 96 Stat. 25 (April 2, 1982).

as the erosion of the statutory presumption of validity that attached to patents upon issue.[94] Perhaps even more important was the widespread perception that patent cases were receiving quite distinct treatment throughout the regional circuits, yielding both confusion concerning the ability to enforce patent rights, as well as rampant forum shopping (and related litigation). The Supreme Court, for its part, had shown little interest in managing the patent law—probably because of increasing demands on its docket, as well as the general perception among the judiciary that patent cases were particularly troublesome or difficult because of the involvement of technology.[95]

Thus, from its inception, the Federal Circuit's exclusive appellate jurisdiction over the patent law has been based on the following line of reasoning:

> First, that the court, in its centralized role, would act as the manager and developer of the patent law,[96] and second, that the imposition of such a structure would yield a clearer, more coherent, and more predictable patent doctrine, reduce or eliminate forum shopping, and at least rationalize—if not strengthen—the patent grant.[97]

While the ultimate success of this foray into centralized judicial authority for the patent law is uncertain (and, indeed, subject to ongoing controversy), Congress' basic structural goals for the Federal Circuit seem to have been realized. There is little doubt that the Federal Circuit has moved briskly into its role as the manager and developer of the patent doctrine.[98] Professor Dreyfuss, in the seminal survey of the Federal Circuit's early development, notes that the court seized the jurisprudential initiative in a number of areas, including the standard for obviousness, the availability of remedies, and procedural issues—though her conclusions as to the success of these efforts are mixed.[99] It is widely perceived that patents are more valuable today than before 1982, and the results

94. See id. at 6.

95. But see Cecil D. Quillen, *Innovation and the Current U.S. Patent System*, 1 Va. L. & Bus Rev. 207 (2006) (arguing that forum shopping and outcome variability were not notable problems in the 1970s). See also Testimony of James W. Geriak, Hearings before the Committee on the Judiciary, Subcommittee on Courts, Civil Liberties and the Administration of Justice on H.R. 2405 (April 1981), 69 (stating it "would be a very, very substantial error for the subcommittee to conclude that all patent lawyers are agreed upon the desirability of the ... Federal Circuit legislation").

96. See, e.g., H.R. Rep. No. 312, at 20–22.

97. See H.R. Rep. No. 312, at 22; S. Rep. No. 275, 97 Cong. 1st Sess. 5.

98. See, e.g., Mark D. Janis, *Patent Abolitionism*, 17 Berkeley Tech. L.J. 899 (2002).

99. See Rochelle Cooper Dreyfuss, *The Federal Circuit: A Case Study in Specialized Courts*, 64 N.Y.U. L. Rev. 1, 7–22 (1989).

in any case are clearly not affected by the regional circuit from which they emanate. In short, the institutional design envisioned by Congress has been realized: the Federal Circuit has, in a variety of doctrinal areas, assumed its central role. Whether the court has been successful in implementing this role to achieve the expected results underlying the Congressional action remains, of course, an open question.[100]

One common view of the basis for the Federal Circuit's exclusive jurisdiction over the patent law is that routing all appeals to the Federal Circuit will reduce or eliminate forum shopping among litigants. This theory has immediate appeal, of course: because of its status as a federal question, liberalized rules for venue and personal jurisdiction, and even the relatively easy availability of declaratory judgment jurisdiction in the patent context, parties in patent disputes have a great many options in choosing the location of the original suit. Indeed, in the paradigmatic example of two large corporations disputing over patent rights, virtually any United States district court is a potential venue. But the anti-forum-shopping theory has some important flaws, perhaps the most significant being that the locus of the Federal Circuit for patent appeals does not change any incentives to shop among district courts.[101] That is, while the appellate court and (more broadly) the governing legal standards are fixed, there remain many reasons that litigants might (and do) select among district courts. Issues of timing, for example, local judicial expertise, or even specialized local patent procedural rules, are all important questions that can be expected to be considered in the high-stakes game of patent litigation. In addition, some district courts—notably the U.S. District for the District of Delaware—are known to be particularly amenable to patent cases, while others may consider the technology and legal complexity, as well as the role of the Federal Circuit, to make patent cases relatively unattractive. Put another way: while the Federal Circuit eliminates forum shopping in patent cases for legal rules, it self-evidently does not do so for procedural rules or other, practical considerations. Indeed, given the limited impact on forum shopping that the Federal Circuit can be expected to have, it seems clear that there must be another, more direct, theory justifying the Federal Circuit. It is to this issue that we now turn.

100. See Craig Allen Nard and John F. Duffy, *Rethinking Patent Law's Uniformity Principle*, 101 Nw. L. Rev. 1619 (2007) (arguing for more decentralization in patent law's judicial appellate architecture).

101. See, e.g., Kimberly A. Moore, *Forum Shopping in Patent Cases: Does Geographic Choice Affect Innovation,* 79 N.C. L. Rev. 934 (2001) (finding significant forum shopping).

C. Managers versus Decision Makers: Two Views of the Federal Circuit

As noted above, the theory of the Federal Circuit must be grounded in its role as the centralized source of legal authority for the patent system—the idea that the court would, via its oversight of the legal doctrine, shape the patent system into a clearer, more consistent, more predictable mechanism for supporting innovation. But understanding this theory does not end the inquiry. There are at least two roles that the Federal Circuit can play when implementing this theory:

First, the *Managerial Approach*. Under this approach, the primary task of the Federal Circuit is to manage the development of the legal doctrine, to ensure that it remains clear, coherent, and consistent.

Second, the *Decision Maker Approach*. Under this view, the primary task of the Federal Circuit is to make coherent, clear, and consistent decisions regarding the patent appeals before them.

Neither of these roles is particularly unique to the Federal Circuit, of course—they broadly describe the roles of any appellate body. Here, however, they take on added significance because of the Federal Circuit's special role with respect to the patent law. The important thing to understand is that these two roles are often in tension, and that the resolution of that tension (e.g., placing one role above the other) will determine much about the shape of the law in this area. When the court acts in its managerial role, the content and description of the legal doctrine takes precedence, even if the outcome of individual cases is not ideal. An example of the Federal Circuit in managerial mode is the 2000 en banc case of *Festo*, wherein a majority of the court determined that the legal doctrine was workable only with a relatively clear line between subject matter that was—and was not—surrendered due to prosecution history estoppel. (See Chapter 10 on the DOE.) As it turned out, the doctrine was short-lived, as the Supreme Court reversed, and put into place a far more open-ended, case-by-case inquiry. Conversely, an example of the Federal Circuit in "decision maker mode" is the 2005 en banc opinion on claim construction in *Phillips*, where the court abandoned an effort championed by what was then a majority of judges to bring additional clarity to the doctrine. Instead, the court eschewed any doctrinal rules in this area, pronouncing the inquiry to be fundamentally contextual.

Selecting between managerial and decision maker roles does more than define whether the legal doctrine will be more or less rule-like (though that is a significant effect)—it also determines the place of the Federal Circuit within the patent system. In the decision maker role, the Federal Circuit becomes the de facto arbiter of virtually every patent case, the only real source of authority to decide the outcome. By contrast, in the managerial role, the Federal Circuit is less of a case-by-case decider, instead focusing on laying down a framework for district courts and the USPTO to follow. In some ways, the court is more "powerful" in the decision making role—its hand can be in virtually every important patent dispute. However, this power comes at a cost to the system as a whole, both in terms of judicial resources—why have extensive district court proceedings when the Federal Circuit will ultimately decide the case on its own?—and the longer-term ability of the court to achieve its original mandate to bring clarity and predictability to the patent doctrine.

This is a live, albeit rather subtle, struggle at the Federal Circuit, and one that is unlikely to be fully resolved.

D. The Future of the Federal Circuit

Looking ahead, the key issues facing the Federal Circuit surround its long-term place at the heart of the U.S. patent system. At least two major challenges have presented themselves in recent years. The first is the question discussed in the section above—whether and how the Federal Circuit resolves the tension between its two roles, and how that resolution fits into the court's ability to fulfill its mandate from the 1982 Federal Courts Improvement Act—indeed, the justification for its very existence.

The second important challenge is—in contrast to the internalized struggle about its proper role—a more direct challenge to the court's place in the patent system. In very recent years, the Supreme Court has returned to the patent law with some vigor, granting *certiorari* at a much higher rate than during the prior twenty years. As part of this renewed activity, the Supreme Court has been increasingly aggressive about asserting its (supreme) role in the development of the doctrine, striking down Federal Circuit law that was settled (injunctive relief, *eBay v. MercExchange*), as well as divisive (prosecution history estoppel, *Festo*). Indeed, in *Holmes v. Vornado*, members of the Supreme Court appeared to question the wisdom of the Federal Circuit's central role in the patent system (or perhaps the implementation of it).[102]

There are several possible reasons for the Supreme Court's renewed attention to the patent law (and thus the Federal Circuit).

102. See *Holmes Group, Inc. v. Vornado Air Circulation Systems, Inc.*, 535 U.S. 826, 839 (2002) (Stevens, J., concurrence) (stating "occasional decisions by courts with broader jurisdiction will provide an antidote to the risk that the

One may be the Court's effort to engage in patent reform. In the late 1990s and early 2000s, there was an increasing sense, especially in the annals of the popular press, that the patent system was in need of serious reform. Two high-profile studies in 2003, by the National Academies of Science and the Federal Trade Commission, identified what were described as serious problems with the patent system, and proposed a number of reform measures.[103] The Federal Circuit's doctrine was fingered as a root cause of some problems, and the Supreme Court may view its more active role as that of a facilitator in the patent reform discussion.

A second possible reason for the Supreme Court's renewed interest in the patent law is a sense among the Justices that the Federal Circuit judges are in need of greater oversight or guidance. In many areas of the patent law, the Federal Circuit's doctrine has strayed afield from that established by earlier (albeit at times much earlier) precedents. For example, issues such as the legal test for non-obviousness under 35 U.S.C. ¶ 103, the role of the "written description" requirement of § 112, and even the standard for patentable subject matter under § 101 are all quite distinct from that established by the Supreme Court prior to 1982. It may be that the Supreme Court is trying to force the Federal Circuit to pay more attention to existing precedent rather than develop the doctrine independently.

Third, it may simply be the time. That is, the Supreme Court may have left the Federal Circuit largely alone for twenty years, to let the court develop the doctrine, its role, etc. Now the Supreme Court is ready to reassert itself, and the recent rise in activity can be understood as a response to the many years of inattention.

In any case, the dramatically increasing role of the Supreme Court in the patent law will pose challenges to the Federal Circuit—not only because that court will have to interpret and implement the at-times vague pronouncements of the higher court, but also because it will directly affect the Federal Circuit's current role as the central player in the U.S. patent system.

specialized court may develop an institutional bias"); See, e.g., *Laboratory Corp. of America Holdings v. Metabolite Labs. Inc.*, 126 S.Ct. 2921, 2929 (2006) (Breyer, J., dissenting from decision to dismiss case as improvidently granted) (stating "a decision from this generalist Court could contribute to the important ongoing debate, among both specialists and generalists, as to whether the patent system, as currently administered and enforced, adequately reflects the 'careful balance' that 'the federal patent laws ... embod[y]' ") (citing *Bonito Boats, Inc. v. Thunder Craft Boats, Inc.*).

103. See *A Patent System for the 21st Century* (The National Academies Press 2004) and *To Promote Innovation: The Proper Balance of Competition, Patent Law and Policy* (FTC 2003). http://www.ftc.gov/os/2003/10/innovationrpt.pdf.

Part II: Obtaining Patents

Chapter Four

An Overview of Patent Prosecution

I. Introduction

Each patent granted by the U.S. Government is done so after being reviewed for compliance with applicable rules and regulations by an administrative agency, the United States Patent and Trademark Office (USPTO).[104] This process of administrative review and approval is called "patent prosecution," and begins with a prospective patentee filing an application for a patent with the USPTO. Patent applications are assigned to employees of the USPTO known as "patent examiners," who evaluate the patent application. Once evaluation is complete, the USPTO will "issue" the final patent, which will be printed in formal format and published. Once a patent is issued, it becomes fully enforceable by the patentee.

The critical thing to understand about the patent prosecution process is its institutional location within the overall scheme of the patent system. In general, it is useful to think of the temporal life of a U.S. patent in two phases: the first phase is patent prosecution; the second phase is patent enforcement. The differences between these two phases are significant, and important to understanding the structure of the U.S. patent system.

Differences of scale. Every patent must go through a prosecution phase, while only a very small percentage of all patents are enforced. In Fiscal Year 2006, over 443,000 patent applications were filed, and about 183,000 patents were issued.[105] Compare this to the amount of litigation, where 2,205 patent enforcement actions were filed during Fiscal Year 2006. Note that filing of litigation need not—and usually does not—result in lengthy litigation. Recent empirical patent litigation scholarship suggests that only about 1% of patents are ever litigated.[106] Of this small percentage, 5% of

104. As should be apparent from the agency's title, it has somewhat similar responsibilities with respect to federally-registered trademarks.

105. Note that because of the average two- to three-year pendency of applications in the prosecution phase, these FY 2006 numbers are not directly comparable.

106. See Mark A. Lemley, *Rational Ignorance at the Patent Office*, 95 Nw. L. Rev. 1495, 1501 (2001). Some scholars have suggested that the small number of patents being litigated is because "[m]any patents are not worth enforc-

patent cases go to trial,[107] an additional 8–9% are resolved on the merits through summary judgment, and the remaining are resolved through some form of settlement.[108]

Differences in resources. The enforcement of patents is an enormously expensive process, consuming vast amounts of time and resources. Looking solely at litigation (which surely understates the costs of enforcement), in 2005 the mean cost of a "medium-sized" patent litigation was at least $2,500,000 per side—and that cost could soar to $5.5 million or more for a substantial litigation.[109] By contrast, the typical private cost of a patent prosecution in 2005 ranged from $4,000 to about $20,000, depending on complexity of the invention and the length of prosecution. Estimates of patent examiner time spent per application range from 15 to 30 hours—again depending on complexity and other factors. Thus, the resources applied per patent in the prosecution context are a mere fraction of those in the enforcement context. (As discussed below, this structure seems likely to be a generally correct allocation of resources.)

Differences in process. While patent enforcement is an open, public, and adversarial process (often involving high-stakes litigation in federal courts), patent prosecution is (generally) subject to secrecy—at least for the first eighteen months, if not more[110]—and is conducted between the prospective patentee and the patent examin-

ing—either because the inventions they cover turn out to be worthless, or because even if the invention has economic value the patent does not." John R. Allison, Mark A. Lemley, Kimberly A. Moore, and R. Derek Trunkey, *Valuable Patents*, 92 GEO. L.J. 435, 436 (2004). Of course, many patents are licensed (or subject to cross-licensing agreements), and can be used to intimidate competitors, or be useful in attractive capital investment. See Shubha Ghosh and Jay Kesan, *What Do Patents Purchase? In Search of Optimal Ignorance in the Patent Office*, 40 HOUS. L. REV. 1219 (2004). But see Lemley, *Rational Ignorance*, *supra* (estimating only 3.5% of patents are licensed for a royalty).

107. See Jean O. Lanjouw and Mark Schankerman, *Protecting Intellectual Property Rights: Are Small Firms Handicapped?* 47 J. L. ECON. 45 (2004); Jay P. Kesan and Gwendolyn G. Ball, *How Art Patent Case Resolved? An Empirical Examination of the Adjudication and Settlement of Patent Disputes*, 84 WASH. U. L. REV. 237 (2006).

108. See Kesan and Ball, *How Are Patent Cases Resolved*, *supra* note 107. These figures, of course, only tell part of the picture. In testimony on patent reform before the House Subcommittee on Courts, the Internet, and Intellectual Property, an Apple Computer representative stated: "[F]or every lawsuit that goes to final judgment, there is [*sic*] 25 more that don't go to final judgment, that get adjudicated or settled ahead of time, and for every one of those, there's [*sic*] 25 [cease and desist] letters that were written that never made it to a lawsuit at all." H.R. Rep. 109–11, pt. 1, at 122 (2005).

109. See *American Intellectual Property Law Ass'n, Report of the Economic Survey* 2005, at 23.

110. Since 2000, patent applications are, by default, published eighteen months after their effective filing date. See 35 U.S.C. § 122 (2005). An exception applies to applicants who do not file outside the U.S.

er only. Further, while the patentee will bear the burden of proving infringement in any enforcement action, the USPTO, not the prospective patentee, bears most of the substantive burdens during patent prosecution—though accused infringers will have the burden of proving the invalidity of the patent if it is challenged.[111]

Patent prosecution is thus at once the "front lines" of the patent system—the entry point and origin of all U.S. patents—as well as a relatively lightly resourced hurdle for patentability. For while the same standards apply (the key criteria of sections 101, 102, 103 and 112 apply equally at the PTO and in the courts), the quantity of resources applied to each patent pales in comparison to the resources expended during post-grant licensing and enforcement activities.

At first glance this disparity between the prosecution and enforcement phases of a patent (especially with respect to resources applied per patent) may seem remarkable, and decidedly unwise: why spend millions of dollars to re-evaluate the patentability and scope of an invention years after the same analysis has been conducted by the USPTO? Yet this structural arrangement—this allocation of resources—may well be appropriate. A critical difference between the prosecution and enforcement phase lies in their timing with respect to the life of the invention. During the prosecution phase, the future marketplace effects of an invention (if any) are rarely known; although the patent law provides for some grace periods,[112] there remain very significant incentives to file a patent application at a relatively early stage, when commercial potential (or even basic feasibility) is likely to be an unknown. By contrast, during the enforcement phase, these questions are answered: almost by definition, those patents subject to litigation or licensing have important commercial effects. This difference in knowledge—whether an invention will be of actual benefit—supports the differences in resources applied. Put more simply, given uncertainty about the actual value of an invention at an early stage, it is not worth committing large amounts of resources to fully evaluating its scope and patentability. On the other hand, when we do know that an invention is valuable, then a more extensive analysis is justified.

Thus, the U.S. patent system exhibits what some academics have described as "rational ignorance," or a "soft look" system.[113] Under these theories, there *should* be a significant difference in

111. See 35 U.S.C. § 282 (2005).

112. See 35 U.S.C. § 102, (2005).

113. See Mark A. Lemley, *Rational Ignorance at the Patent Office*, 95 Nw. U. L. Rev. 1495 (2001); F. Scott Kieff, *The Case for Registering Patents and the Law and Economics of Present Patent-Obtaining Rules*, 45 B.C. L. Rev. 55 (2003).

resources applied at the prosecution and enforcement phase; for the reasons noted above, basic efficiency dictates that greater resources be applied to those patents that actually matter. The USPTO, then, stands as a sort of gatekeeper, or filter, separating out those inventions clearly unpatentable—and granting a patent to the rest. The marketplace (and, in some cases, the courts) will sort out the "true" value, scope, and validity of patents; this is not (and should not be) the USPTO's job.

However, even if one accepts that the U.S. patent system will not, and should not, have a perfect patent office—one that thoroughly and accurate evaluates each and every patent applied for—there remains a good deal of room for debate about the role of the USPTO. The optimal allocation of resources is unknown: while it is a cliché among commentators to suggest that the USPTO needs additional resources, there is remarkably little known about how resources should be distributed between prosecution and enforcement. And if the USPTO is to remain under-resourced, at least in comparison to litigation/enforcement, what things should it do to best enhance the overall system's goal of promoting progress? On this last point, one school of thought holds that the most important function of the prosecution process is to force patentees to disclose as much meaningful information as possible about their inventions, as well as commit themselves to relatively clear (and thus binding) assertions about the scope of their patents and its relationship to the prior art.[114] This is not uncontroversial: for the same temporal reasons noted above, patentees may not be well positioned to either disclose fully or make binding commitments during the prosecution process, so such rules may result in some unfairness or uncertainty.[115]

The role of the patent prosecution process in the structure of the patent system remains a topic of substantial controversy. Does its location as the key—and for the vast majority of patents, the *only*—review of compliance with the requirements for patentability justify a vast increase in resources, so as to ensure that granted patents are valid? Or should we understand patent prosecution to be an opportunity to implement a coarse filtering mechanism, perhaps one where the goal of measuring validity is second to the goal of memorializing a patentee's understanding of her invention? Should the USPTO be given more resources and power, or less? While the answers to these questions (and many other, related

114. See generally, R. Polk Wagner, *Reconsidering Estoppel: Patent Administration and the Failure of Festo*, 51 U. Pa. L. Rev. 159 (2002).

115. See *Festo Corp. v. Shoketsu Kinzoku Kogyo Kabushiki Co.*, 535 U.S. 722, 739 (2002).

ones) are unclear, the important role of patent prosecution in the overall patent system makes it an area ripe for reform efforts in the future.

II. The U.S. Patent and Trademark Office

The USPTO is an administrative agency of the United States Government, organizationally located within the Department of Commerce. With its main headquarters just outside Washington, D.C., in Alexandria, Virginia, the USPTO employs about 8,200 people, about 4,800 of them as patent examiners.[116] In Fiscal Year 2006, the USPTO spent about $1.7 billion on its operations.[117]

The USPTO describes its mission as:

> . . . to foster innovation and competitiveness by providing high quality and timely examination of patent and trademark applications, guiding domestic and international intellectual property policy, and delivering intellectual property information and education worldwide.[118]

Its core mission with respect to patents, of course, is to examine patent applications for compliance with the various validity requirements.

A. Prosecution Rules, Regulation, and Procedures

As one might expect of any administrative process, patent prosecution is conducted according to a detailed set of rules, regulations, and procedures. At the top of the regulatory hierarchy is the Patent Statute, Title 35 of the United States Code, as well as the court decisions interpreting the statutory language. The patent statute establishes the basic requirements for patentability, which is the core of patent prosecution. Next is Title 37 of the Code of Federal Regulations, which codifies the formal rules by which patent prosecution is to be conducted. Finally, the USPTO publishes a multi-volume manual, The Manual of Patent Examining Procedure (MPEP), which both collects and interprets the statutory and regulatory sources, as well as establishing in substantial detail the procedures by which prosecution will be conducted. The MPEP in particular does not have the force of law, but because it establishes the rules that examiners must follow when evaluating patent applications, it is in essence the governing document for most patent prosecution.

116. See USPTO, Performance and Accountability Report: Fiscal Year 2006, at 150.

117. Id. at 80.

118. Id.

Broadly speaking, patent prosecution includes the following steps:

1. Drafting the Application

In the typical case, the inventor will meet with his patent attorney or agent to begin the drafting of a patent application. Under USPTO rules, only those who have passed an exam (known as "the patent bar") covering prosecution procedures can represent others before the USPTO. (Hiring an agent or attorney is the norm, but not required; inventors are also allowed to file and prosecute applications on their own behalf.) In addition to passing the exam, the USPTO requires that its registered agents and attorneys have a technical education or background; an undergraduate degree in a science or engineering discipline is sufficient, and at times other technical qualifications (such as work experience in a technical field) can be substituted for formal education. The designation of "patent attorney" or "patent agent" specifies whether the individual has also passed a bar exam administered by a U.S. state, and is thus an "attorney."[119]

The basic content of a patent application is broadly specified by 35 U.S.C. § 111, which requires that it have a specification (defined by § 112); a drawing where necessary for understanding the patented subject matter (defined by § 113); and an oath signed by the inventor(s) (defined by § 115). The oath is a formal (notarized) declaration that the inventor "believes himself to be the original and first inventor of the process, machine, manufacture, or composition of matter, or improvement thereof, for which he solicits a patent." The specification, of course, is the primary source of the disclosure, and includes (at its end) the text of the claims which the patentee seeks to obtain.

Drafting patent applications is a specialized skill, involving a number of critical considerations and trade-offs. Because of the centrality of the text of the patent document to virtually all patent doctrines, the choices made during the drafting of an application will have fundamental implications for the life of the patent. Most patent drafting seeks to walk along a series of narrow lines: for example, providing a disclosure that satisfies the "enablement" and "written description" requirements of 35 U.S.C. § 112 without providing detail that would lead a court to later construe the patent claims more narrowly; or drafting claims that are at once broad

119. For information about the patent bar, see http://www.uspto.gov/web/offices/dcom/gcounsel/oed.htm.

enough to provide real power in the marketplace, and not so broad that they ensnare the prior art under sections 102 or 103. It is also important to remember that patent applications are formal legal documents, not technical reports or academic papers; they have very different purposes, very different audiences, and will therefore be created and understood very differently. Although legally they are to be understood through the eyes of "a person having ordinary skill in the art" (a "PHOSITA" in patent jargon), their primary purpose is not merely to teach. Instead, a patent application might be analogized to the formal title document for a piece of real estate: the formally, carefully drafted document that both locates the property and establishes its boundaries. (Obviously, because describing the borders of an intellectual creation—an invention—is considerably more difficult than marching off a set of lot lines, patent applications are far more complex and involved than title documents. But the basic purpose is similar.)

2. Submission, Classification and Initial Proceedings

Once an application is drafted, and the oath made, the application can be filed with the USPTO. Typically this means sending the documents—along with the appropriate filing fee (which for 2006 starts at $300 for large companies and $150 for small companies and individuals)[120] via the U.S. mail, though work is underway to make patent prosecution an all-electronic process in the relatively near future. Upon arrival at the USPTO, the application will be quickly checked for compliance with section 111, and then submitted for classification.

As part of its administrative responsibilities, the USPTO maintains a detailed system of technological classification (entitled the U.S. Patent Classification System, or "USPC System"). Each patent application is categorized according to this system, which includes more than 450 "classes" of technology, and about 15,000 "subclasses." These classes and subclasses are numerically coded: a designation of 482/10 means that the invention is within the "Exercise Devices" class (482) and the "For Head or Neck" subclass. Typically, inventions will fall within multiple class/subclass pairs; in this case, one set will be designated as the "primary classification." An application's primary classification determines its allocation within the corps of patent examiners (who are also organized into "art units" according to technological categories). Note that the USPC System is not only useful to the PTO in allocating applications—because it categorizes every U.S. patent, it

120. 37 C.F.R. § 1.16(a) (2005).

provides an extremely useful mechanism for searching for patents by technological area.

3. Examination Proceedings

After being assigned to an art unit, and then eventually an examiner, the examiner will begin the analysis of the application. The examination includes an evaluation of the disclosure of the patent, a search of the relevant prior art, and a comparison of the prior art to the claims of the patent application. Typically, the examiner will (if necessary) issue what is known as an "Office Action," which is an official correspondence between the examiner and the applicant. In most cases, the examiner will issue "rejections" to the claims of the application as drafted, usually based on the statutory standards for patentability. (Each claim is analyzed individually, so different claims may prompt different responses from the examiner.) The applicant then has several months to respond to the Office Action (in a "Response to Office Action"). A variety of responses are possible, ranging from amendment of the claims to meet the rejections, arguments to the examiner concerning the appropriate understanding of the invention or the prior art, and even abandonment of the application altogether.

This pattern of Office Action, then Response to Office action, can repeat itself for some time, depending on the circumstances of the individual case. At some point, the examiner can declare any rejections "final," which essentially reduces the applicant's options to two: abandonment of the application (and, usually, re-filing as a related application); or an appeal to the Board of Patent Appeals and Interferences (or "BPAI"), which is an internal USPTO appellate process. An unsuccessful appeal to the BPAI can be followed by an appeal to the U.S. Court of Appeals for the Federal Circuit.

When the examiner feels that all the claims are patentable, and the disclosure of the patent is in proper form, she will issue a "Notice of Allowance," and the patent application will be reformatted, printed, and formally "issued" via a notice in the USPTO's weekly "Official Gazette."

4. Continuation Practice

The patent statute and USPTO procedures allow applicants to file related applications, usually in order to allow revisions, to otherwise continue prosecution of the application even after the examiner has issued final rejections to the claims, or to separate distinct inventions from one another. These related applications are called continuations, continuations-in-part, and divisional applications. Continuation applications contain the identical disclosure as the original (parent) application, and are thus accorded the same filing date. Continuations-in-part (CIPs) contain both old matter (from the parent application) and new matter. Claims supported by old matter are given the original (parent) filing date, while claims supported by new matter are given the filing date of the CIP application. Divisional applications are similar to continuation applications, except that they contain claims to distinct inventions; primarily for administrative convenience, the USPTO requires each patent application to contain claims to a single invention (though there is no limit on the number of claims that may be drawn to that invention).

The use of continuations and CIPs is very common in modern prosecution practice, but is somewhat controversial.[121] One concern is that the liberal use of continuations means that applicants can endlessly argue with the examiner about the patentability of claims, and possibly wear down the rejections.[122] (Note that some measures of the performance of examiners include the quantity of applications processed, so examiners may have incentives to approve applications quickly.) Lengthy continuation practice also allows applicants to alter their claims for a longer period of time, which might encourage strategic behavior.[123] And simply extending prosecution, which can in some cases keep the existence and scope of a prospective patent secret, might confer surprise or uncertainty in the marketplace.[124] Indeed, in early 2006, the USPTO, in a move controversial with patent practitioners, proposed to severely limit continuation practice, generally seeking to limit applicants to a single related application.[125]

B. Post–Grant Practice: Maintenance, Reissues and Reexaminations

The issuance of a patent does not end the USPTO's involvement. First and most simply, patentees are required to pay maintenance fees after 3.5 years (currently $900), 7.5 years (currently $2,300) and 11.5 years (currently $3,800) from filing. Failure to pay

121. For discussion of this issue, and an argument to abolish or curtail continuation applications, see Mark A. Lemley and Kimberly A. Moore, *Ending Abuse of Patent Continuations*, 84 B.U. L. Rev. 63 (2004).

122. See id. at 74.

123. Id. at 76.

124. See id. at 71, 79.

125. USPTO, *Changes to Practice for Continuing Applications, Requests for Continued Examination Practice, and Applications Containing Patentably Indistinct Claims*, 71 Fed. Reg. 1 (Jan. 3, 2006), at 48–49.

these fees will result in the expiration of the patent; well more than one-half of U.S. patents expire as a result of nonpayment of these fees.

Second, in some cases, granted patents may be reexamined by the USPTO via two types of proceedings, reissue and reexamination. A reissue proceeding is instigated by the patentee herself, and is offered as an opportunity to correct an error of patentability or claiming in the patent that occurred "without deceptive intent."[126] Such a proceeding can allow patentees to broaden their claims, though only within two years of issue.[127] A reexamination proceeding, by contrast, may be requested by anyone (including the patentee). The basis of a reexamination is "the existence of a substantial new question of validity."[128] Whether to conduct the reexamination is at the discretion of the USPTO; most requests are not granted.

In either case—reissue or reexamination—the patent is essentially analyzed anew, under the same basic proceedings as apply for original prosecution.[129] One exception is that a party requesting reexamination may request *inter-partes* proceedings, which allows her continued involvement during the course of the reexamination. Inter-partes reexamination thus resembles a form of trial concerning a patent's validity, with opposing sides (patentee and inter-partes requestor) making arguments to a neutral decision maker (the examiner).[130] However, the inter-partes reexamination process is relatively seldom invoked—the USPTO reported just 70 requests in FY 2006, as compared to 511 requests for the ex-parte reexamination proceedings.[131] This is in large measure because a party to inter-partes reexamination is estopped from raising the invalidity of the patent upon any ground that was or could have been raised during the reexamination proceeding.[132] Thus, inter-partes reexamination proceedings are seen as relatively high risk.

C. Challenges at the Patent Office

As its role as a key institutional component of the patent system suggests, the USPTO faces significant policy and administrative challenges going forward. We outline a few here.

126. See 35 U.S.C. § 251 (2005).
127. See id.
128. See 35 U.S.C. § 303 (2005).
129. See 35 U.S.C. § 305 (2005).
130. See 35 U.S.C. § 314 (2005).
131. See USPTO, Performance and Accountability Report: Fiscal Year 2006, at 133.
132. See 35 U.S.C. § 315 (2005).

1. Responding to the Rise in Patenting Activity

One important challenge facing the USPTO is related to a major trend noted in Chapter 3: the dramatic rise in patenting activity. There, we reported that while patent grants had risen 140 percent in two decades, the number of applications had risen over 240 percent. The gap between these two numbers foretells a third key statistic: that the number of patent applications pending at the USPTO has exploded. See Figure 4–1. As of 2006, over 1,000,000 patent applications were undergoing prosecution at the USPTO, with no end in sight.[133]

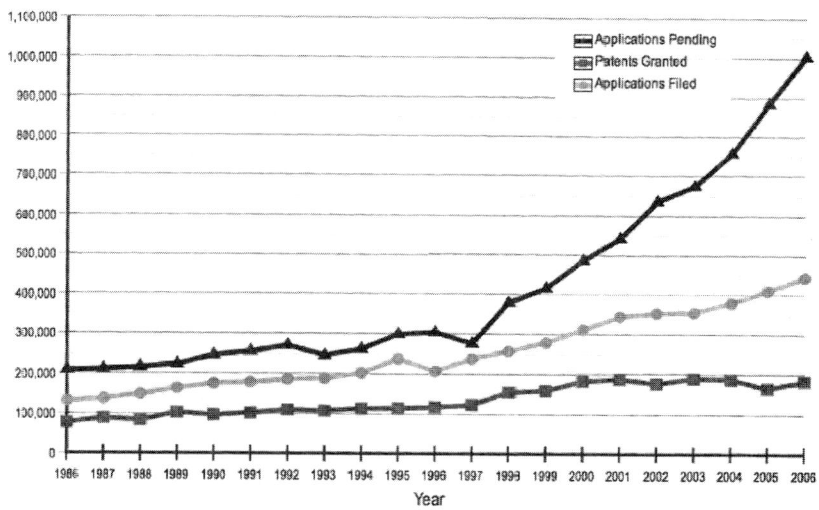

Figure 4–1. Patent Applications Pending, Filed, Granted, 1986–2006[134]

This vast increase in application pendency places enormous pressure on the operations of the Patent Office, generates widespread dissatisfaction among patent applicants, and—depending upon how the problem is (or is not) resolved, has serious consequences for the future of the patent prosecution system.

The vast growth of patent pendency harms all concerned. For applicants, it adds costs, delays the beginning of the enforcement period of their patents, and reduces the effective term of the patent.[135] For the USPTO, the growth of pendency places enormous

133. See U.S. Patent & Trademark Office, Performance & Accountability Report 2006.

134. U.S. Patent & Trademark Office, Performance & Accountability Reports (annual series).

135. Patent terms are measured as of the filing date of the application, yet

pressures on its operations, and creates very serious political problems, generating widespread dissatisfaction among patent applicants (as well as, perhaps, a sense that the agency is not up to the task).

Further, from a general policy perspective, additional pendency can: (1) make patenting less attractive than alternative means of protection, such as trade secrecy; (2) distribute the benefits of the patent system away from those with fewer resources (those with more resources will be able to absorb the delays and costs); (3) provide a lengthened window wherein patent applicants can engage in strategic behavior, such as altering pending claims to fit a competitor's product;[136] and (4) increase the pressure on the PTO to simply issue more patents with less stringent review, leading to a diminishment in the quality of patents overall.

Clearly, one way to address the growth of patenting activity is to greatly expand the patent examiner corps. This is already a major goal of the USPTO. It is important to realize, however, that the scale of the problem—the mismatch between the growth of examination capacity and the influx of new applications—seems likely to be beyond any reasonable long-term hiring increase. (At the approximately 10 percent yearly growth rate for applications, the effort to correspondingly add new examiners would quickly balloon the PTO workforce, creating a host of other problems, not to mention the basic problem of recruiting, hiring, and training that many new employees per year.)

How to respond to the patenting explosion is, without question, the most pressing problem facing the USPTO. And while some elements of a solution are clear (e.g., hire more examiners), there is plainly no magic formula. In all likelihood, the solution will have to be multi-pronged, involving additional PTO resources, gains in efficiency, additional costs placed on patent applicants (via prior art searches, etc.), and perhaps even more radical approaches, such as outsourcing of examination.

2. Resolving a Regulatory Role

Another key issue facing the USPTO surrounds the question of its regulatory role in the U.S. patent system. Unlike many federal

enforcement actions cannot be undertaken until the patent is granted. Thus, extending the time of prosecution (when the term is running, but enforcement is impossible) reduces the effective enforcement time of the patent.

136. There has been a recent emergence of the doctrine of "prosecution history latches."

administrative agencies, the PTO does not have what is known as "substantive rulemaking authority."[137] That is, while the PTO is free to promulgate rules and regulations governing its own operations (most importantly, the patent prosecution process)—and prescribing procedures by which patent applicants interact with the PTO—the agency cannot establish substantive rules concerning the application and interpretation of the patent law.

Endowing the PTO with substantive rulemaking power would greatly elevate its role in patent policy.[138] Indeed, one might even expect that, over time, the PTO could become as central to innovation policy in the U.S. as the Federal Communications Commission or Federal Trade Commission are with respect to telecommunications and competition policy, respectively. One might imagine the PTO establishing rules on various key patent law issues, such as the ways in which claim construction is to be conducted,[139] or the binding legal framework for the analysis of "nonobvious" inventions under 35 U.S.C. § 103.[140] And under rules of administrative law, such interpretations of the patent law would be binding on the judiciary, meaning that the PTO could in theory become the major authority on aspects of the patent law.

Whether the PTO should be granted additional regulatory authority is a complicated question. Certainly many critics of the Federal Circuit's role in the development of the patent law might view the entry of the PTO into the field as an opportunity for new thinking.[141] On the other hand, the PTO does not have a tradition of policy analysis, and at this point does not seem well equipped to play a central role in patent policy. Further, the possibility that the USPTO could be captured by various interest groups (especially the patent applicants and patent holders who are the core users of PTO services) should give advocates of this change pause.[142] In any event,

137. See Stuart Benjamin and Arti Rai, *Who's Afraid of the APA? What the Patent System Can Learn from Administrative Law*, 95 GEO. L. J. 269, 271 (2007) (noting this fact). Cf. Craig Allen Nard, *Deference, Defiance and the Useful Arts*, 56 OHIO ST. L.J. 1415 (1995).

138. See James F. Holderman, *Judicial Patent Specialization: A View from the Trial Bench*, 2002 U. ILL. J.L. TECH. & POL'Y 425, 427–28 (proposing this approach). As of mid–2007, this approach was among the items in the Patent Reform Act of 2007, HR 1908 (110th Congress, 1st Session), § 11.

139. See Chapter 10 for a detailed discussion of claim construction.

140. See Chapter 7 on the challenges surrounding § 103 analysis.

141. See, e.g. Craig Allen Nard and John F. Duffy, *Rethinking Patent Law's Uniformity Principle,* 101 Nw. L. Rev. ___ (2007) (forthcoming) (critiquing the Federal Circuit's development of the patent law, and proposing that multiple appellate courts should be responsible for reviewing patent cases).

142. See Benjamin and Rai, *Who's Afraid of the APA? supra* note 137, at 310 (noting this concern).

the PTO's regulatory role in the patent system is an important issue for the future.

3. Defining the Constituency

A third challenge facing the USPTO is not its substantive role in the patent system, but instead how the PTO itself *perceives* its role. That is, due to its key position in the patent system—for example, on the "front lines" of the overwhelming majority of patent analyses—the PTO has a complicated set of interests. One key question is to define the constituencies of the PTO, and understand how their incentives might impact the PTO's activities.

On the one hand, it seems unquestionable that the PTO, as a federal agency, is intended to serve the interests of the general public. On the other hand, the core (patent-related) mission of the PTO is to evaluate and process patent applications (in a timely and effective manner), which means that to no small degree, the PTO is providing services to a relatively small class of the public: patent applicants. These two groups are not necessarily aligned on matters of relevance to the patent law. While the general public wants patents to be issued only when they meet the standards established by Title 35, patent applicants have an interest in seeing their applications granted as quickly and easily as possible. Thus, this question is no small concern.

Taking the growth of patent pendency as an example illustrates the potential conflicts facing the PTO. All can agree that 1,000,000 pending applications is a bad circumstance; the proposed solutions, however, are likely to be very different. Patent applicants would encourage the PTO to ease the backlog by either relaxing or at least not increasing the standards for patentability. From a public policy perspective, however, this would be problematic, for the diminishment of the quality of issued patents would likely create a more negative scenario than the growth of pendency.

Therefore, the USPTO faces an ongoing challenge in navigating a path between two potentially conflicting constituencies—the general public and patent applicants—as it carries out its administrative tasks.

Chapter Five

DISCLOSURE REQUIREMENTS

It would be difficult to overstate the importance of patent law's disclosure requirements, which are contained in the first two paragraphs of 35 U.S.C. § 112. The patent's disclosure provides the foundation for the claims and hence for the scope of patent protection. On the one hand, § 112 requires the patentee to give the public "fair notice of what the patentee and the USPTO have agreed constitute the metes and bounds of the claimed invention."[143] On the other hand, § 112 requires the patentee to disseminate to the public information concerning the patented subject matter. This dual notice/dissemination function is intended to assist third parties from engaging in conduct that would infringe the patent while providing the interested public with information that enlarges the storehouse of knowledge, and may also help others to improve upon or design around the claimed invention—thus leading to further technological progress. As the Supreme Court stated in *Markman v. Westview Instruments, Inc.*, "[t]he limits of a patent must be known for the protection of the patentee, the encouragement of the inventive genius of others and the assurance that the subject of the patent will be dedicated ultimately to the public." Without establishing clear guideposts, "a zone of uncertainty which enterprise and experimentation may enter only at the risk of infringement claims would discourage invention only a little less than unequivocal foreclosure of the field, and [t]he public [would] be deprived of rights supposed to belong to it, without being clearly told what it is that limits these rights."[144]

The first two paragraphs of § 112 set forth four distinct disclosure requirements: (1) enablement; (2) written description; (3) best mode; and (4) definiteness. The first three requirements are found in the first paragraph of § 112, while the fourth is provided by the second paragraph. Section 112 reads as follows:

> The specification shall contain a [1] written description of the invention, and [2] of the manner of making and using it, in such full, clear, concise, and exact terms as to enable any person skilled in the art to which it pertains, or with which it is most nearly connected, to make and use the same, and [3] shall

143. *London v. Carson Pirie Scott & Co.*, 946 F.2d 1534, 1538 (Fed.Cir.1991).

144. 517 U.S. 370, 390 (1996).

set forth the best mode contemplated by the inventor of carrying out his invention.

The specification shall conclude with [4] one or more claims particularly pointing out and distinctly claiming the subject matter which the applicant regards as his invention. . . .[145]

Section 112 expressly states the specification includes the written description as well as the claims. But it should be noted that, although technically incorrect, the terms "written description" and "specification" are often used interchangeably. Moreover, regardless of which term is employed, common usage always distinguishes the claims from the specification or written description. So, it is common to hear patent attorneys, for example, refer to the specification (or "spec") and the claims.

The following sections address these four requirements.

A. Enablement

The enablement requirement demands the inventor provide sufficient information in the specification to enable a person skilled in the relevant art to make and use the claimed invention without "undue experimentation." The enablement requirement is often considered to be at the heart of the *quid pro quo* between the government and the inventor. In exchange for the powerful right to exclude, the inventor must inform the public how to make and use the invention so others, namely competitors of the inventor, can improve upon the claimed invention.[146]

Although § 112 does not expressly resolve the question of what time the disclosure must be enabling, the Federal Circuit has held that the sufficiency of the patent's disclosure "must be judged as of its filing date."[147] Information that is developed or becomes available after the filing date cannot be considered in determining disclosure sufficiency. Similarly, post-filing date developments that enable previously unknown variations cannot be relied upon to establish non-enablement.[148]

1. Enablement and "Undue Experimentation"

145. 35 U.S.C. § 112, ¶¶ 1 and 2.

146. This policy was first expressed by Chief Justice Marshall in *Grant v. Raymond*, 31 U.S. (6 Pet.) 218 (1832) (stating the enablement requirement "is necessary in order to give the public, after the privilege shall expire, the advantage for which the privilege is allowed, and is the foundation of the power to issue the patent").

147. See *In re Glass*, 492 F.2d 1228 (CCPA 1974).

148. See *United States Steel Corp. v. Phillips Petroleum Co.*, 865 F.2d 1247, 1251 (Fed.Cir.1989); *In re Hogan*, 559 F.2d 595 (CCPA 1977).

The test for compliance with the enablement requirement is whether "undue experimentation" is required to make and use the claimed invention. Under a standard of reasonableness, the Federal Circuit will consider several factors in determining whether undue experimentation is needed, including: (1) the quantity of experimentation necessary, (2) the amount of direction or guidance presented, (3) the presence or absence of working examples, (4) the nature of the invention, (5) the state of the prior art, (6) the relative skill of those in the art, (7) the predictability or unpredictability of the art, and (8) the breadth of the claims.[149] The experimentation must be "undue," implying that some routine experimentation—trial and error—is permissible.[150] Moreover, a patent specification need not disclose information within the knowledge of a PHOSITA.[151] But when nascent technology is involved, the breadth and depth of PHOSITA's database of knowledge is not as great. Therefore, given PHOSITA's almost exclusive reliance on the patentee's specification, nascent technology "must be enabled with a specific and useful teaching."[152]

The Federal Circuit's application of the enablement requirement to specific types of inventions has been recently explored by scholars. Some commentators, for instance, have suggested that the court has weakened the requirement for software inventions. They cite to *Northern Telecom, Inc. v. Datapoint Corp.*[153] as an example, wherein, in reversing a district court's finding of invalidity under § 112, the Federal Circuit stated that "computer language is not a conjuration of some black art; rather, the conversion of a complete thought ... into a language a machine understands is necessarily a mere clerical function to a skilled programmer."[154] As such, an

149. See *In re Wands*, 858 F.2d 731, 737 (Fed.Cir.1988). See also *Liebel–Flarsheim Co. v. Medrad, Inc.*, 481 F.3d 1371 (Fed.Cir.2007) (applying *Wands* factors).

150. See *W.L. Gore & Assocs. v. Garlock, Inc.*, 721 F.2d 1540, 1557 (Fed.Cir. 1983) ("Assuming some experimentation were needed, a patent is not invalid because of a need for experimentation. A patent is invalid only when those skilled in the art are required to engage in undue experimentation to practice the invention.").

151. See *Chiron Corp. v. Genentech, Inc.*, 363 F.3d 1247, 1254 (Fed.Cir.2004). See also *National Recovery Technologies v. Magnetic Separation Systems, Inc.*, 166 F.3d 1190 (Fed.Cir.1999) (stating "[t]he scope of enablement ... is that which is disclosed in the specification plus the scope of what would be known to one of ordinary skill in the art without undue experimentation"). Nonetheless, the specification must enable a PHOSITA "to practice the full scope of the claimed invention." Liebel–Flarsheim Co. v. Medrad, Inc., 481 F.3d 1371, 1378 (Fed. Cir. 2007).

152. Chiron, *supra*. See also *Genentech, Inc. v. Novo Nordisk, A/S*, 108 F.3d 1361, 1368 (Fed.Cir.1997).

153. 908 F.2d 931 (Fed.Cir.1990).

154. Id. at 942 (quoting *In re Sherwood*, 613 F.2d 809, 817 n.6 (CCPA 1980)). See *Dan L. Burk and Mark A. Lemley, Policy Levers in Patent Law*, 89 VA. L. REV. 1575 (2003) (criticizing Fed-

applicant need only disclose the functional characteristics of the software, and not necessarily the source code, algorithms, or flow charts. But the Federal Circuit has refrained from expressly stating that source code and information do not have to be disclosed to comply with the enablement requirement. To make that determination, the court will examine the level of skill in the particular art and the level of complexity of the software at issue. The court in *Northern Telecom* stated:

> Although there have been circumstances wherein production of the computer program was not routine, as in *White Consol. Indus.*, where the production of the program required one and one half to two person-years of work, such circumstances were not shown or suggested for the '375 invention. The great weight of the expert testimony on both sides was that a programmer of reasonable skill could write a satisfactory program with ordinary effort. This requires the conclusion that the programs here involved were, to a skilled programmer, routine.[155]

2. Enablement and Claim Scope

In addition to serving as an information dissemination device, the enablement requirement also requires the specification's enablement be commensurate with the scope of the claims. A patentee cannot claim more than he discloses.[156] An example of the claim-limiting function of the enablement requirement can be found in the famous case of *O'Reilly v. Morse*.[157] Samuel Morse, known principally for his work in telegraphy, owned a patent that had eight claims. The patent described "a new and useful apparatus for, and a system of, transmitting intelligence between distant points by means of electro-magnetism, which puts in motion machinery for producing sounds or signs, and recording said signs upon paper or other suitable material, which invention I denominate the American Electro–Magnetic Telegraph." The patent also set forth the instruments to carry out the transmission and the famous "Code."

eral Circuit's application enablement requirement to software inventions); Ronald J. Mann, *Do Patents Facilitate Financing in the Software Industry*, 83 TEX. L. REV. 961, 1026 (2005) (criticizing Federal Circuit's "steadfast determination . . . to weaken enablement standard for software").

155. 908 F.2d 942–43.

156. See *National Recovery*, *supra* note 151, at 1195–96 ("The enablement requirement ensures that the public knowledge is enriched by the patent specification to a degree at least commensurate with the scope of the claims. The scope of the claims must be less than or equal to the scope of the enablement.").

157. 56 U.S. 62 (1853).

Claims 1–7 covered the machinery for "transmitting intelligence" by employing principles of electromagnetism. But claim 8 was more expansive:

> I do not propose to limit myself to the specific machinery, or parts of machinery, described in the foregoing specifications and claims; *the essence of my invention being the use of the motive power of the electric or galvanic current, which I call electro-magnetism, however developed*, for making or printing intelligible characters, letters, or signs, at any distances, being a new application of that power, of which I claim to be the first inventor or discovered.[158]

The Supreme Court held claim eight invalid because the breadth of this claim was not commensurate with the specification. The specification did not disclose all uses and improvements of the motive power of the electric or galvanic current. In other words, Morse claimed "an exclusive right to use a manner and process which he has not described and indeed had not invented, and therefore could not describe when he obtained his patent." The Court was particularly concerned with stifling the ability or willingness of others to improve on Morse's invention. According to the Court:

> If this claim can be maintained, it matters not by what process or machinery the result is accomplished. For aught that we now know some future inventor, in the onward march of science, may discover a mode of writing or printing at a distance by means of the electric or galvanic current, without using any part of the process or combination set forth in the plaintiff's specification.... But yet if it is covered by this patent the inventor could not use it, nor the public have the benefit of it without the permission of this patentee. [W]hile he shuts the door against inventions of other persons, the patentee would be able to avail himself of new discoveries in the properties and powers of electro-magnetism which scientific men might bring to light.[159]

Morse demonstrates the importance of determining optimal claim scope.[160] The Court employed the enablement requirement to limit Morse to his first seven claims. The Court was very concerned that Morse's claim eight would easily capture future improvements

158. Emphasis added.

159. Id. at 113. See also *The Incandescent Lamp Patent*, 159 U.S. 465 (1895) (finding claims not commensurate with specification).

160. The process of interpreting claims is discussed in Chapter 9.

or alternatives that Morse did not invent or describe in his patent. But determining the proper scope of Morse's patent (or any patent) is very difficult. A court must ascertain how much improvement activity patentees such as Morse should be able to capture vis-à-vis improver-competitors. Morse, by all accounts, made a significant inventive contribution, something upon which the dissent focused in urging the majority to provide Morse with a broader proprietary scope. According to the dissent, Morse's invention was "not only 'a new and useful art,' but a most wonderful and astonishing invention, requiring tenfold more ingenuity and patient experiment to perfect it, than the art of printing with types and press, as originally invented."[161]

Cases such as *Morse* highlight that a critical and difficult balance must be struck regarding claim scope, keeping in mind patent law's incentives to invent and commercialize, coordinate improvement activity, and manage transaction costs (i.e., the costs associated with identifying owners of patents, negotiating licensing terms, etc.). A narrower claim scope may allow for more vigorous improvement activity and competition, but detract from the incentive to invent in the first instance or to see a product through to commercialization. A particular concern is that future innovators may unduly benefit from the first invention's disclosure that allows for enabling follow-on research and lower research costs. In contrast, a broader claim scope may lend itself to efficient coordination of improvement activity and allow a patentee to efficiently commercialize the claimed invention, but may limit competition and the pace of technologic advancement due to high transaction costs. Professor Suzanne Scotchmer succinctly captures the aforementioned scope dilemma when she writes, "the challenge is to reward early innovators fully for the technological foundation they provide to later innovators, but to reward later innovators adequately for their improvements and new products as well."[162]

B. Written Description

The first paragraph of § 112 provides that the "specification shall contain *a written description of the invention*." The written description requirement ("WD") serves a signaling function, per-

161. 56 U.S. at 134.

162. Suzanne Scotchmer, *Standing on the Shoulders of Giants: Cumulative Research and the Patent Law*, 5 J. Econ. Perspectives 29, 30 (Winter 1991). See also Robert P. Merges and Richard Nelson, *On the Complex Economics of Claim Scope*, 90 Colum. L. Rev. 839 (1990); Edmund W. Kitch, *The Nature and Function of the Patent System,* 20 J.L. & Econ. 265 (1977). Indeed, some commentators have argued that the Federal Circuit has weakened the enablement requirement for software inventions.

mitting third parties to ascertain whether the inventor had "possession" of the claimed invention at the time the original filing date. The policy underlying the requirement becomes clear when we consider the significance of the filing date. The filing date is deemed constructive reduction to practice, which is the applicant's latest date of invention. In this capacity, the WD requirement assures the applicant's claimed invention is entitled a particular priority date (date of invention) and "prevent[s] an applicant from later asserting that he invented that which he did not."[163]

The WD requirement is most often at issue when an applicant amends his claims during prosecution or files subsequent applications while trying to retain his original filing date.[164] For instance, in the well known case of *Vas–Cath Inc. v. Mahurkar*,[165] Mahurkar appealed a partial summary judgment ruling in favor of Vas–Cath that declared Mahurkar's two utility patents invalid as anticipated under 35 U.S.C. § 102(b). The district court concluded that Mahurkar's patents were not entitled to a filing date of an earlier filed application, which had the same drawings as the two patents, because the earlier-filed application did not provide a "written description of the invention." To avoid the § 102(b), Mahurkar needed to prove his two patents were entitled to an earlier priority date. The Federal Circuit reversed, and held that the drawings could provide enough support to satisfy the written description requirement.

The test for compliance with the WD requirement is "whether the disclosure of the application relied upon 'reasonably conveys to the artisan that the inventor had possession at that time of the later claimed subject matter.' "[166] But the specification does not have to disclose "*in haec verba*" (verbatim) support to satisfy the requirement.[167] For instance, in *Application of Wertheim*,[168] the patent claimed a particular range, "at least 35%," that was narrow-

163. *Amgen Inc. v. Hoechst Marion Roussel, Inc.*, 314 F.3d 1313, 1330 (Fed. Cir.2003).

164. See *In re Wright*, 866 F.2d 422, 424 (Fed.Cir.1989) ("When the scope of a claim has been changed by amendment in such a way as to justify an assertion that it is directed to a different invention than was the original claim, it is proper to inquire whether the newly claimed subject matter was described in the patent application when filed as the invention of the applicant. That is the essence of the so-called 'description requirement' of § 112, first paragraph.").

165. See *Vas–Cath Inc. v. Mahurkar*, 935 F.2d 1555 (Fed.Cir.1991) (stating "the cases indicate that the 'written description' requirement most often comes into play where claims not presented in the application when filed are presented thereafter").

166. *Ralston Purina Co. v. Far–Mar–Co, Inc.*, 772 F.2d 1570, 1575 (Fed. Cir.1985) (quoting *In re Kaslow*, 707 F.2d 1366, 1375 (Fed.Cir.1983)).

167. See *Cordis Corp. v. Medtronic Ave, Inc.*, 339 F.3d 1352 (Fed.Cir.2003).

168. 541 F.2d 257, 265 (CCPA 1976).

er than what was disclosed in the specification, which read "25% to 60%." The Court of Customs and Patent Appeals (CCPA) held that the specification supported the claim even though the precise range claimed was not exactly set forth in the specification.

This "possession" test suggests that the written description and enablement requirements are closely related,[169] and indeed they are. The key difference, however, is that written description focuses on what the applicant actually invented, proof of which requires a level of specificity in the specification that may be unnecessary for enablement purposes.[170] Thus, it is possible for a specification to enable a skilled artisan to make and use claimed subject matter yet fall short of satisfying the written description requirement. As the Court of Customs and Patent Appeals noted in *In re DiLeone*,[171] a specification that only discloses compound A with no broadening language "might very well enable one skilled in the art to make and use compounds B and C; yet the class consisting of A, B and C has not been described."[172] Thus, an applicant who later amends his claims to add B and C may comply with enablement, but not WD.

Interestingly, the WD requirement has recently been applied to *originally* filed, un-amended claims, particularly claims related to biotechnology inventions, where priority was not at issue. In *Regents of the Univ. of California v. Eli Lilly & Co.*,[173] for example, the University of California (UC) claimed in its '525 patent a cDNA sequence for vertebrate or mammalian insulin. But at the time the '525 was filed, UC only ascertained and isolated the cDNA sequence in rats, not humans. The Federal Circuit invalidated the vertebrate claims, holding that the '525 patent's disclosure of the cDNA sequence of the insulin gene of a rat did not adequately describe the cDNA sequence of the insulin gene of every vertebrate. According to the court, the WD requirement demands more than a functional recitation of the DNA; it demands a "precise definition" of the DNA itself "such as by structure, formula, chemical name, or physical properties," not a "mere wish or plan for obtaining the claimed chemical invention."[174] It should be noted that when ap-

169. The written description and definiteness requirements are also closely related. This relationship is explored in Section D of this chapter.

170. See *In re Ruschig*, 379 F.2d 990, 995 (CCPA 1967) ("[T]he question is not whether [one skilled in the art] would be so enabled but whether the specification discloses the compound to him, specifically, as something appellants actually invented.").

171. 436 F.2d 1404 (CCPA 1971).

172. Id. at 1405.

173. 119 F.3d 1559 (Fed.Cir.1997).

174. Id. at 1566. In *Enzo Biochem v. Gen–Probe Inc.*, 323 F.3d 956, 964 (Fed. Cir.2002), the court refined its *Eli Lilly* decision, noting that not all functional descriptions of genetic material run afoul of the WD requirement. The court stated that the WD requirement may be satisfied if it is known in the art that the disclosed function is sufficiently cor-

plied in a non-priority context, the WD requirement looks very close to the enablement requirement. Indeed, some Federal Circuit judges have expressed concern about this doctrinal overlap.[175]

C. Best Mode

The last phrase of the first paragraph of § 112 provides that the specification "shall set forth the best mode contemplated by the inventor of carrying out his invention." This provision requires the inventor to disclose not only how to make and use the claimed invention, but the *best* way to do so. The purpose of the best mode requirement is to prevent inventors from obtaining patent protection while concealing (perhaps as a trade secret) from the public preferred embodiments of their claimed invention.

The Federal Circuit has constructed a two-part test to determine compliance with the best mode requirement. The first part is subjective, and asks whether at the time of filing the inventor "knew of a mode of practicing his claimed invention that he considered to be better than any other." If indeed the inventor contemplated a "best mode," the second part of the test is objective and compares what the inventor knew with what was disclosed. The key inquiry is whether the disclosure is "adequate to enable one skilled in the art to practice the best mode or, in other words, has the inventor 'concealed' his preferred mode from the public?"[176] The critical time for complying with the best mode requirement is the filing date of the application. An inventor need not amend an application to add a best mode discovered after the filing date; best mode compliance for a continuation application will be measured as of the filing date of the original application.[177]

The subjective nature of the first part of the best mode inquiry

related to a particular, known structure. See also *Amgen Inc. v. Hoechst Marion Roussel, Inc.*, 314 F.3d 1313, 1332–33 (Fed.Cir.2003) (noting that *Enzo* "clarified" *Eli Lilly* holding); *Moba, B.V. v. Diamond Automation, Inc.*, 325 F.3d 1306, 1320 (Fed.Cir.2003) (same). For commentary on this issue, see Arti K. Rai, *Intellectual Property Rights in Biotechnology: Addressing New Technology*, 34 Wake Forest L. Rev. 827 (1999) (same); Janice M. Mueller, *The Evolving Application of the Written Description Requirement to Biotechnological Inventions*, 13 Berkeley Tech. L.J. 615 (1998) (same).

175. See *Enzo Biochem*, 323 F.3d at 976 n.2 (Rader, J., dissenting from denial of petition to rehear case en banc) ("When applied outside the priority context as a general disclosure doctrine, however, [written description] cannot depart from the enablement test without replacing it. Thus, the United States advocates application of the statutory standard of enablement.").

176. *Chemcast Corp. v. Arco Industries Corp. Inc.*, 913 F.2d 923, 927–28 (Fed.Cir.1990).

177. See *Transco Products Inc. v. Performance Contracting, Inc.*, 38 F.3d 551, 557–58 (Fed.Cir.1994).

was reaffirmed in *Glaxo Inc. v. Novopharm Ltd.*[178] Glaxo owned the '431 patent, which claimed a specific crystalline form of the compound ranitidine hydrochloride, a salt that Glaxo marketed as an antiulcer medication under the brand name Zantac. The inventor, Derek Crookes, developed a process to prepare crystalline ranitidine hydrochloride that was visibly different from all previous batches of the salt. Tests revealed that the new product was a crystalline form, or polymorph, of ranitidine hydrochloride. Glaxo referred to this polymorph as "Form 2." While Form 2 had superior qualities to other forms of the salt, it suffered from poor flow properties, which made it difficult to measure and dispense in pure form. To resolve this problem, Glaxo scientists, not including the inventor Crookes, developed an azeotroping process (a technique for separating a chemical mixture) to granulate the Form 2 salt, which facilitated the formation of Form 2 into a pharmaceutical composition. Glaxo decided not to disclose the azeotroping process in the specification, which Novopharm asserted violated the best mode requirement.

The Federal Circuit held there was no best mode violation because the inventor, Crookes, was not aware of the azeotroping process. The court stated that the "statutory language could not be clearer" in requiring that "the best mode of carrying out an invention, indeed if there is one, to be disclosed is that 'contemplated by the inventor.' "[179] The court elaborated on the knowledge requirement by contrasting best mode to enablement:

> That the best mode inquiry is grounded in knowledge of the inventor is even more evident upon contrasting the best mode requirement of § 112 with the enablement requirement of that section. Enablement looks to placing the subject matter of the claims generally in the possession of the public. Best mode looks to whether specific instrumentalities and techniques have been developed by the inventor and known to him at the time of filing as the best way of carrying out the invention.... The enablement requirement, thus, looks to the objective knowledge of one of ordinary skill in the art, while the best mode inquiry is a subjective, factual one, looking to the state of the mind of the inventor.[180]

Glaxo illustrates the difficulties that non-U.S. inventors and companies face in pursuing U.S. patents. The intricate best mode disclosure requirement is unique to the United States, but to establish a right of priority in the United States, an applicant filing

178. 52 F.3d 1043 (Fed.Cir.1995).

179. Id. at 1049.

180. Id. at 1050.

an application in another country must fully comply with U.S. disclosure requirements, including the best mode requirement. Thus, an applicant who intends to pursue patent rights in the U.S. must, before filing a priority application in his own country, predict what must be disclosed to comply with the U.S. best mode requirement.[181]

The second part of the best mode test is only employed if the first part is satisfied. Thus, assuming the inventor did contemplate a best mode, the inquiry turns to the adequacy of the disclosure—an objective analysis. In *Great Northern Corp. v. Henry Molded Products, Inc.*,[182] the Federal Circuit explored what does and does not have to be disclosed. Henry Molded was the owner of the '314 patent, which relates to elongated bar members—a so-called roll stacker—that may be used to support rolls of material such as cellophane or steel. The '314 patent disclosed a roll stacker made of molded pulp, an environmentally friendly material. Henry Molded sued Great Northern for patent infringement, and Great Northern in turn asserted that the '314 patent was invalid for failing to comply with the best mode requirement. According to Great Northern, the '314 patent does not disclose the use of diamond indentations, which provided strength to the molded pulp, in part to prevent it from collapsing while still wet. Henry Molded argued that the use of diamond indentations was a "production detail," and therefore, did not have to be disclosed.

The Federal Circuit acknowledged that production details do not have to be disclosed, but found that the use of diamond indentations was not a production detail. In making this determination, the court first discussed what is meant by a production detail:

> We have used the term [production detail] to refer to commercial considerations such as the equipment on hand, or prior relationships with suppliers that were satisfactory. Such commercial considerations do not constitute a best mode of practicing the claimed invention because they do not relate to the quality or nature of the invention. Our cases have also used "production details" to refer to details which do relate to the quality or nature of the invention but which need not be disclosed because they are routine, i.e., details of production about which those of ordinary skill in the art would already know. In this latter scenario, the omitted detail constitutes a

181. As the United States continues to trend toward harmonizing its patent laws, the best mode requirement is likely to be eliminated.

182. 94 F.3d 1569 (Fed.Cir.1996).

best mode but the disclosure is deemed adequate because the detail is routine.[183]

Thereafter, the court turned its attention to the diamond indentations, noting that whether the diamonds are a production detail requires a determination of whether the diamonds related to the claimed invention or to commercial considerations. The court found that the claimed invention, which was designed to support large diameter rolls, could not be produced without use of the diamond indentations. Therefore, the diamonds were not commercial considerations.[184]

The best mode requirement as applied to software inventions has provoked a good deal of commentary. The Federal Circuit has held that compliance with the best mode requirement demands that only the function of the software be disclosed, not the source code. The rationale underlying this arguably more relaxed application of best mode (and enablement) is that the source code is readily discernable from the software's functional aspects. In *Fonar Corp. v. General Electric Co.*,[185] the patent related to a technique of using magnetic resonance imaging (MRI) to obtain multiple image slices of a patient's body. GE argued that the patent failed to disclose two software routines that the inventors conceded were the best means they knew to accomplish the imaging. The court held that although the inventors had a best mode in mind regarding the routines, the disclosure of functional aspects of the software was sufficient to satisfy the best mode requirement:

> As a general rule, where software constitutes part of a best mode of carrying out an invention, description of such a best mode is satisfied by a disclosure of the functions of the software. This is because, normally, writing code for such software is within the skill of the art, not requiring undue experimentation, once its functions have been disclosed. It is well established that what is within the skill of the art need not be disclosed to satisfy the best mode requirement as long as that mode is described. Stating the functions of the best mode software satisfies that description test. We have so held previously and we so hold today. Thus, flow charts or source code listings are not a requirement for adequately disclosing the functions of software.[186]

183. Id. at 1572. For more discussion on production details, see *Wahl Instruments, Inc. v. Acvious, Inc.*, 950 F.2d 1575, 1579–81 (Fed.Cir.1991).

184. Id.

185. 107 F.3d 1543, 1549 (Fed.Cir. 1997).

186. Id. at 1549. See also *In re Hayes Microcomputer Prods., Inc. Patent Litigation*, 982 F.2d 1527, 1537–38 (Fed.Cir. 1992); *Moba B.V. v. Diamond Automa-*

D. Definiteness

Section 112, ¶ 2 requires that the patentee to particularly point out and distinctly claim the invention. This requirement, known as the "definiteness" requirement, serves two purposes. First, a distinctly drafted claim puts the public, particularly the patentee's competitors, on notice of where the patentee's proprietary boundaries reside, thereby informing the competitors of what activity may constitute infringement; and second, a distinctly drafted claim distinguishes the invention from the prior art; in other words, it sets forth exactly what the invention is. In the late 19th century, the Supreme Court captured the policies underlying the notice function:

> Accurate description of the invention is required by law, for several important purposes: (1) That the government may know what is granted, and what will become public property when the term of the monopoly expires; (2) That licensed persons desiring to practice the invention may know during the term how to make, construct, and use the invention; [and] (3) That other inventors may know what part of the field of invention is unoccupied.[187]

An assertion of indefiniteness "requires an analysis of whether those persons skilled in the art would understand the bounds of the claim when read in light of the specification,"[188] and the "degree of precision necessary for adequate claims is a function of the nature of the subject matter."[189] Thus, a patentee does not have to "define his invention with mathematical precision" to comply with the definiteness requirement;[190] indeed, terms of degree such as "substantially" are frequently and properly used in claim drafting.[191] In

tion, Inc., 325 F.3d 1306, 1325 (Fed.Cir. 2003) (Rader, J., concurring) (noting the low disclosure threshold for software inventions); *Robotic Vision Systems, Inc. v. View Engineering, Inc.*, 112 F.3d 1163, 1166 (Fed.Cir.1997) (stating "when disclosure of software is required, it is generally sufficient if the functions of the software are disclosed, it usually being the case that creation of the specific source code is within the skill of the art"). Some commentators have criticized the Federal Circuit's best mode jurisprudence in the software area. Indeed, two commentators suggested that the "Federal Circuit has essentially excused software inventions from compliance with the enablement and best mode requirements." Dan L. Burk and Mark A. Lemley, *Policy Levers in Patent Law*, 89 VA. L. REV. 1575, 1593 (2003).

187. *Bates v. Coe*, 98 U.S. 31, 39 (1878).

188. *Credle v. Bond*, 25 F.3d 1566, 1576 (Fed.Cir.1994).

189. *Miles Laboratories, Inc. v. Shandon Inc.*, 997 F.2d 870, 875 (Fed. Cir.1993).

190. *Oakley, Inc. v. Sunglass Hut Intern.*, 316 F.3d 1331, 1341 (Fed.Cir. 2003).

191. See *Andrew Corp. v. Gabriel Electronics, Inc.*, 847 F.2d 819, 821 (Fed. Cir.1988).

short, only claims "not amenable to construction" or "insolubly ambiguous" are indefinite.[192]

Reflecting this reluctance to demand precision is the case of *Bancorp Services, L.L.C. v. Hartford Life Insurance Co.*[193] Bancorp owned a patent related to a system for administering and tracking the value of life insurance policies in several accounts. All of the independent claims of the patent referred to "surrender value protected investment credits," and it is this phrase that Hartford asserted was indefinite. Hartford argued that the term was not defined in the patent and it did not have a commonly understood meaning by persons having ordinary skill in the art. The court agreed with Hartford that "surrender value protected investment credits" was not defined in the patent and Bancorp did not provide an industry publication that defines the term. Nevertheless, said the court, "the components of the term have well-recognized meanings, which allow the reader to infer the meaning of the entire phrase with reasonable confidence."[194] The court, citing the presumption of validity that accompanies issued patents, expressed a reluctance to invalidate claims that are not "insolubly ambiguous." For the court, a claim is not indefinite "if the meaning of the claim is discernible, even though the task may be formidable and the conclusion may be one over which reasonable persons will disagree."[195]

192. See *Datamize, LLC v. Plumtree Software, Inc.*, 417 F.3d 1342 (Fed.Cir. 2005) (finding claim term "aesthetically pleasing" indefinite).

193. 359 F.3d 1367 (Fed.Cir.2004).

194. Id. at 1372.

195. Id. at 1371 (quoting *Exxon Research & Eng'g Co. v. United States*, 265 F.3d 1371, 1375 (Fed.Cir.2001)). Another case where the court was reluctant to invalidate a claim based on indefiniteness was *Athletic Alternatives v. Prince Mfg.*, 73 F.3d 1573 (Fed.Cir.1996). There the court believed the claim language in question was subject to two interpretations, one narrower than the other, but both supported under § 112, ¶ 1. In this situation, the court adopted the narrower interpretation instead of invalidating the claim. The court based its decision on the notice function of the patent claim. That is, a PHOSITA faced with this scenario will know that a court will opt for a narrow interpretation.

Chapter Six

Novelty and Statutory Bars

A. Novelty

The novelty requirement precludes a patent from issuing on claimed subject matter that was not new at the time of invention. The novelty provisions pertain to third-party knowledge or activity prior to the applicant's date of invention. The reason for the novelty requirement is straightforward: it makes no sense to grant someone a patent on an invention that already exists or is in the public domain free for all to use. If an invention is not new, it is said to be *anticipated* by the prior art. Anticipation of a patent claim must be proven by showing that each limitation of the claim is present, either expressly or under principles of inherency,[196] in a single prior art reference.[197] Anticipation does not demand that the prior art be reduced to practice or actually created.[198] But the single anticipatory reference requirement must be sufficient to enable a person of ordinary skill in the art to make and use the claimed invention.[199] This requirement borrows from § 112, but instead of focusing on the claimed invention as enabling, anticipatory enablement asks whether the prior art is enabling.

The principal novelty section in Title 35 is § 102(a).[200] Section 102(a) states that a patent shall issue "unless the invention was known or used by others in this country, or patented or described in a printed publication in this or a foreign country, before the invention thereof by the applicant for patent." There are several terms in this section that need to be defined. We will explore four of

196. Inherency is discussed in Section A.4, *infra*.

197. *See Minnesota Mining & Mfg. Co. v. Johnson & Johnson Orthopaedics*, 976 F.2d 1559, 1565 (Fed.Cir.1992) (stating one reference rule); See *In re Bond*, 910 F.2d 831, 832 (Fed.Cir.1990) (same). Unlike a § 103 non-obviousness determination, it is impermissible to combine prior art references. See Chapter 7 for a discussion of non-obviousness,

198. See *Schering Corporation v. Geneva Pharmaceuticals, Inc.*, 339 F.3d 1373, 1380 (Fed.Cir.2003).

199. *Minnesota Mining. & Mfg. Co. v. Chemque, Inc.*, 303 F.3d 1294, 1301 (Fed.Cir.2002). Sometimes the Federal Circuit speaks in terms of putting a person of ordinary skill in the art "in possession" of the claimed invention. See *In re Donohue*, 766 F.2d 531, 533 (Fed.Cir. 1985).

200. There are two additional novelty provisions, §§ 102(e) and (g)(2), which will be discussed later in this section.

them: "date of invention," "known," "used," and "printed publication."

1. Date of Invention

The temporal focus in § 102(a) is before "date of invention". Thus, it becomes quite important to define when invention occurs. There are two important concepts relating to date of invention: reduction to practice and conception.

The date of invention is shown by proving *reduction to practice* (RTP). RTP can be either constructive, which occurs when a patent application is filed (assuming it satisfies § 112's disclosure requirements), or actual, which occurs when the inventor determines that the invention works for its intended purpose.[201] An inventor must have a contemporaneous appreciation that the invention worked for its intended purpose.[202] Whether actual testing is required to prove actual RTP depends on the character and complexity of the invention and the problem it addresses.[203] Indeed, some inventions may be "so simple and their purpose and efficacy so obvious that their complete construction is sufficient to demonstrate workability."[204] The benefit of proving actual RTP, rather than relying on constructive RTP (i.e., filing date) is obvious; the inventor may be able to antedate prior art that came into existence before his filing date but after actual RTP.

An inventor may be able to move the date of invention date back further if he can show he conceived of the invention prior to his reducing it to practice. Conception is a term of art in patent law that means the inventor had in his mind "a definite and permanent idea of the complete and operative invention, as it is hereafter to be applied in practice."[205] That is, the inventive idea was "so clearly defined in the inventor's mind that only ordinary skill would be necessary to reduce the invention to practice, without extensive research or experimentation."[206] Corroboration is required if the inventor is only relying on oral testimony to prove conception,

201. See *Cooper v. Goldfarb,* 154 F.3d 1321, 1327 (Fed.Cir.1998).

202. See *Estee Lauder Inc. v. L'Oreal, S.A.*, 129 F.3d 588, 594–95 (Fed.Cir. 1997); *Mycogen Plant Science, Inc. v. Monsanto Co.*, 252 F.3d 1306, 1314 (Fed. Cir.2001).

203. See *Mahurkar v. C.R. Bard, Inc.*, 79 F.3d 1572, 1578 (Fed.Cir.1996).

204. Id.

205. *Burroughs Wellcome Co. v. Barr Labs., Inc.*, 40 F.3d 1223, 1228 (Fed.Cir.1994).

206. Id. See also *Kridl v. McCormick*, 105 F.3d 1446, 1449 (Fed.Cir. 1997) ("Conception is the formation 'in the mind of the inventor of a definite and permanent idea of the complete and operative invention, as it is therefore to be applied in practice.' ").

rather than documentation or physical exhibits.[207] (As will be explored below in Section C, conception only comes into play when the inventor is trying to antedate a prior art reference or he was not the first to reduce the invention to practice.)

A case that nicely illustrates these concepts is *Mahurkar v. C.R. Bard.*[208] In this case, Mahurkar sued Bard for infringing the '155 patent, which claimed and disclosed that the double-lumen catheter simultaneously removes and restores fluids to the human body during a transfusion. The '155 patent was entitled to a filing date of October 24, 1983. Bard asserted that the '155 patent was non-novel, and therefore, invalid under § 102(a). Bard relied on a prior art publication known as the Cook catalog that was published in July 1983. Because the Cook catalog antedated Mahurkar's filing date of October 24, 1983, Mahurkar was forced to show he actually reduced the '155 claimed invention to practice or conceived of such prior to July 1983. The Federal Circuit held that Mahurkar, through a combination of corroborated oral testimony,[209] test results, and physical exhibits, successfully proved a date of invention prior to July 1983. For instance, Mahurkar showed that he constructed and tested several prototype catheters in his kitchen before July 1983.

One more point about proving date of invention is in order. Prior to the implementation of the North American Free Trade Agreement (NAFTA) and the international agreement on the Trade–Related Aspects of Intellectual Property Rights (TRIPS) of the General Agreement on Tariffs and Trade (GATT), inventive activity (i.e., conception and reduction to practice) outside of the United States could not be used to prove date of invention under 35 U.S.C. § 104. For example, prior to these international treaties, an inventor who filed his application in the U.S., but conceived in France and reduced the invention to practice in Germany would not be able to offer his conception and reduction to practice activity as proof of date of invention because it occurred outside the U.S. This form of economic nationalism has historically been a part of

207. See *Mahurkar*, 79 F.3d at 1577–78.

208. 79 F.3d 1572 (Fed.Cir.1996).

209. Regarding corroboration, the court stated:

> Dr. Mahurkar confidentially disclosed the catheter prototype tips of his '155 invention to Geoffrey Martin, President of Vas–Cath Inc. in 1981, and Brian L. Bates of Cook, Inc. Mr. Martin testified that he received the [a] prototype from Dr. Mahurkar in 1981. Dr. Mahurkar also produced a letter from Stephen Brushey, an employee of Vas–Cath, dated April 21, 1981, that described several of his catheters. Additionally, Dr. Mahurkar presented a letter from Brian L. Bates of Cook, Inc., dated October 23, 1981. In this letter, Cook was "impressed with the thought and technology which has gone into the fabrication of the prototype material." (*Id.* at 1578–79).

American patent law. (For instance, foreign applicants were not permitted to obtain U.S. patents under the 1793 Patent Act, and while foreigners could obtain patent rights under the 1836 Act, British citizens were required to pay $500 and other aliens had to submit $300.)

The later twentieth century witnessed a strong push towards patent harmonization. Consistent with this trend, § 104 was amended to permit patent applicants to rely on inventive activity in any NAFTA or World Trade Organization (WTO) member country.[210] The amendments to § 104 became effective for NAFTA and WTO countries on December 8, 1993 and January 1, 1996, respectively. Nonetheless, inventive activity occurring before December 8, 1993 in NAFTA countries and before January 1, 1996 in WTO countries cannot be used to prove date of invention. These dates are important because there remain thousands of patents that were issued prior to the creation of NAFTA and the WTO.

2. "Known or Used"

The words "known or used" are not as straightforward as they seem. Although not expressed in § 102(a), courts have held prior knowledge and use must be accessible to the public.[211] For instance, in *Woodland Trust v. Flowertree Nursery, Inc.*[212] the '440 patent, owned by Woodland Trust, related to a method and apparatus for protecting a plot of foliage plants from freezing, by establishing an insulating covering of ice over ground level watering. The patent was filed on July 1, 1983 and issued on August 16, 1988. Flowertree asserted the '440 patent was invalid under § 102(a) because the invention was known and used prior to 1983 by Joseph Burke and William Hawkins, who owned Flowertree. Four witnesses, including the son of William Hawkins, testified that the claimed invention was known (and is still known) and in use in the 1960s and 1970s in Flowertree's Florida nurseries, but the use was discontinued in

210. As of February 16, 2005, there were 146 member countries to the WTO. For more information about the WTO, *see* www.wto.org.

211. See, e.g., *Carella v. Starlight Archery,* 804 F.2d 135, 139 (Fed.Cir. 1986) (stating "the § 102(a) language 'known or used by others in this country' means knowledge or use which is accessible to the public"); P.J. Federico, *Commentary on the New Patent Act* (1954) reprinted in 75 J. Pat. Trademark Off. Soc'y 161, 178 (1993) (noting that § 102(a) excludes "private knowledge not known to the public"). When asking whether an invention was "known or used" under § 102(a), we are really asking whether the invention was "known or used" by someone other than the inventor. As Justice Story explained in *Pennock v. Dialogue*, 27 U.S. (2 Pet.) 1, 18 (1829), "known or used cannot mean knowledge or use by the inventor because that would prohibit him from the only means to obtain a patent."

212. 148 F.3d 1368 (Fed.Cir.1998).

the late 1970s. The court did not find this evidence persuasive because it failed to prove that knowledge and use of the claimed invention was publicly accessible prior to Woodland Trust's date of invention. In particular, the court cited the lack of physical evidence of prior knowledge, the relationship of the witnesses, and the extensive passing of time (20 years) between the asserted prior uses and trial.[213]

A similar scenario was present in *Gayler v. Wilder*,[214] a mid–19th century case replete with important policy statements. Wilder, the assignee of the patent, brought an action against Gayler and Brown for an alleged infringement of a patent right for the use of plaster of Paris in the construction of fire-proof chests. The claimed invention was developed by Daniel Fitzgerald, who received a patent in 1843. The defendants asserted the claimed invention was known since at least 1829 when James Conner developed a similar safe for his own use. There was evidence that Conner used the safe until 1838, but it was not known what became of Conner's safe and there was "nothing in the testimony from which it [could] be inferred that its mode of construction was known to the person into whose possession it fell."[215] The trial court instructed the jury:

> . . . that if Conner had not made his discovery public, but had used it simply for his own private purpose, and it had been finally forgotten or abandoned, such a discovery and use would be no obstacle to the taking out of a patent by Fitzgerald or those claiming under him, if he be an original, though not the first, inventor or discoverer.

The jury instruction and the Supreme Court assumed that Conner invented a safe substantially the same as Fitzgerald. The issue was whether the Conner safe was prior art for purposes of the Fitzgerald invention. Referring to the statutory language of § 102(a)'s predecessor, the Court answered in the negative:

> Upon a literal construction of these particular words, the patentee in this case certainly was not the original and first inventor or discoverer, if the Conner safe was the same as his, and preceded his discovery. But we do not think that this construction would carry into effect the intention of the legislature. . . . The clause in question [i.e., 102(a)'s predecessor] qualifies the words before used, and shows that by knowledge and use the legislature meant knowledge and use existing in a manner accessible to the public.

213. Id. at 1373.

214. 51 U.S. (10 How.) 477 (1850).

215. Id. at 495.

> For if the Conner safe had passed away from the memory of Conner himself, and of those who had seen it, and the safe itself had disappeared, the knowledge of the improvement was as completely lost as if it had never been discovered. The public could derive no benefit from it until it was discovered by another inventor. And if Fitzgerald made his discovery by his own efforts, without any knowledge of Conner's, he invented an improvement that was then new, and at that time unknown; and it was not the less new and unknown because Conner's safe was recalled to his memory by the success of Fitzgerald's.[216]

As *Gayler* points out, an invention may have been known or used by others, but such knowledge or use will not anticipate the claimed invention if the prior knowledge or use is not publicly accessible. Why? One reason may be the public policy favoring the person who is the first to disclose the invention to the public, even though someone else may have made the discovery earlier. Public disclosure is a firmly embedded policy underlying our patent system.[217] Recall, the Court in *Gayler* stated that "[i]t is the inventor here that brings [the invention] to [the public], and places it in their possession." In the eyes of our patent law, Conner, the prior user, did not contribute anything to the public; and although Fitzgerald's invention was not novel in the strictest sense of the word, he was the first to disclose the invention to the public, and "the law regards him as the first and original inventor."[218]

Cases such as *Woodland Trust* and *Gayler* show that public accessibility is an important concept under § 102(a) and serves one of patent law's functions. But some cases reveal that the extent of accessibility can be slight and still satisfy § 102(a) publicity requirement. For instance, in *Rosaire v. Baroid Sales Division*,[219] Rosaire and Horvitz held patents related to methods of prospecting for oil or other hydrocarbons. Rosaire, to whom Horvitz assigned his patented interest, testified that he and Horvitz invented these methods in 1936. The alleged infringers asserted that the patents were invalid under § 102(a) in the light of work performed by Mr. Teplitz for the Gulf Oil Corporation prior to 1936. Rosaire conceded that Teplitz conceived of the claimed methods before Rosaire and Horvitz, but argued that Teplitz's activity was not prior art because

216. Id. at 498.

217. Of course, public disclosure could be achieved by means other than filing a patent application. Indeed, § 102(a) bars patentability if the claimed invention were publicly accessible, regardless of means of disclosure. Thus, Fitzgerald would be denied a patent if Conner's safe, for which he did not receive a patent, were publicly known

218. Id. at 497.

219. 218 F.2d 72 (5th Cir.1955).

"Gulf did not apply for patent until 1939, did not publish Teplitz's ideas, and did not otherwise give the public the benefit of the experimental work."[220] Rosaire also emphasized that Teplitz's work was discontinued. Nevertheless, the trial court ruled, and the appellate court affirmed, that Teplitz's activity was invalidating prior art. According to the trial court, Teplitz's "work was a successful and adequate field trial of the prospecting method involved and a reduction to practice of that method. The work was performed in the field under ordinary conditions without any deliberate attempt at concealment or effort to exclude the public and without any instructions of secrecy to the employees performing the work."[221] The appellate court also addressed the fact that Teplitz and Gulf never published Teplitz's work, and therefore, failed to convey a benefit on society:

> [W]e find no case which constrains us to hold that where such work was done openly and in the ordinary course of the activities of the employer, a large producing company in the oil industry, the statute is to be so modified by construction as to require some affirmative act to bring the work to the attention of the public at large.
>
> While there is authority for the proposition that one of the basic principles underlying the patent laws is the enrichment of the art, and that a patent is given to encourage disclosure of inventions, no case we have found requires a holding that, under the circumstances that attended the work of Teplitz, the fact of public knowledge must be shown before it can be urged to invalidate a subsequent patent.[222]

To what extent knowledge or use must be publicly accessible is difficult to articulate, which perhaps explains why the Federal Circuit recently stated that its "decisions have not decided what degree of public accessibility is required."[223] We do know that it does not take much to satisfy the publicity requirement of § 102(a). The work of Teplitz in *Rosaire*, from a practical standpoint, was inaccessible to the public, yet it served as prior art. So the publicity requirement of § 102(a) is perhaps best understood as an absence of secrecy. In *Gayler*, Conner's knowledge of his invention was not complete enough to serve as prior art. The Court upheld the Fitzgerald patent even though he was not the first inventor and awarded him because he was the person who first disclosed the

220. Id. at 73.

221. Id. at 74.

222. Id.

223. *Aspex Eyewear, Inc. v. Concepts In Optics, Inc.*, 111 Fed.Appx. 582, 586 (Fed.Cir.2004).

invention to the public. Did Teplitz contribute anything more to society than Conner?

3. "Printed Publication"

Section 102(a) states that no patent shall issue if the invention was patented or "described in a printed publication" before the date of invention. (Section 102(b) also has the phrase "described in a printed publication.") The courts have held that public accessibility is the key to determining whether a reference constitutes a printed publication.[224] In particular, accessibility focuses on members of the public who are interested in the art, so that by examining the reference, one could make the claimed invention without further research or experimentation. There is no requirement that particular members of the public actually receive the printed publication or the information be disseminated.[225] And the public accessibility requirement may be satisfied even though access is "restricted to a part of the public, so long as accessibility is sufficient 'to raise a presumption that the public concerned with the art would know of' " the invention.[226]

An oft-cited case for the public accessibility doctrine is *In re Hall*, wherein the Federal Circuit held that a single doctoral thesis deposited and indexed in a German library was sufficiently accessible to be a "printed publication." But the "indexing" system in another frequently cited case, *In re Cronyn*, was not sufficient. In *Cronyn*,[227] the alleged printed publications were student theses filed in Reed College's main library and in the library of the particular department in which the student's work was done. The theses were listed on individual cards that displayed the student's name and the title of the thesis. The cards were filed alphabetically by the author's name, and the titles were sometimes descriptive. The Federal Circuit held the theses were not publicly accessible because, unlike *In re Hall*, the theses were not indexed, catalogued, or shelved in "a meaningful way."[228]

224. *In re Hall*, 781 F.2d 897, 899 (Fed.Cir.1986) ("The proponent of the publication bar must show that prior to the critical date the reference was sufficiently accessible, at least to the public interested in the art, so that such a one by examining the reference could make the claimed invention without further research or experimentation.").

225. See *In re Wyer*,655 F.2d 221, 226 (CCPA 1981) (Australian patent application kept on microfilm at the Australian Patent Office was "sufficiently accessible to the public and to persons skilled in the pertinent art to qualify as a 'printed publication,' " even though court did not determine whether there was "actual viewing or dissemination" of the patent application).

226. *In re Bayer,* 568 F.2d 1357, 1361 (CCPA 1978).

227. 890 F.2d 1158 (Fed.Cir.1989).

228. Id. at 1161. The court continued: "Although the titles of the theses were listed on 3 out of 450 cards filed

Although indexing is an important component to a finding of public accessibility, it is not a requirement. In *In re Klopfenstein*,[229] a slide presentation continuously displayed at a conference over a period of three consecutive days was held to be a printed publication. The court disagreed with appellant's argument that indexing or distribution is a requirement to qualify as a printed publication. According to the Federal Circuit, "the key inquiry is whether or not a reference has been made 'publicly accessible.' "[230] Because the presentation was temporary and not indexed or distributed, the court looked to other factors to determine whether the public accessibility requirement was met. These factors included the "[1] length of time the display was exhibited, [2] the expertise of the target audience, [3] the existence (or lack thereof) of reasonable expectations that the material displayed would not be copied, and [4] the simplicity or ease with which the material displayed could have been copied."[231] Duration of display, expertise of the audience, and ease with which the displayed material could be copied are important because they measure the likelihood the audience processed and retained the information. The court held these three factors lend themselves to a finding of public accessibility because the duration was for three consecutive days to a target audience comprised of persons having ordinary skill in the art, namely cereal chemists and agriculture, and of the 14 slides presented, only eight were substantive. Most of the eight, however, recited information already known in the art, leaving "only a few slides presented [that] would have needed to have been copied by an observer to capture the novel information presented by the slides."[232] Lastly, appellants neither took measures (e.g., non-disclosure agreements) to maintain the secrecy of the slide presentation, nor were there

alphabetically by author in a shoebox in the chemistry department library, such 'availability' was not sufficient to make them reasonably accessible to the public. Here, the only research aid was the student's name, which, of course, bears no relationship to the subject of the student's thesis."

229. 380 F.3d 1345 (Fed.Cir.2004).

230. Id. at 1348. As an example, the court provided that "a public billboard targeted to those of ordinary skill in the art that describes all of the limitations of an invention and that is on display for the public for months may be neither 'distributed' nor 'indexed'—but it most surely is 'sufficiently accessible to the public interested in the art' and therefore, under controlling precedent, a 'printed publication.' "

231. Id. at 1350.

232. Id. at 1351–52. The fact that there were slides is of significance. As the court noted regarding scientific presentations, "an entirely oral presentation at a scientific conference that includes neither slides nor copies of the presentation is without question not a 'printed publication' for the purposes of 35 U.S.C. § 102(b)," and "a presentation that includes a transient display of slides is likewise not necessarily a 'printed publication.' " Id. at 1349, n.4.

professional norms that would entitle appellants to a reasonable expectation that the displayed information not be copied.

4. Novelty Under §§ 102(e) and 102(g)(2)

a. Section 102(e) Prior Art

Under § 102(e), prior art may assume two forms. First, the American Inventors Protection Act of 1999 amended the patent code to require patent applications filed on or after November 29, 2000, to be published "promptly after the expiration of a period of 18 months from the earliest filed date."[233] Under section 102(e)(1), once a United States patent application is *published* in the United States, its prior art effect is triggered, and its effective date as a prior art reference reverts to its date of filing.

Of perhaps greater significance, however, is that an international patent application filed pursuant to the Patent Cooperation Treaty (PCT) that designates the United States and is ultimately published in English will have prior art effect under § 102(e)(1) as of its international filing date, which is the date the PCT application is filed. The international filing date is no more than 12 months from the priority date (i.e., the date of first filing in a PCT member country); and, under Article 21(2)(a) of the PCT, a PCT application is published 18 months after its priority date. Of note is that a PCT application, which satisfies the English language and designation requirements, can serve as a prior art reference as of its international filing date, even though an application is never subsequently filed in the United States.[234] Consider the following example:

> Inventor files a patent application in France on January 2, 2001. Ten months later, on November 2, 2001, he files a PCT application designating the United States and several other PCT member countries. The PCT application will be published on July 2, 2002, 18 months after the priority date (i.e., French filing date). If the PCT publication is in English, it can serve as prior art under § 102(e)(1) as of its international filing date (not the priority date), which is November 2, 2001, even

233. There are exceptions to the publication rule. The most noteworthy exception to publication is when an applicant certifies that the disclosed invention "has not and will not be the subject of an application filed in another country, or under a multilateral international agreement." 35 U.S.C. § 122(b)(2)(B)(i). Other exceptions are set forth in 35 U.S.C. § 122(b)(2)(A)(i)–(iv). Also, under 37 C.F.R. 1.219, an applicant can have his application published "earlier" than 18 months from the earliest filing date.

234. See 35 U.S.C. § 374.

though Inventor may choose not to file an application in the United States.

The other prior art scenario under § 102(e) relates to unpublished patent applications. Unlike "publicly accessible" prior art under § 102(a), an applicant may be the victim of so-called secret prior art under § 102(e)(2). If an application is not published, it will be kept confidential pursuant to § 122(a). But the confidential application may nevertheless serve as prior art under § 102(e)(2) if the application discloses the claimed subject matter and ultimately issues as a patent. The most famous case illustrating this doctrine is *Alexander Milburn Co. v. Davis–Bournonville Co.*,[235] which was codified in § 102(e)(2). In *Milburn*, plaintiff owned a patent on an invention related to a welding and cutting apparatus invented by Whitford. Plaintiff's patent was filed on March 4, 1911, this date being plaintiff's earliest date of invention. The patent issued June 4, 1912. The defendant asserted that plaintiff's patent is not novel in the light of a patent to Clifford that was filed on January 31, 1911. Clifford did not claim the same invention as the plaintiff, and therefore, the issue is not one of priority or who is entitled to a patent on the same invention. Rather, the Clifford patent is being used as prior art for what its specification discloses, namely the invention that plaintiff claims in his patent. The concern here is that no matter how painstaking a prior art search plaintiff would have conducted, Clifford's patent application would not have been discovered because patent applications by law, at that time, were held in confidence. (Thus, the Clifford patent was so-called secret prior art.) At the same time, it is clear that Whitford was not the first to invent the welding and cutting apparatus as claimed. The Supreme Court, in an opinion by Justice Holmes, held that Clifford was prior art:

> The delays of the patent office ought not to cut down the effect of what has been done. The description shows that Whitford was not the first inventor. Clifford had done all that he could do to make his description public. He had taken steps that would make it public as soon as the Patent Office did its work.... We see no reason in the words or policy of the law for allowing Whitford to profit by the delay and make himself out to be the first inventor when he was not so in fact.[236]

The delays of the patent office Justice Holmes was referring to were the same delays that are experienced today, principally administrative delays accompanying the examination of patent applica-

235. 270 U.S. 390 (1926).

236. Id. at 401.

tions. But these delays should not "cut down" the fact that the Clifford patent rendered Whitford's invention not novel. As Justice Holmes stated, "if Whitford had not applied for his patent until after the issue to Clifford, the disclosure by the latter would have had the same effect as the publication of the same words in a periodical."[237] Thus, under section 102(e)2, to serve as prior art, the patent application must ultimately issue.

Two important requirements for section 102(e)(2) prior art are worth emphasizing. First, unlike § 102(e)(1), prior art under 102(e)(2) is limited to United States patent applications that ultimately issue as patents. Consider the following: one month before inventor Y files her U.S. patent application, X files a patent application in France disclosing inventor Y's claimed invention. X eventually receives a French patent. X's French patent is not prior art as of its filing date. Why not? Given the policy of *Milburn*, what is the difference between X filing his application in France and Clifford filing in the U.S.? Certainly patent offices outside the United States have inefficiencies and experience delays. Is there a U.S. bias in § 102(e)(2), or are Congress and the courts simply unwilling, regardless of geography, to extend the secret prior art provision of § 102(e)? In *In re Hilmer* (*Hilmer I*),[238] the Court of Customs and Patent Appeals addressed the issue of whether foreign filing dates can be used for prior art purposes under § 102(e). The court answered in the negative, largely based on its discomfort with the secret nature of § 102(e) prior art and the *Milburn* case:

> What has always been pointed out in attacks on the *Milburn* rule, or in attempts to limit it, is that it uses, as prior knowledge, information which was secret at the time *as of which* it is used—the contents of U.S. patent applications which are preserved in secrecy, generally speaking, 35 U.S.C. 122. This is true, and we think there is some validity to the argument that that which is secret should be in a different category from knowledge which is public. Nevertheless we have the rule. However, we are not disposed to extend that rule, which applies to the date of filing applications *in the United States*, the actual filing date when the disclosure is on deposit in the U.S. Patent Office and on its way, in due course, to publication in an issued patent.[239]

The other important requirement to remember under § 102(e)(1) and (2) is that patents and published patent applications are prior art only for what they disclose, not what they claim.

237. Id. at 400.

238. 359 F.2d 859 (CCPA 1966).

239. Id. at 877.

If a previously filed patent application claims the same subject matter as a later filed application, § 102(g) would be applicable, because now we are talking about who *invented* first. Remember, it is the claims that define the property interest.

b. Section 102(g)(2) Prior Art

Section 102(g) serves dual purposes. Section 102(g)(1) is the basis for what is known as a priority dispute or "interference." When an application is made for a patent claiming the same subject matter as another application or an issued patent, an interference may be declared by the Patent and Trademark Office. An interference is a procedural mechanism to determine who is the first inventor (i.e., who has priority of invention). Priority and interferences are discussed in Section C, *infra*. Second, and for present purposes, section 102(g)(2) provides another novelty-based statutory foundation for "secret" prior art. Under this section, a patent will not issue if the claimed invention "was made in this country by another inventor who had not abandoned, suppressed, or concealed it" before the patent applicant's date of invention. Unlike § 102(g)(1), § 102(g)(2) contemplates a scenario whereby the first inventor has opted not to pursue a patent, but is making or using the claimed invention.[240]

Section 102(g)(2) does not render § 102(a) superfluous, even though the former incorporates public and secret knowledge and use. A basic distinction is that § 102(a) does not require continued use like § 102(g); that is, under § 102(g), the invention must not be abandoned, suppressed or concealed to act as prior art, whereas under § 102(a) only prior knowledge (as in *Rosaire*) will suffice for prior art purposes regardless of continued use.[241]

Prior art under § 102(g)(2) is thought of as "secret" because it is very difficult to uncover, particularly process-related inventions. But at what point does the secrecy of the prior use become so great as to constitute concealment under § 102(g)? The issue is whether inventive activity of the first inventor practiced under secrecy conditions can be used as prior art. Does it matter if the first

240. See *Corona Cord Tire Co. v. Dovan Chemical Corp.*, 276 U.S. 358, 384 (1928) (noting that first inventor who decides not to pursue a patent may still use his inventive activity as prior art); Thomson S.A. v. Quixote Corp., 166 F.3d 1172 (Fed. Cir. 1999).

241. See *International Glass Co. v. United States*, 408 F.2d 395, 402 (Ct.Cl. 1969) ("[U]nlike a defense under § 102(a) where prior knowledge and use must be 'public' at the time the patented invention is made, ... prior invention under § 102(g) requires only that the invention be complete, i.e., conceived and reduced to practice, and not abandoned, suppressed or concealed ...").

inventor commercially exploits the secret invention (e.g., a secret process from which products are sold)? The circumstances and rationale have yet to be fully developed by the courts and have been treated somewhat inconsistently. But there are certain distinctions that can be discerned from the case law. For instance, in *Gillman v. Stern*,[242] Judge Learned Hand wrote of non-informing public uses and secret uses,[243] and somewhat reluctantly embraced the notion that non-informing public uses, unlike secret uses, can serve as prior art.[244] Judge Hand held that the prior use in *Gillman* was not anticipatory prior art, because the prior user, Haas, "kept his machine absolutely secret from the outside world."

The non-informing public use/secret use distinction was applied by the Seventh Circuit in *Dunlop Holdings Ltd. v. Ram Golf Corp.*[245] Dunlop held a patent on a golf ball that was highly durable due to its covering, which was made of a synthetic material called "Surlyn" that possessed improved cut-resistant properties. Prior to Dunlop's invention date, Butch Wagner began experimenting with Surlyn-covered golf balls, which led to his developing a formula that adjusted the weight and texture of the golf ball cover. Although Wagner was careful to keep his formula secret, he sold thousands of golf balls covered with Surlyn. The accused infringer, Ram, asserted that Dunlop's patent was invalid in the light of Wagner's prior inventive activity.

The court, in an opinion by then Judge Stevens, held that Wagner's inventive activity was a non-informing public use, and therefore, invalidating prior art. Judge Stevens distinguished *Gillman* by noting that "Haas had used the machine in his own factory under tight security" and although "the output from the machine had been sold, the public had not been given access to the machine itself."[246] In contrast, "the evidence clearly demonstrates that Wagner endeavored to market his golf balls as promptly and effectively

242. 114 F.2d 28 (2d Cir.1940).

243. Id. at 31.

244. Id. Judge Hand was apparently dissatisfied with this distinction, but felt constrained by the statute. He wrote of non-informing public use and secret use:

> It is true that in each case the fund of common knowledge is not enriched, and that might indeed have been good reason originally for throwing out each as anticipations. But when the statute made any "public use" fatal to a patent, and when thereafter the court held that it was equally fatal, whether or not the patentee had consented to it, there was no escape from holding—contrary to the underlying theory of the law—that it was irrelevant whether the use informed the public so that they could profit by it.

245. 524 F.2d 33 (7th Cir.1975).

246. Id. at 36. The court also distinguished *Palmer v. Dudzik*, 481 F.2d 1377 (CCPA 1973), on the basis that *Palmer*, like *Gillman*, involved a machine and "the benefits of using the machine were not made available to anyone except the inventor." *Dunlop*, 524 F.2d at 37.

as possible.... Therefore, at best, the evidence establishes a non-informing public use of the subject matter of the invention."[247] The court concluded by offering an explanation as to why Wagner's non-informing public use forecloses a finding of concealment. The court explained that even though Wagner's use does not disclose his discovery to the public, he nonetheless gave "the public the benefit of the invention" by introducing the discovery into the marketplace, a fact that militates against a finding of suppression "in an economic sense."[248] Building upon the marketplace rationale, the court stated that despite a lack of express disclosure "when the article itself is freely accessible to the public at large, it is fair to presume that its secret will be uncovered by potential competitors long before the time when a patent would have expired if the inventor had made a timely application and disclosure to the Patent Office."[249] In a footnote to this point, the court stressed that it is likely that a competitor would soon reverse engineer the golf ball covering, revealing its "secret ingredient."

Thus, the fact that the prior use is practiced as a trade secret does not necessarily lead to a finding of suppression or concealment under § 102(g)(2).[250] The focus is on whether the prior user engaged in a non-informing public use or a secret use. Judge Stevens provided a rationale for the distinction between non-informing public uses and secret uses. First, by emphasizing the importance of introducing the product into the market, the court invoked patent law's Constitutional purpose of promoting the progress of the useful arts. Of course, an express disclosure would be more consistent with Article I, Section 8, Clause 8. And second, Judge Stevens stressed that by introducing the product, Wagner provided an impetus for competition and improvement activity. Is this second rationale consistent with patent law's incentive structure? Does it inadequately recognize the contribution of Dunlop, the second inventor in the tradition of Daniel Fitzgerald in *Gayler v. Wilder*—someone who made an express disclosure to society?

247. *Dunlop*, 524 F.2d at 36.

248. Id. at 37.

249. Id.

250. See *Friction Division Products, Inc. v. E.I. DuPont de Nemours & Co.*, 658 F.Supp. 998, 1013–14 (D.Del.1987), further proceedings, 693 F.Supp. 114 (D.Del.1988), aff'd, 883 F.2d 1027 (Fed. Cir.1989) (finding trade secret processes prior art and stating "[p]ublic use of the invention, without disclosing the details of it, is sufficient to negate any intention to abandon, suppress or conceal."). The *Friction Division* court relied heavily on *Dunlop Holdings*.

c. Prior User Rights

Section 102(g) was drafted in 1952 for the purpose of serving as an interference provision.[251] In the decades that followed, more thought was given to whether § 102(g) could also be used as a prior art provision, yet there remained a great deal of uncertainty regarding this issue. This uncertainty was settled in *Thomson v. Quixote*.[252] In footnote 3 of *Thomson*, the court acknowledged the historical ambiguity surrounding § 102(g)'s prior art status, and concluded that allowing § 102(g) prior art "makes sense" because "[t]he first to invent who has invested time and labor in making and using the invention—but who might have opted not to apply for a patent—will not be liable for infringing another's patent on that same invention, while the public will have benefited because the invention was not abandoned, suppressed or concealed."[253] Importantly, to serve as prior art under § 102(g)(2), the prior art invention must be made in the United States. In the second *Hilmer* decision, the Court of Customs and Patent Appeals held that inventive activity outside the United States cannot serve as patent-defeating prior art.[254] But foreign inventive activity can be used to obtain patent rights.

Footnote 3 of the *Thomson* case portrayed a zero-sum game. If the court decided not to use § 102(g) for prior art purposes, the first inventor becomes an infringer and the patent's validity is maintained. But, as the court held, employing § 102(g) allowed the first inventor to escape infringement, but the patent was rendered invalid. Each result is arguably unsatisfactory. In the first scenario, the first inventor is benefiting society by practicing the invention and should not be punished for failing to obtain a patent.[255] In the second scenario, the patentee is also benefiting society by disclosing the invention to the public and should not be punished based on secret prior art. To address this winner-take-all situation, some have proposed the United States should adopt prior user rights—a doctrine that forms a part of the European patent system as well as

251. See P.J. Federico, *Commentary on the New Patent Act* at 19, 35 U.S.C. § 1 *et seq.* (1954 ed., discontinued in subsequent volumes) (reprinted in 75 J. Pat. Trademark Off. Soc'y 161, 180 (1993)); Giles S. Rich, Speech to the New York Patent Law Association (Nov. 6, 1951).

252. 166 F.3d 1172 (Fed.Cir.1999).

253. Id. at 1176.

254. See *In re Hilmer*, 424 F.2d 1108 (CCPA 1970) (*Hilmer II*).

255. Judge Stevens in *Dunlop Holdings* took note of this unfairness, which was a factor in the court's finding that Wanger, the prior user, did not suppress or conceal the invention. According to the court, "the inventor is under no duty to apply for a patent; he is free to contribute his idea to the public, either voluntarily by an express disclosure, or involuntarily by a noninforming public use. In either case, although he may forfeit his entitlement to monopoly protection, it would be unjust to hold that such an election should impair his right to continue diligent efforts to market the product of his own invention." *Dunlop Holdings*, 524 F.2d at 37. *See also Checkpoint Systems,* 54 F.3d at 762 (no duty to apply for patent).

others.[256] Prior user rights are also seen as an important component of a first-to-file patent system, one that awards patent rights to the party who was the first to file a patent application. There are certain inequities in a first-to-file system because the first person to invent may not be the first to file a patent application. Giving the first inventor a prior user right is a way to ameliorate this concern.

A prior user right would permit the prior user to continue using the patented invention without fear of infringement, but would also preclude the prior use from invalidating the patent. What are the advantages and disadvantages of the first inventor defense, from both practical and policy viewpoints? A first inventor defense provides the court with the option of maintaining the patent's validity but exempts the prior user from infringement liability. The public continues to benefit from the prior user's domestic investment and commercialization of the invention *and* obtains an enabling disclosure of the claimed subject matter from the patent.

Are there any disadvantages to prior user rights? Would they encourage the first user to avoid disclosure via the patent system? Would the second inventor also avoid the patent system, having lost the possibility of exclusivity? Are prior user rights a form of compulsory licensing? Should they be *in personam*, non-transferable rights? Would prior user rights benefit larger corporations at the expense of small inventor patentees in that the former can use their resources to tie up the latter in court?

In 1999, the American Inventors Protection Act (AIPA) enacted the "First Inventor Defense Act of 1999," which is a mild form of prior user rights. Under newly created § 273,

> It shall be a defense to an action for infringement under § 271 of this title with respect to any subject matter that would otherwise infringe one or more claims for a *method* in the patent being asserted against a person, if such person had, acting in good faith, actually reduced the subject matter to practice at least 1 year before the effective filing date of such

256. By way of a representative European example, the prior use defense in the United Kingdom can only be invoked if the prior acts are committed in the UK and carried out in good faith. Moreover, the "defense is available where the defendant had done the acts or made 'serious and effective preparations' before the priority date of the patent to do an act which would be infringing if it was carried out after the grant of the patent." Lionel Bently and Brad Sherman, INTELLECTUAL PROPERTY 508–09 (2001). Importantly, the right can be assigned to an entity that acquires "that part of the business in the course of which the act was done or the preparations were made." Id. at 509. But licensees are excluded from enjoying the defense.

patent, and commercially used the subject matter before the effective filing date of such patent.[257]

Note that the defense is limited to method patents, but § 273(a)(3) limits the defense even more by defining "method" as "a method of doing or conducting business." The reason for limiting the defense to business method patents relates to the controversy surrounding the *State Street Bank* decision that expressly allowed for the patenting of business methods.

For purposes of § 102(g) prior art, it is important to note that § 273(b)(6) states that the first inventor defense "may be asserted only by the person who performed the acts necessary to establish the defense" and this defense, absent a transfer or assignment of patent rights, "cannot be licensed or assigned or transferred to another person." Furthermore, § 273(b)(9) states a "patent shall not be deemed to be invalid under §§ 102 or 103 of this title solely because a defense is raised or established under this section." Thus, establishment of the first inventor defense does not invalidate the patent-in-suit.

d. Patent–Obtaining v. Patent–Defeating Activity

The distinction between patent-obtaining and patent-defeating activity under §§ 102(e) and (g) can be confusing. It may be helpful to think of the following when encountering this issue. Section 102(e) may be used to defeat Inventor's patent rights when a third party's United States patent application *discloses* (but does not claim) the subject matter sought to be patented by Inventor prior to Inventor's date of invention. If the third party application is published, then § 102(e)(1) applies; if not published, then § 102(e)(2) applies. Under *Hilmer I*, § 102(e) cannot be used to defeat patent rights if the third party application that discloses Inventor's invention is based on a foreign filing date. If the application *claims* the same subject matter sought to be patented by Inventor, then § 102(g)(1) applies and an interference proceeding is invoked to determine who is entitled to the patent on the subject matter. In addition, under the Paris Convention,[258] a party who files a patent application in a member country can receive the benefit of an earlier filed application in another member country if the applicant

257. 35 U.S.C. § 273(b)(1) (emphasis added).

258. The full name is the Paris Convention for the Protection of Industrial Property, a treaty that was originally signed by 11 countries in 1883 with the purpose of harmonizing the patent laws of various countries. There are currently 169 member states. For more on the Paris Convention, see http://www.wipo.int/treaties/en/ip/paris/index.html.

filed the later application within 12 months after filing the original. For example, X files in France on January 10, 1996, and thereafter files in the U.S. on January 9, 1997. Under 35 U.S.C. § 119, X can claim January 10, 1996 as his priority date for obtaining patent rights.

Section 102(g)(2) may be used to defeat patent rights if Inventor's claimed invention was invented in the United States by a third party before Inventor's date of invention, and the third party does not file a patent application claiming the invention. If the third party does files a patent application, then § 102(g)(1) applies and an interference proceeding is invoked to determine who is entitled to the patent on the subject matter. Moreover, under § 104, a third party who files a patent application can use foreign inventive activity in WTO and NAFTA countries to obtain patent rights. But if a patent application is not filed, *Hilmer II* holds that § 102(g)(2) cannot be used to defeat patent rights if the inventive activity occurred outside of the United States.

B. Statutory Bars: Public Use and On–Sale Activity

Section 102(b) is a statutory bar provision. Under this section, even if the inventor is the first to invent something new, he may be statutorily barred from obtaining a patent if he or a third party does one of the following things: sell, offer for sale, publicly use, patent, or describe in a printed publication the claimed invention (or an obvious variation thereof) more than one year before filing a patent application. The one-year period is known as the grace period.[259] The date that is one year before the filing date is known as the *critical date*.

The Federal Circuit has identified four policies underlying § 102(b): (1) the policy "against removing inventions from the public which the public has justifiably come to believe are freely available to all as a consequence of prolonged sales activity;" (2) the policy "favoring prompt and widespread disclosure of new inventions to the public;" (3) the policy preventing "the inventor from

259. The patent code did not always provide for a grace period. The 1836 Act barred a patent if the invention was, "at the time of his application, in public use or on sale with consent or allowance" of the inventor. The 1839 Patent Act broke new ground and introduced a period of "grace" by providing that pre-application purchase, sale or use would not invalidate a patent "except on proof ... that such purchase, sale, or prior use has been for more than two years prior to such application for a patent." Note that the 1839 Act did away with the "consent or allowance" language. Two additional changes brought the statutory provision into its current form. In 1897, Congress specified that barring public use or sale must be "in this country," but added patenting and description in a printed publication anywhere as bars. In 1939, exactly a century after the two-year grace period was introduced, Congress lowered the period to one year.

commercially exploiting the exclusivity of his invention substantially beyond the" statutory term; and (4) the policy giving "the inventor a reasonable amount of time following sales activity (set by statute as one year) to determine whether a patent is a worthwhile investment."[260] Judge Learned Hand captured the essence of statutory bar policy when he wrote "it is a condition upon an inventor's right to a patent that he shall not exploit his discovery competitively after it is ready for patenting; he must content himself with either secrecy, or legal monopoly."[261]

There are two important differences between the novelty provisions and the statutory bar provision in § 102(b). First, statutory bars focus on activity of both the inventor and third parties, whereas novelty pertains only to third-party activity. Second, the critical date for statutory bars is one year before the application was filed; the critical date for novelty is the date of invention.

This section will explore the on-sale bar, public use, experimental use, and third-party activity that can lead to a statutory bar. Recall that what constitutes a "printed publication," which appeals in both §§ 102(a) and 102(b), was discussed under Novelty in Section A.3, *supra*. The term "printed publication" assumes the same meaning for both statutory sections.

1. On–Sale Bar

Section 102(b) prevents a patent from issuing (or invalidates a patent) if the claimed invention was on sale in the United States more than one year before the patent application was filed. There are several issues relating to the on-sale bar that need to be unpacked, including what constitutes a sale or offer to sell and at what development stage (e.g., reduction to practice, mere conception, or something in between) must the invention be before the one-year clock begins to run.

In *Pfaff v. Wells Electronics, Inc.*,[262] the Supreme Court set forth two conditions that must be satisfied before the on-sale bar applies. First, the product must be the subject of a commercial offer for sale. The Court viewed this condition as consistent within the control of the inventor because that "inventor can both understand and control the timing of the first commercial marketing of his

260. *General Electric Co. v. United States*, 654 F.2d 55, 61 (Ct.Cl.1981).

261. *Metallizing Engineering Co. v. Kenyon Bearing & Auto Parts Co.*, 153 F.2d 516, 520 (2d Cir.1946).

262. 525 U.S. 55 (1998).

invention."[263] In interpreting this condition, the Federal Circuit in *Group One, Ltd. v. Hallmark Cards, Inc.*,[264] applied traditional contract principles and held that "the offer must meet the level of an offer for sale in the contract sense, one that would be understood as such in the commercial community."[265]

The second condition is that the invention must be "ready for patenting." This condition relates to the requisite developmental stage of the invention at the time the offer for sale was made. The Court noted that "ready for patenting" can be shown by proof that "prior to the critical date the inventor had prepared drawings or other descriptions of the invention that were sufficiently specific to enable a person skilled in the art to practice the invention." Reduction to practice of the invention, although certainly satisfying the "ready for patenting" condition, is not required for application of the on-sale bar. And there needs to be more than just conception. Rather, "the inventor must be able to prepare a patent application, that is, to provide an enabling disclosure as required by 35 U.S.C § 112."[266] The inventor's confidence in whether the invention would work for its intended purpose is irrelevant in determining whether the invention is "ready for patenting."[267]

A few more points about the commercial sale condition are in order. The *Pfaff* case did not remove the requirement that the subject matter of the commercial offer for sale be something within the scope of the claim. In other words, for the on-sale bar to apply, the subject matter of the offer for sale must either fully anticipate or render obvious what is eventually claimed. For example, in *Sparton v. U.S.*,[268] the Navy entered into a contract with Sparton for the procurement of a sonobuoy, a device that is used to detect, locate, and classify the source of underwater sounds, such as those generated by submarines. Sparton subsequently submitted an Engineering Change Proposal ("ECP") to the Navy under its existing contract, proposing to incorporate dual depth operating capability into the existing sonobuoy by modifying the design. The sonobuoy device described in the ECP included a *multi-piece release plate* for either retaining or deploying the sonobuoy internal components within or from the sonobuoy housing. But shortly after the ECP was issued, Sparton developed, and later tested, a sonobuoy having

263. Id. at 67.

264. 254 F.3d 1041 (Fed.Cir.2001).

265. Id. at 1046–47.

266. *Space Systems/Loral, Inc. v. Lockheed Martin Corp.*, 271 F.3d 1076, 1080 (Fed.Cir.2001).

267. See *Robotic Vision Systems, Inc. v. View Engineering, Inc.*, 249 F.3d 1307, 1312 (Fed.Cir.2001) (stating "notably absent from [the *Pfaff*] test is a requirement that an inventor have complete confidence that his invention work will work for its intended purpose").

268. 399 F.3d 1321 (Fed.Cir.2005).

a *single-piece release plate*. This single-piece release plate performed better than previous release plates and was ultimately used in the sonobuoy Sparton delivered to the Navy under the contract.

Sparton obtained two patents that each contained claim limitations drawn to a single piece release plate for a sonobuoy. In 1992, Sparton filed suit in the Claims Court against the United States to recover money damages for the government's unlicensed use of Sparton's patented inventions. The government maintained that the patents were invalid under § 102(b)'s on-sale bar. The Federal Circuit held that the patented invention was not the subject of the offer for sale prior to the critical date. According to the court, the offer for sale was the submission of an ECP incorporating dual depth operating capability. The ECP included a description of the dual depth sonobuoy deployment design, including drawings. This description and drawings contained a release plate mechanism. But the court noted that:

> [t]he parties disagree as to what type of release plate was identified. The specific release plate mechanism proposed in the ECP is not relevant to our analysis, because, as the Claims Court noted, the government concedes, and the parties do not dispute, the release plate mechanism described in the [patents-in-suit] is not the release plate that was part of the original design proposed in the ECP; in other words, the ... contract does not include a release plate that meets the description of the release plate limitation of the claimed inventions. This fact is of utmost importance, as both sides agree that what was offered in the ECP was not the patented invention.... Accordingly, there is nothing to suggest that prior to the critical date of March 29, 1972, Sparton made an offer for anything other than dual-depth sonobuoys having the release plate mechanism described in the ECP.[269]

In addition, an inventor who sells his patent rights (assigns the invention) to raise money to develop and perfect the invention does not invoke the on-sale bar.[270] Also, a transfer of know-how requiring further development or an offer to license the patent does not

269. Id. at 1323.

270. See *Moleculon Research Corp. v. CBS, Inc.*, 793 F.2d 1261, 1267 (Fed. Cir.1986) (noting "an assignment or sale of the rights in the invention and potential patent rights is not a sale of 'the invention' within the meaning of 102(b).... Such a result comports with the policies underlying the on sale bar ... and with the business realities ordinarily surrounding a corporation's prosecution of patent applications for inventors."); *U.S. Electric Lighting Co. v. Consolidated Electric*, 33 F. 869, 870 (C.C.N.Y.1888) (stating "what was put on sale, if anything was, was the patent itself, and not the thing patented. The patent is the mere right to exclude others from practicing the invention. The invention itself is another thing.").

typically give rise to the on-sale bar because 102(b) bars a sale, not a license, of the patented product, and a license usually involves prospective activity.[271] Moreover, the Federal Circuit has held that there was no commercial offer for sale where the patentee had provided potential customers with samples of a product without providing any contract terms, because the patentee had not manifested sufficient willingness to be contractually bound under general contract law.[272]

Lastly, for the commercial offer condition of *Pfaff* to be satisfied, the court applies an objective standard with respect to whether the seller and buyer appreciated the nature of the subject matter being sold. The court has held, for instance, that "there is no requirement that the offer specifically identify the [claim] limitations.... Nor is there a requirement that [the patentee] must have recognized the significance of these limitations at the time of offer."[273] And in *Abbott Laboratories v. Geneva Pharmaceuticals, Inc.*,[274] the patentee argued that the on-sale bar does not apply because the seller did not have knowledge of the exact nature of the invention sold, and therefore, there was no conception. The Federal Circuit disagreed, stating "[i]t is well settled in the law that there is no requirement that a sales offer specifically identify all the characteristics of an invention offered for sale or that the parties recognize the significance of all these characteristics at the time of the offer."[275]

2. Public Use

The party asserting public use has the burden of showing that "the subject of the barring activity met each of the limitations of the claim, and thus was an embodiment of the claimed invention."[276] That is, what was ultimately claimed must have been the

271. See *In re Kollar*, 286 F.3d 1326, 1330–31 (Fed. Cir. 2002). ("We have held that merely granting a license to an invention, without more, does not trigger the on-sale bar") (citing *Mas–Hamilton Group v. LaGard, Inc.*, 156 F.3d 1206, 1216–7 (Fed.Cir.1998)).

272. See *3M v. Chemque*, 303 F.3d 1294 (Fed.Cir.2002). But see *In re Kollar*, 286 F.3d at 1331 n.3 ("We use the term 'license' here to refer to rights under a patent, not to describe a commercial transaction arranged as a 'license' or a 'lease' of a product or a device that may or may not have been patented. In certain situations, a 'license' in the latter sense of the word may be tantamount to a sale (e.g., a standard computer software license), whereupon the bar of § 102(b) would be triggered because '[t]he product is ... just as immediately transferred to the "buyer" as if it were sold'" (quoting *Group One*, 254 F.3d at 1053 (Lourie, J. concurring))).

273. *Scaltech Inc. v. Retec/Tetra,* 178 F.3d 1378, 1383 (Fed.Cir.1999).

274. 182 F.3d 1315 (Fed.Cir.1999).

275. Id. at 1318–19.

276. *Scaltech Inc. v. Retec/Tetra, L.L.C.,* 178 F.3d 1378, 1383 (Fed.Cir. 1999).

subject of what was used publicly or an obvious variation thereof.[277] This statement of law leaves many questions unanswered. For instance, what is public? Do a certain number of people have to use the claimed invention before the use is considered public? Does the nature of the invention have to be such that its use can be readily observed? How many of the patented articles have to be used to be public? The Supreme Court in *Egbert v. Lippmann*[278] addressed these questions. In *Egbert*, Samuel Barnes invented an improvement for corset springs between January and May 1855. There was testimony from Frances Barnes that Samuel presented her with a pair of corset steels sometime in 1855 and again in 1858. Frances wore the corset steels for more than two years under no obligation of secrecy and not for the purpose of experimentation. A patent was not applied for until 1866, 11 years after the date of invention and first use by Frances. The Supreme Court held the claimed invention was in public use, and therefore, invalid. The Court enunciated three important principles. First, "it is not necessary that more than one of the patented articles should be publicly used."[279] Second, "whether the use of an invention is public or private does not necessarily depend upon the number of persons to whom its use is known;" indeed, "the use and knowledge of the use may be confined to one person."[280] And third, the fact that some inventions cannot be seen "by the public eye" is irrelevant to a finding of public use.[281] The Court was particularly concerned that during the 11 years from date of invention to filing of the patent application, "the invention had found its way into general, and almost universal, use," and that "[i]t is fair to presume that having learned from this general use that there was some value in his invention, [Samuel Barnes] attempted to resume, by his application, what by his acts he had clearly dedicated to the public."

What if the invention is used for a commercial purpose, but under conditions of deliberate secrecy? Judge Hand faced this question in *Metallizing Engineering Co. v. Kenyon Bearing and*

277. See, e.g., *Juicy Whip, Inc. v. Orange Bang, Inc.*, 292 F.3d 728, 739 (Fed.Cir.2002) (holding the defendant did not provide an element-by-element comparison between the public use subject matter and the claimed limitations).

278. 104 U.S. 333 (1881).

279. Id. at 336.

280. Id.

281. The Court gave as examples "lever or spring, hidden in the running gear of a watch, or of a ratchet, shaft, or cog-wheel covered from view in the processes of a machine for spinning or weaving." See *New Railhead Mfg., LLC v. Vermeer Mfg. Co.*, 298 F.3d 1290, 1297 (Fed.Cir.2002) (invention related to a drill bit used for horizontal drilling of rock formations, and thus not visible when in use. Court stated " 'public use' does not necessarily mean open and visible in the ordinary sense; it includes any use of the claimed invention by a person other than the inventor who is under no limitation, restriction, or obligation of secrecy to the inventor.").

Auto Parts Co.[282] This case established that commercial exploitation by the inventor of a machine or process constitutes a public use even though the machine or process is held secret. As Judge Hand stated in this regard, an inventor "forfeits his right regardless of how little the public may have learned about the invention." Thus, a secretly used process, which is used to make a commercially exploited product, is a public use under § 102(b). The *Metallizing* principle is now well established.[283]

It is clear from the pertinent Supreme Court decisions that very little use and very little publicity are required to constitute a public use under 35 U.S.C. § 102(b). The Federal Circuit has adopted this minimalist approach.

3. Experimental Use

A court will not find public use if the inventor can show that he was engaging in experimental use. In other words, the experimental use doctrine allows a patent owner to negate public use. Experimental use is an important doctrine because it provides the inventor time to test and perfect his invention and to assess its utility in operation, which results in social benefits. When public use begins is usually straightforward, thus, most disputes relating to public use are really focused on whether the use was experimental—a more difficult determination.

The statutory language, including § 102(b) and its predecessors, does not expressly mention experimental use, but beginning with *Pennock v. Dialogue*[284] in 1829 and later *City of Elizabeth v. American Nicholson Pavement Company*,[285] the courts recognized that such use by an inventor should not create a bar. In *City of Elizabeth*, Nicholson invented and received a patent for a new type of wooden pavement. Upon being sued for patent infringement, defendant alleged that Nicholson's patent was invalid because the invention was in public use for six years before Nicholson applied for a patent. Nicholson admitted that he used his wooden pavement invention on Mill-dam Avenue in Boston for several years, but he argued that this use was experimental. The Court found while

282. 153 F.2d 516 (2d Cir.1946).

283. See *TP Laboratories v. Professional Positioners, Inc.*, 724 F.2d 965, 972 (Fed.Cir.1984) (public use may bar patent "if the inventor is making commercial use of the invention under circumstances which preserve its secrecy"); *Torpharm, Inc. v. Ranbaxy Pharmaceuticals, Inc.*, 336 F.3d 1322 (Fed.Cir.2003) (stating that if the patentee owner "sold improved Form 1 ranitidine made by the claimed process, then its process claims would be invalid under § 102(b) regardless of whether the process was disclosed to the public or not").

284. 27 U.S. (2 Pet.) 1 (1829).

285. 97 U.S. (7 Otto) 126 (1877).

Nicholson's use of the pavement "was public in one sense cannot be disputed," it was not public use as a matter of law. The Court emphasized that Nicholson exercised control over the experimentation, citing testimony that Nicholson would examine the pavement on a daily basis, ask questions, and walk over the pavement, "striking it with his cane." The Court also took note of the nature of the invention and the fact that durability was an important consideration:

> If durability is one of the qualities to be attained, a long period, perhaps years, may be necessary to enable the inventor to discover whether his purpose is accomplished.... Nicholson wished to experiment on his pavement. He believed it to be a good thing, but he was not sure; and the only mode in which he could test it was to place a specimen of it in a public roadway. He did this at his own expense, and with the consent of the owners of the road. Durability was one of the qualities to be attained. He wanted to know whether his pavement would stand, and whether it would resist decay.... The public had the incidental use of the pavement, it is true; but was the invention in public use, within the meaning of the statute? We think not.[286]

In *Lough v. Brunswick Corporation*,[287] the Federal Circuit enunciated several factors that form an experimental use determination. Steven G. Lough was a repairman for a boat dealership in Sarasota, Florida. While working on Brunswick inboard/outboard boats, he noticed that the upper seal assembly in the stern drives often failed due to corrosion. To address this problem, Lough designed a new upper seal assembly. He made six prototypes in 1986, installing one in his own boat and then gave the rest away. He gave one to a friend who installed it in his own boat. Lough also installed a prototype in the dealership owner's boat and one in the boat of a customer. And he gave the remaining two prototypes to friends who were employees at another marina, who in turn installed one on the boat of someone unknown to Lough. Lough received no compensation, but he also neither asked for nor received comments about the operability of the prototypes.

Upon receiving a patent, which was applied for on June 6, 1988, Lough sued Brunswick for patent infringement. Brunswick asserted that the claimed invention was in public use more than one year before the filing date of the patent. Lough responded the use was for experimental purposes. In finding that Lough's use was

286. Id. at 136.

287. 86 F.3d 1113 (Fed.Cir.1996).

not experimental, the court examined the following factors in addressing the public/experimental use issue: (1) "number of prototypes and duration of testing" (2) "whether records or progress reports were made concerning the testing" (3) "the existence of a secrecy agreement between the patentee and the party performing the testing" (4) "whether the patentee received compensation for the use of the invention" and (5) "the extent of control the inventor maintained over the testing." The court emphasized that the control factor "is critically important, because if the inventor has no control over the alleged experiments, he is not experimenting."

The court noted that the structure of experimentation may be formal for large corporations, which may employ contracts and written obligations, and informal for individuals and small entities. But the court emphasized that regardless of structure, the party asserting experimental use must "demonstrate the presence of the same basic elements that are required to validate any experimental program." Lough did not meet this threshold, according to the court. The court cited the lack of recordkeeping and inspection of the prototypes after they were installed. There was no follow-on involvement by Lough, and at least one prototype was installed in a boat that was later sold to strangers. Thus, said the court, "Lough did not maintain any supervision and control over the [prototypes] during the alleged testing." The court concluded:

> We do not dispute that it may have been desirable in this case for Lough to have had his prototypes installed by mechanics of various levels of skill in boats that were exposed to different conditions. Moreover, Lough was free to test his invention in boats of friends and acquaintances to further verify that his invention worked for its intended purpose; however, Lough was required to maintain some degree of control and feedback over those uses of the prototypes if those tests were to negate public use . . . Lough in effect provided the prototype seal assemblies to members of the public for their free and unrestricted use. The law does not waive statutory requirements for inventors of lesser sophistication. When one distributes his invention to members of the public under circumstances that evidence a near total disregard for supervision and control concerning its use, the absence of these minimal indicia of experimentation require a conclusion that the invention was in public use.[288]

A number of factors contributed to the holding in *City of Elizabeth*. First, the nature of the invention (road paving) was such

288. Id. at 1122.

that any testing necessarily had to be to some extent in public. Second, for similar reasons, the testing had to be for a substantial period of time (long-term durability being the object of road paving). Third, the section of paving was at least to some extent under the control of the inventor. It was laid on private land belonging to a company of which the inventor was an officer. Fourth, the inventor regularly inspected the road during the period of use to determine its performance. In *Lough*, experimental use was not found because the court thought that even allowing for Lough's lack of commercialization, recordkeeping and inventor control were lacking.[289] Indeed, control is the most important factor in an experimental use determination.

When does experimental use end? The Federal Circuit has stated on numerous occasions that experimental use ends when the invention is reduced to practice.[290] And a public use bar may not be overcome even though the invention may be later refined or improved. But the environment in which the invention will be used must be taken into consideration. For example, in the *City of Elizabeth*, Nicholson had to test the pavement in its intended environment. As Judge Hand noted in *Aerovox Corp. v. Polymet Mfg.*,[291] "it did not appear that Nicholson, the inventor, delayed for any other reason than to learn how well his pavement would wear; apparently it was already as good as he hoped to make it." In this regard, consider *Manville Sales Corp. v. Paramount Systems, Inc.*[292] In *Manville*, the court held that a public use bar did not arise when the inventor installed the invention, an iris arm luminaire pole, in a highway rest stop for testing in Wyoming winter weather conditions, even though the inventor previously tested the invention in an R & D center. According to the court: "Prior to its testing in the winter environment, there really was no basis for confidence by the

289. Compare *Lough* with *Lisle Corp. v. A.J. Mfg. Co.*, 398 F.3d 1306 (Fed.Cir.2005) (inventors gave four prototypes of invention to mechanics with no confidentiality agreement or restrictions on how mechanics could use prototypes. Nonetheless, the court found experimental use based, in part, on evidence of control, namely visits by inventors to mechanics every two to three weeks to obtain feedback).

290. See *SmithKline Beecham Corp. v. Apotex Corp.*, 365 F.3d 1306, 1318 (Fed.Cir.2004) (stating "after the invention is reduced to practice, further testing will not qualify as experimental use for purposes of negating a bar under § 102(b)"); *Continental Plastic Containers v. Owens Brockway Plastic Prods.*, 141 F.3d 1073, 1079 (Fed.Cir.1998) ("The policy behind experimental use negation is to give the inventor an opportunity to reduce the invention to practice.... Thus, experimental use can not occur after a reduction to practice."); *RCA Corp. v. Data Gen. Corp.*, 887 F.2d 1056, 1061 (Fed.Cir.1989) ("[E]xperimental use, which means perfecting or completing an invention to the point of determining that it will work for its intended purpose, ends with an actual reduction to practice.").

291. 67 F.2d 860, 863 (2d Cir.1933).

292. 917 F.2d 544 (Fed.Cir.1990).

inventor that the invention would perform as intended, and hence no proven invention to disclose.... When durability in an outdoor environment is inherent to the purpose of an invention, then further testing to determine the invention's ability to serve that purpose will not subject the invention to a § 102(b) bar."[293]

4. Third–Party Activity

Whether commercial use or on-sale activity by one without the knowledge or consent of the first inventor constitutes a statutory bar is a question of considerable difficulty. Certainly, the language of § 102(b) does not distinguish between inventor-applicant-patentee activity and third-party activity. Regarding third-party use or on-sale activity, Justice Story, in *Pennock v. Dialogue*,[294] stated that "it can scarcely be supposed, that the legislature had within its contemplation such knowledge and use."[295] And Judge Hand, in *Metallizing Engineering Co. v. Kenyon Bearing & Auto Parts Co.*,[296] distinguished between inventor and third-party "exploitation." Notably, *Pennock,* which was decided in 1829, was interpreting the 1793 Patent Act. The 1836 Act codified *Pennock* in this regard by stating that invalidating use must be conducted with the "consent and allowance" of the inventor.

Since the 1839 Act, which adopted a two-year grace period and eliminated the "consent and allowance" language of the 1836 Act, the Supreme Court, on numerous occasions, indicated that the statutory bar standards are the same, whether the use or sale is by the inventor or by someone else without the inventor's consent. For example, the Court in *Andrews v. Hovey*,[297] noted that Congress, by eliminating the "consent or allowance," intended to adopt a certain standard requiring only a calculation to time:

> It is very plain that under the act of 1836, if the thing patented had been in public use or on sale, with the consent or allowance of the applicant, for any time, however short, prior to his application, the patent issued to him was invalid. Then came § 7 of the act of 1839, which was intended as an amelioration in favor of the inventor, in this respect, of the strict provisions of the act of 1836 [because it introduced a two-year grace period]....
>
> [But by eliminating the "consent or allowance" language,] [t]he evident intention of congress was to take away the right

293. Id at 550–51.

294. 27 U.S. (2 Pet.) 1 (1829).

295. Id. at 19.

296. 153 F.2d 516 (2d Cir.1946).

297. 123 U.S. 267 (1887).

(which existed under the act of 1836) to obtain a patent after an invention had for a long period of time been in public use, without the consent or allowance of the inventor; it limited that period to two years, whether the inventor had or had not consented to or allowed the public use. The right of an inventor to obtain a patent was in this respect narrowed, and the rights of the public as against him were enlarged, by the act of 1839.[298]

Perhaps Congress felt comfortable eliminating the "consent and allowance" language because, as an off-setting measure, it introduced a two-year grace period, thus retaining a degree of protection for inventors from third-party activity, but one based on time, not consent.

The Federal Circuit has followed *Andrews*, stating that "it is of no consequence that the sale was made by a third party, not by the inventor."[299] But a third-party sale of a product made from the patented process is treated differently.[300] One could speculate that third-party use of the patented process is much more difficult to detect than use or sale of a product. Nonetheless, the rationale for this distinction remains controversial.

Of the four policies underlying § 102(b), only two are served by allowing third-party use to act as a statutory bar: the policy against removing inventions from the public that the public has come to enjoy, and the policy of encouraging prompt filings.[301] If you accept that these policies are furthered by recognizing legitimate third-party activity, ask if an exception should be made if the invention

298. Id. at 274.

299. See *Zacharin v. United States*, 213 F.3d 1366, 1371 (Fed.Cir.2000); *Abbott Laboratories v. Geneva Pharmaceuticals, Inc.*, 182 F.3d 1315 (Fed.Cir. 1999); *In re Epstein*, 32 F.3d 1559, 1564 (Fed.Cir.1994) ("The § 102(b) 'public use' and 'on sale' bars are not limited to sales or uses by the inventor or one under the inventor's control, but may result from activities of a third party which anticipate the invention, or render it obvious.").

300. See *Torpharm, Inc. v. Ranbaxy Pharmaceuticals, Inc.*, 336 F.3d 1322, 1327 (Fed.Cir.2003) (stating "if the product were sold by one other than the patentee, and the process of making remained unknown, then sale of the product would not pose a statutory bar to a claim on the process"); *W.L. Gore & Associates, Inc. v. Garlock, Inc.*, 721 F.2d 1540 (Fed.Cir.1983) (court indicated that secret third party use of a process was not a bar).

301. See *General Electric v. United States*, 654 F.2d 55, 61 (Ct.Cl.1981) (Stating that "Congress should be held to have concluded ... that the policy against removing inventions from the public domain and the policy favoring early patent filing are of sufficient importance in and of themselves to invalidate a patent where the invention is sold by one other than the inventor or one under his control"); *Baxter International, Inc. v. COBE Laboratories, Inc.*, 88 F.3d 1054, 1058 (Fed.Cir.1996) (noting "the most applicable policy underlying the public use bar here is discouraging removal from the public domain of inventions that the public reasonably has come to believe are freely available").

were stolen or pirated from the inventor and thereafter publicly used or sold. The courts have not recognized an exception. In *Lorenz v. Colgate–Palmolive–Peet Co.*, the court reasoned:

> There is not a single word in the statute which would tend to put an inventor, whose disclosures have been pirated, in any different position from one who has permitted the use of his process.... As Judge Coxe said in the *Eastman* case, isolated instances of injustice may result if the law be strictly applied, but the inventor's remedy is sure. He is master of the situation and by prompt action can protect himself fully and render the defense of prior public use impossible: "If (the inventor) fails to take so simple and reasonable a precaution why should it not be said that the risk is his own and that he cannot complain of the consequences of his own supineness?"

The Federal Circuit has cited *Lorenz* with approval. In *Evans Cooling Systems, Inc. v. General Motors Corp.*,[302] the patentee argued that the on-sale bar should not apply when its invention was misappropriated by the alleged infringer which led to an offer for sale by third parties not involved in the theft. The Federal Circuit disagreed. Quoting from *Lorenz*, the court held that a patent is barred when " 'a public use arises from any source whatsoever.' " But the court was particularly persuaded by the fact that the offers were made by innocent third parties:

> Even if we were to create an exception to the on sale bar such that third parties accused of misappropriating an invention could not invalidate a patent based upon sales by the guilty third party, GM correctly asserts that ... activities of third parties uninvolved in the alleged misappropriation raise the statutory bar, even if those activities are instigated by the one who allegedly misappropriated the invention.[303]

With respect to available remedies for the inventor, the courts have indicated that a state law cause of action for misappropriation of trade secrets can be pursued.

C. Priority of Invention

Priority of invention in the United States is based on a *first to invent* system. The United States is unique in this regard among industrialized nations in that other countries have adopted a *first to*

302. 125 F.3d 1448 (Fed.Cir.1997). See also *Abbott Laboratories v. Geneva Pharmaceuticals, Inc.*, 182 F.3d 1315, 1318 (Fed.Cir.1999) (stating "the statutory on-sale bar is not subject to exceptions for sales made by third parties either innocently or fraudulently").

303. Id. at 1453.

file system of priority.[304] Thus, a party who is second to file may nevertheless be awarded the patent if he can prove that he was the first to invent. The procedure by which priority is determined is called an *interference*, which is an *inter partes*, administrative proceeding within the PTO. As you can imagine, an interference can be quite convoluted and cumbersome given the potential for numerous dates and parties, different types of inventive activity, and potentially complex technology.

As a general rule, priority is awarded to the inventor who first reduced the invention to practice. But there are two exceptions to this rule: (1) an inventor who was the first to conceive the invention, but the last to reduce it to practice will be deemed the first inventor if he exercised *reasonable diligence* in reducing his invention to practice from a time just prior to when the other party conceived;[305] and (2) the second inventor will be awarded priority if the first inventor abandoned, suppressed, or concealed the invention. Conception and reduction to practice were discussed in Section A.1 of this chapter. This section will discuss abandonment and reasonable diligence.

1. Abandonment, Suppression, and Concealment

Consistent with the patent policy favoring prompt disclosure, an inventor who was the first to reduce to practice may lose his right of priority if he abandons, suppresses, or conceals his invention. There are two types of conduct that can give rise to a finding of abandonment, suppression, or concealment ("ASC"). The first is when an inventor withholds the invention from the public "designedly, and with the view of applying it indefinitely and exclusively for his own profit."[306] And second, when "abandonment, suppression, or concealment may be inferred based upon the prior inventor's unreasonable delay in making the invention publicly known."[307] With respect to inferential ASC, there are no set time

304. See the "Comparative Perspective" on first to file v. first to invent, *infra*.

305. See *Singh v. Brake*, 317 F.3d 1334, 1340 (Fed.Cir.2003). Section 102(g) states that: "In determining priority of invention under this subsection, there shall be considered not only the respective dates of conception and reduction to practice of the invention, but also the reasonable diligence of one who was first to conceive and last to reduce to practice, *from a time prior to conception by the other*" (emphasis added). Sometimes the party who was the first to reduce to practice is unable to prove prior conception. As such, the courts have held the second party to reduce to practice must show diligence from a time just prior to when the first party "entered the field."

306. *Fujikawa v. Wattanasin*, 93 F.3d 1559, 1567 (Fed.Cir.1996).

307. *Dow Chem. Co. v. Astro–Valcour, Inc.*, 267 F.3d 1334, 1342 (Fed.Cir. 2001).

limits on when an inventor must publicly disclose his invention having first made it. The Federal Circuit has stated that after first making the invention, an inventor's failure to file a patent application, describe the invention in a published document, or publicly use the invention within a "reasonable time" may result in ASC.[308] But mere delay is not enough.[309]

The Federal Circuit will also find abandonment when an inventor is "spurred" into acting. For example, in *Paulik v. Rizkalla*,[310] the court held that ASC could be negated by renewed inventive activity prior to an opposing party's effective date. In *Paulik*, the inventor, Paulik, reduced his invention to practice and submitted an invention disclosure to his employer's patent department. The patent department sat on the invention for four years. But just two months before Rizkalla's effective date (i.e., the earliest date to which Rizkalla was entitled), the patent department began working on a patent application and ultimately filed it with the PTO.[311] The court held that Paulik could rely on the date of renewed activity in his priority contest with Rizkalla even though four years transpired between the initial invention disclosure and the renewed activity. The court was concerned that denying Paulik the benefit of his renewed activity might "discourage inventors and their supporters from working on projects that had been 'too long' set aside, because of the impossibility of relying, in a priority contest, on either their original work or their renewed work."[312] But if Paulik did not renew activity until after Rizkalla's effective date, the court would have held Paulik was spurred into action, and therefore, abandoned the invention.

308. Id.

309. See *Checkpoint Systems, Inc. v. U.S. Int'l Trade Comm'n*, 54 F.3d 756, 761 (Fed.Cir.1995) (stating that "there is no particular length of delay that is per se unreasonable"). But see *Peeler v. Miller*, 535 F.2d 647, 654 (CCPA 1976) (in response to applicant's assertion that mere delay, without more, is not sufficient for a finding of abandonment, court stated a four-year delay is "prima facie unreasonably long" and the word "mere is a chameleonic word, whose meaning depends on the circumstances"). One commentator has observed that after *Peeler*, the "pattern" in court and PTO decisions "was to find abandonment, suppression, or concealment if, but only if, the delay period equaled or exceeded about two years." Chisum on Patents § 10.08[3][b][i], p. 10–284 (2005). The Federal Circuit has also frowned upon delay that results from commercial refinements or improvements not reflected in the patent application. See *Lutzker v. Plet*, 843 F.2d 1364, 1367 (Fed.Cir.1988).

310. 760 F.2d 1270 (Fed.Cir.1985).

311. Id. at 1271–72, 226.

312. Id. at 1275–76. See also *Fujikawa v. Wattanasin*, 93 F.3d 1559, 1562 (Fed.Cir.1996) (stating "right to rely on renewed activity for purposes of priority would encourage the decisionmaker to fund the additional research").

2. Diligence

Diligence only comes into play when a party is the first to conceive, but the second to reduce to practice. There is no "race of diligence" between or among the parties vying for a patent. Diligence of the party who was the first to reduce to practice is irrelevant. And diligence does not come into play if a party is both the first to conceive and first to reduce to practice.

The diligence requirement is one way to ask what Party A, for example, was doing given the fact that another party (Party B) was the second to conceive, but the first to reduce to practice. In this scenario, Party A can only be deemed the first inventor if he can show continuous and reasonable diligence from just prior to Party B's conception. The connection between Party A's conception and his reduction to practice must be "substantially one continuous act."[313]

While a showing of constant effort is not required to prove diligence, the inventor must account for the entire critical period. There are a variety of ways to prove diligence, including ongoing laboratory experimentation. The question is whether the applicant was pursuing his goal in a reasonable manner. Thus, periods of inactivity may not be fatal to a showing of diligence if the inventor has an adequate excuse such as (1) poverty or illness of the inventor, (2) obligations of the inventor's regular employment, or (3) excessive workload of the inventor's patent attorney.

3. Comparative Perspective: First-to-Invent versus First-to-File

Proving date of invention for novelty purposes (as well as for determining who is entitled to a patent between two or more parties claiming the same invention) is unique to American patent law. Other industrialized nations are first-to-file countries, meaning that their focus is on the *priority date* (not the invention date), which is the earliest *filing* date of the patent application. For example, in determining novelty, Article 54(2) of the European Patent Convention looks to the "state of the art ... before the *date of filing of the European patent application*" (emphasis added). And Article 29(1) of the Japanese Patent Law recites that one is entitled to a patent unless the invention was "publicly known in Japan or elsewhere *prior to the filing of the patent application*" (emphasis added).

The pros and cons of the first-to-invent vis-à-vis a first-to-file system have been well mined. Those who advocate a first-to-invent

313. *Mahurkar v. C.R. Bard, Inc.*, 79 F.3d 1572, 1577 (Fed.Cir.1996) (quoting *Christie v. Seybold*, 55 F. 69, 76 (6th Cir.1893)).

approach frequently assert that it provides a more equitable basis for giving rewards and fear a first-to-file system would unfairly burden the independent and small inventor class, those individuals who do not have the resources to file as promptly as larger entities. Moreover, first-to-invent advocates assert that a first-to-file system would encourage the filing of sloppy or incomplete patent applications. The first-to-file devotees point out that a vast majority of the interferences (i.e., procedural mechanism for determining priority of invention) are won by the party who was the first-to-file, and therefore, the U.S. already has a de facto first-to-file system. Moreover, they claim that a first-to-file system is cleaner in that one is not subjected to the burdens and arcana associated with proving date of invention.[314]

314. There has been much discussion in recent years among commentators and members of the bar as to whether the United States should adopt a first-to-file system. Indeed, legislation was introduced in 2005 that would change U.S. patent law to a first-to-file system. See, e.g., Mark A. Lemley and Colleen V. Chien, *Are the U.S. Patent Priority Rules Really Necessary?* 54 HASTINGS L.J. 1299 (2003) (conducting extensive empirical study of priority disputes); Dana Rohrabacher and Paul Crilly, *The Case for a Strong Patent System*, 8 HARV. J.L. & TECH. 263 (1995) (advocating first-to-invent system); Toshiko Takenaka, *Rethinking the United States First-to-Invent Principle From a Comparative Law Perspective*, 39 HOUS. L. REV. 621 (2002) (advocating that global patent systems harmonize to include first-to-file system).

Chapter Seven

NON-OBVIOUSNESS

In addition to being novel, an invention must be non-obvious to be patentable. Novelty and non-obviousness protect the public domain from claims of exclusivity. As the Supreme Court stated, both requirements "are grounded in the notion that concepts within the public grasp, or those so obvious that they readily could be, are the tools of creation available to all."[315] The non-obviousness requirement, embodied in § 103 of the patent code, lies at the heart of our patent system and, in many ways, is the most significant obstacle that a patent applicant faces. Indeed, it has been called the "final gatekeeper of the patent system."[316] Although the novelty requirement of § 102 casts a watchful eye over the public domain so as to prevent a patent applicant from obtaining protection on an invention that a person of ordinary skill in the art could retrieve from the technical literature or other available sources, the test for novelty is rather confining in that each and every limitation of the claimed invention must be present in a single prior art reference. The non-obviousness requirement, in contrast, casts a broader net and recognizes that the limitations of a claimed invention may be scattered throughout more than one prior art reference, and it would be "obvious" to a person of ordinary skill in the art to assemble these elements in the form of the claimed invention.

A. The *Graham* Framework

1. The Non–Obviousness Test

The seminal case in 20th century obviousness jurisprudence is *Graham v. John Deere Co.*[317] The *Graham* Court embraced the objectives of the drafters of § 103, and laid down a test for a non-obviousness analysis based on this section. The Court noted that while the issue of patent validity is one of law, several factual determinations must be made under § 103. For instance, the "[1] scope and content of the prior art are to be determined; [2] differences between the prior art and the claims at issue are to be

315. *Bonito Boats, Inc. v. Thunder Craft Boats, Inc.*, 489 U.S. 141, 156 (1989).

316. Robert Patrick Merges and John Fitzgerald Duffy, PATENT LAW AND POLICY (4th ed. 2007).

317. 383 U.S. 1 (1966).

ascertained; [3] and the level of ordinary skill in the pertinent art resolved. Against this background, the obviousness or non-obviousness of the subject matter is determined."[318] The Federal Circuit has emphasized to district courts the need for express findings of the *Graham* factual inquiries in an ordered and systematic manner.[319]

The *Graham* court conceded "[w]hat is obvious is not a question upon which there is likely to be uniformity of thought in every given factual context."[320] The drafters of § 103 knew that eliminating uncertainty was impossible. Thus, instead, they sought to cabin judicial discretion by establishing parameters and requiring a more demanding factual accounting. These goals, recognized by *Graham*,[321] did result in greater uniformity and predictability in the application of the non-obviousness standard. And due to the fact that judges continue to have flexibility when deciding non-obviousness, § 103 can serve as an important policy tool in promoting the progress of the useful arts.[322]

After establishing what has become know as the *Graham* test, the Court applied the test to the facts before it. The patent in *Graham*—the '798 patent—related to a spring clamp that was fixed to a plow and permitted plow shanks to be pushed upward when they hit obstructions in the soil, and then sprung the shanks back into normal position when the obstruction was passed over. The focus of the validity analysis was on the shank and the hinge plate. In the '798 patent, the shank ran underneath the hinge plate. A key prior art reference was the '811 patent. The principal difference between the '811 and '798 patents was that the shank position was above the hinge plate in the '811 patent. The Court found that reversing the shank position would have been obvious to a person having ordinary skill in the art.

318. *Id.* at 17.

319. See, e.g., *Specialty Composites v. Cabot Corp.*, 845 F.2d 981, 990 (Fed. Cir.1988) ("Failure to base an examination of obviousness on the factual findings required by *Graham* can require that the case be remanded for those findings to be made.... In this case the district court's discussion of obviousness does not mention *Graham*. It would have been preferable if the court had enumerated the *Graham* factors and systematically presented its analysis in terms of these factors.").

320. *Graham*, 383 U.S. at 17.

321. The Court noted that despite the subjectivity inherent in a § 103 determination, "[w]se believe that strict observance of the requirements laid down here will result in that uniformity and definiteness which Congress called for in the 1952 Act." *Id.*

322. See Section C, *infra*.

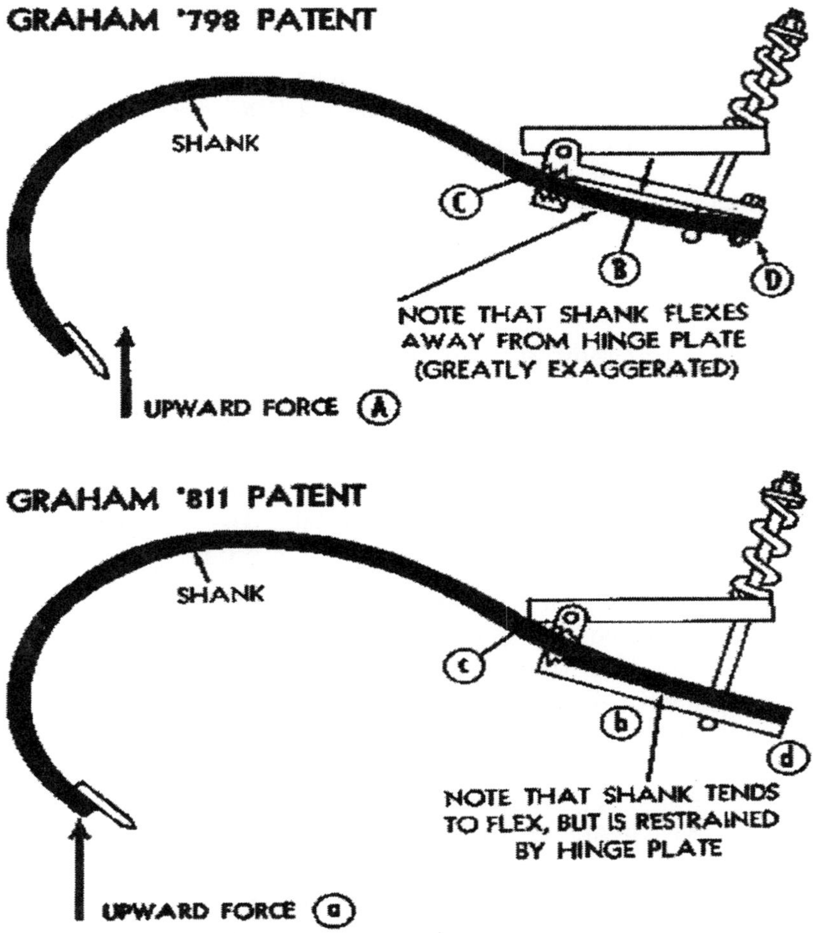

Figure 7–1. Comparison of '798 and '811 patents

2. Scope and Content of the Prior Art

The *Graham* decision requires the courts and the PTO to make several "factual inquiries." One of the most important of these factual determinations is the ascertainment of the "scope and content of the prior art." Prior art "scope" and "content" are different inquiries. With respect to scope, we have to make the initial foundational determination of what exactly *is* the prior art to which to compare the subject matter sought to be patented. Only when the prior art is identified for § 103 purposes can we then explore the content question, which focuses on what the prior art discloses.

a. Analogous and Non-Analogous Art

Under Federal Circuit law, there are two distinct tests for defining the scope of analogous art: (1) whether the art is from the same field of endeavor, regardless of the problem addressed and, (2) if the reference is not within the field of the inventor's endeavor, whether the reference still is reasonably pertinent to the particular problem with which the inventor is involved.[323]

In *KSR Int'l Co. v. Teleflex Inc.*,[324] the Supreme Court expressly stated the Federal Circuit erred "by holding that courts and patent examiners should look only to the problem the patentee was trying to solve."[325] According to the Court, the Federal Circuit "failed to recognize that the problem motivating the patentee may be only one of many addressed by the patent's subject matter."[326] Are these statements consistent with the analogous art doctrine expressed above? It is arguable that *KSR* expanded the scope of the analogous arts doctrine. In *In re Icon Health & Fitness, Inc.*, the Federal Circuit, quoting *KSR*, stated "familiar items may have obvious uses beyond their primary purposes," and that "any need or problem known in the field of endeavor at the time of invention and addressed by the patent can provide a reason for combining the elements in the manner claimed, *KSR*, 127 S.Ct. at 1742."[327]

But even prior to *KSR*, the Federal Circuit noted, "[a] reference is reasonably pertinent if, even though it may be in a different field from that of the inventor's endeavor, it is one which, because of the matter with which it deals, logically would have commended itself to an inventor's attention in considering his problem."[328] In short, "familiar items may have obvious uses beyond their primary purposes."[329] For example, *In re Paulsen*,[330] cited by *Icon Health*, involved prior art that was not within the same field of endeavor of the claimed invention. In *Paulsen*, the patent related to a portable computer contained within a compact metal case. A salient feature of the claimed invention was the "clam shell" configuration, in which the computer's display housing was connected to the computer at its midsection by a hinge assembly that enables the display to

323. *In re Bigio*, 381 F.3d 1320, 1325 (Fed.Cir.2004) (finding toothbrush art analogous to Bigio's hairbrush). See also *In re Clay*, 966 F.2d 656, 658 (Fed.Cir. 1992); *In re Deminski*, 796 F.2d 436, 442 (Fed.Cir.1986); *In re Wood*, 599 F.2d 1032, 1036 (CCPA 1979).

324. 127 S.Ct. 1727 (2007).

325. Id. at 1742.

326. Id. at 1742.

327. 496 F.3d 1374, 1380 (Fed. Cir. 2007).

328. *In re Clay*, 966 F.2d 656, 659 (Fed.Cir.1992).

329. *KSR*, 127 S.Ct. at 1742.

330. 30 F.3d 1475 (Fed.Cir.1994).

swing from a closed, latched position for portability and protection to an open, erect position for viewing and operation. In other words, the patent claimed the design of a "laptop" computer. During a reexamination, the PTO rejected the claims under § 103 in the light of references directed to hinges and latches used in a desktop telephone directory, a piano lid, a kitchen cabinet, a washing machine cabinet, a wooden furniture cabinet, or a two-part housing for storing audiocassettes. The Federal Circuit, in affirming the PTO, rejected the applicant's argument that the prior art was non-analogous. The court agreed that the prior art was not in the same field of endeavor as computers, but the "problems encountered by the inventors of the '456 patent were problems that were not unique to portable computers." *Id.* at 1482.

> They concerned how to connect and secure the computer's display housing to the computer while meeting certain size constraints and functional requirements. The prior art cited by the examiner discloses various means of connecting a cover (or lid) to a device so that the cover is free to swing radially along the connection axis, as well as means of securing the cover in an open or closed position. We agree with the Board that given the nature of the problems confronted by the inventors, one of ordinary skill in the art "would have consulted the mechanical arts for housings, hinges, latches, springs, etc."

b. Suggestion in the Art and Reasonable Expectation of Success

Recall that under § 102, an invention is anticipated if only a *single* prior art reference discloses each and every limitation of the claimed invention. That is, one cannot combine references under § 102. There is no such restriction imposed upon § 103. In fact, an overwhelming majority of obviousness decisions involve more than one prior art reference. But the Federal Circuit has made it perfectly clear on numerous occasions that before prior art references can be combined under § 103, the references as a whole must teach, suggest, or motivate ("TSM") a person of ordinary skill in the art to make the invention and, once made, would have a reasonable expectation of success ("RES").[331] This requirement

331. See *In re Vaeck*, 947 F.2d 488, 493 (Fed.Cir.1991). See also *Life Technologies, Inc. v. Clontech Labs, Inc.*, 224 F.3d 1320, 1326 (Fed.Cir.2000) ("It is axiomatic that the claimed invention is not obvious solely because it is composed of elements that are all individually found in the prior art."); *Symbol Technologies, Inc. v. Opticon, Inc.*, 935 F.2d 1569, 1576 (Fed.Cir.1991) ("We do not 'pick and choose among the individual elements of assorted prior art references to recreate the claimed invention,' but rather, we look for 'some teaching or

highlights another important distinction between a § 102 anticipation analysis and § 103; although § 103, unlike § 102, permits one to combine prior art references, one must have a reason to do so.

Because what is obvious today may not have been obvious yesterday, the Federal Circuit has repeatedly stated that the policy behind the TSM and RES requirement is to prevent the invalidation of claims based on hindsight.[332] The time frame for an obviousness determination is at the time the invention was made.[333] Once the person having ordinary skill in the art casts his mind back to the time of invention, he may consult several sources to satisfy the suggestion and RES requirement, including (1) "the references themselves;" (2) "knowledge of those skilled in the art that certain references, or disclosures in the references, are known to be of special interest or importance in the particular field;" and (3) "the nature of a problem to be solved, leading inventors to look to references relating to possible solutions to that problem."[334] The problem itself is particularly applicable to simple mechanical technologies.[335] Importantly, the applicant's disclosure cannot be a source of suggestion.[336]

suggestion in the references to support their use in the particular claimed combination.' ").

332. See, e.g., *McGinley v. Franklin Sports, Inc.*, 262 F.3d 1339, 1351 (Fed. Cir.2001) (stating "[t]he genius of invention is often a combination of known elements which in hindsight seems preordained" and "[t]o prevent hindsight invalidation of patent claims, the law requires some 'teaching, suggestion or reason' to combine cited references"); *In re Dembiczak*, 175 F.3d 994, 999 (Fed. Cir.1999) ("Our case law makes clear that the best defense against the subtle but powerful attraction of a hindsight-based obviousness analysis is rigorous application of the requirement for a showing of the teaching or motivation to combine prior art references.")

333. See 35 U.S.C. § 103. See also *Panduit Corp. v. Dennison Mfg. Co.*, 774 F.2d 1082, 1090–91 (Fed.Cir.1985) ("The test is whether the subject matter of the claimed invention would have been obvious to one skilled in the art at the time the inventions were made, not what would be obvious to a judge after reading the patents in suit and hearing the testimony."); *W.L. Gore & Assoc., Inc. v. Garlock, Inc.*, 721 F.2d 1540, 1553 (Fed.Cir.1983) ("It is difficult but necessary that the decision-maker forget what he or she has been taught at trial about the claimed invention and cast the mind back to the time the invention was made (often as here many years), to occupy the mind of one skilled in the art who is presented only with the references, and who is normally guided by the then-accepted wisdom of the art.").

334. *Pro–Mold & Tool Company v. Great Lakes Plastics, Inc.*, 75 F.3d 1568, 1573 (Fed.Cir.1996). See also *Ruiz v. A.B. Chance Co.*, 357 F.3d 1270, 1276 (Fed.Cir.2004) (noting that the warning against using hindsight "does not provide a rule of law that an express, written motivation to combine must appear in prior art references before a finding of obviousness. Stated differently, this court has consistently stated that a court or examiner may find a motivation to combine prior art references in the nature of the problem to be solved.") (citing *Pro–Mold*).

335. See *Ruiz*, 357 F.3d at 1276.

336. *Noelle v. Lederman*, 355 F.3d 1343, 1352 (Fed.Cir.2004) (quoting *In re Vaeck*, 947 F.2d at 493); *In re Dow Chem. Co.*, 837 F.2d 469, 473 (Fed.Cir. 1988).

An illustrative case is *Pro–Mold & Tool Company v. Great Lakes Plastics, Inc.*[337] *Neugebauer* obtained a patent on a card holder for baseball cards that was only slightly larger than a standard card, allowing the stored card to fit in a conventional storage box. Neugebauer developed his invention after conversations with his son, who collected sports cards and was familiar with the card market. The son stored his more valuable cards in individual card holders, but these individual holders did not fit in the conventional storage box the son was using, prompting the son to tape the individual cards to the top of the storage box so that the entire set could be stored together. The son's experience led Neugebauer to design the claimed invention, which had the advantage of allowing entire sets of cards to be stored together because cards that were held in an individual card holder could now be stored with cards that were not in such holders.

The Federal Circuit held that the claimed invention was obvious in the light of two prior art references, the "Squeeze Tite" card holder and the "Classic Line Thick and Thin" card holder. The Squeeze Tite was a two-piece holder with a friction fit cover. The Classic Line Thin holder was only slightly larger than the stored card and was designed to hold one card. The Federal Circuit stated that the Squeeze Tite contained all of the claim limitations except for size, but the Classic Line Thin holder, because it was only slightly larger than the stored card, provided this missing limitation.

Pro–Mold, Neugebauer's company and owner of the patent, argued that there was no reason to combine the two prior art references. The court disagreed, noting that the subject matter of the claimed invention provided the reason to combine. According to the court:

> The suggestion or motivation to combine these features of the prior art was ... evident from the very size of the card itself. Card holders larger than the card had already been designed, as evidenced at least by the Squeeze Tite card holder. On the other hand, a card holder no larger than necessary clearly was desirable in order to enable the card holders to fit in a set box.... Accordingly, the size of the card provided the motivation to combine the features of the prior art card holders and hence modify the size of the Squeeze Tite card holder so that it was not larger or smaller than the card, but rather substantially the size of the card.[338]

337. 75 F.3d 1568 (Fed.Cir.1996).

338. Id. at 1571. But the fact that a problem or need is identified does not necessarily make the claimed invention obvious. See *Cardiac Pacemakers, Inc. v. St. Jude Medical, Inc.*, 381 F.3d 1371, 1377 (Fed.Cir.2004) (stating that although identification of the problem can itself be the invention, "[r]ecognition of a need does not render obvious the

Another interesting scenario is when the claimed invention falls within a range disclosed by the prior art. In *Iron Grip Barbell Co., Inc. v. USA Sports, Inc.*,[339] the '015 patent, owned by Iron Grip Barbell, claimed a "weight plate for physical fitness including: a plate body formed with a central throughbore and . . . further formed with solely a triad of spaced apart elongated handle openings." The '015 patent, by disclosing three elongated openings near the periphery of the plate (a three-grip plate), addressed problems associated with grasping and transporting traditional weight plates that typically had only one hole in the center of the plate for insertion of a barbell. The '015 patent is depicted in Figure 3, below. USA Sports, a competitor of Iron Grip Barbell, also manufactured a three-grip plate and was sued by Iron Grip for patent infringement. USA Sports in turn asserted that the '015 is obvious in the light of the prior art, namely the '502 and '183 patents, which disclosed a two-grip and four-grip plate, respectively. See Figures 1 and 2.

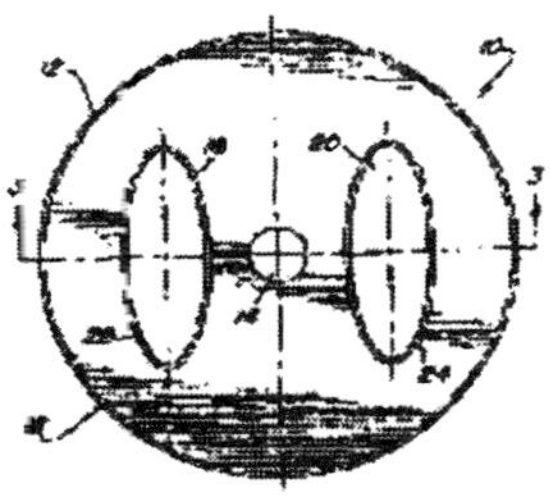

Fig. 1. The '502 patent's two-grip plate.

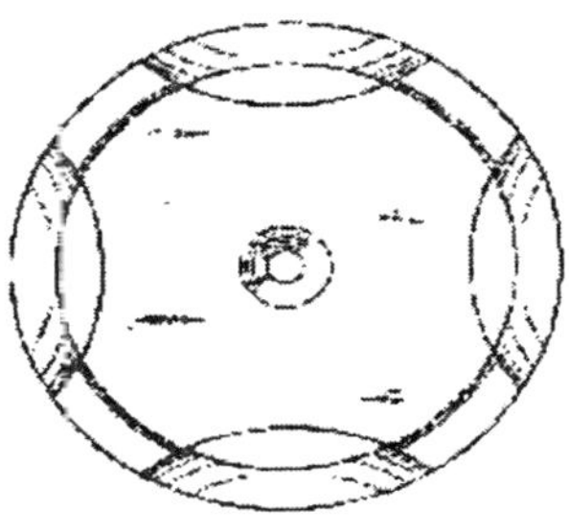

Fig. 2. The '183 patent's four-grip plate.

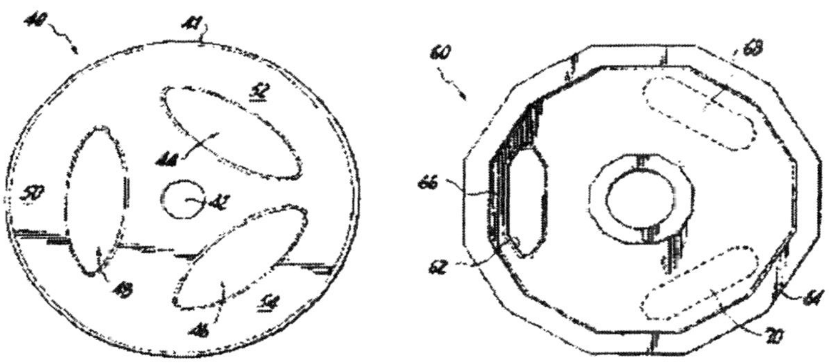

Fig. 3. The '015 patent's three-grip plates.

achievement that meets that need. There is an important distinction between the general motivation to cure an uncured disease (for example, the disease of multiple forms of heart irregularity), and the motivation to create a particular cure.").

339. 392 F.3d 1317 (Fed.Cir.2004).

The Federal Circuit held that because the claimed three-grip of the '015 patent fell within the range of the prior art patents, there is a presumption of obviousness.[340] This presumption could be rebutted if Iron Grip Barbell could show the prior art taught away from the claimed invention or the claimed three-grip plate possessed unexpected properties—something Iron Grip Barbell was unable to do.[341]

In May 2007, the Supreme Court issued its long-awaited opinion in *KSR v. Teleflex*,[342] which both returned the Supreme Court to the question of obviousness after a 31-year hiatus, and directly addressed the Federal Circuit's TSM analysis. The Supreme Court, as was widely expected in the bar, reversed the Federal Circuit's decision in that case, concluding that the invention-at-issue was obvious under 35 U.S.C. § 103. But while the outcome on the merits was as expected, the substance of the Court's opinion—which now represents the latest teachings concerning the analytic structure of the obviousness inquiry—might well have been a remarkable surprise to many.

The *KSR* dispute concerned relatively simple mechanical technology, and a clear example of technological innovation being driven by the adaptation of new technologies to solve old problems—both of these facts, of course, seem likely to have influenced the Supreme Court's interest in the case, as well as the result.

The patent-at-issue in *KSR* claimed an adjustable electronic gas pedal for an automobile with an electronic sensor attached to the pivot-point of the pedal, where the structural arrangement was such that the pivot-point of the pedal did not change as the pedals were adjusted to fit larger or smaller drivers. Figures 2 and 3 of the Engelgau patent are reproduced below.

The Engelgau invention at issue in *KSR* was a paradigmatic case of a combination invention. Each of the various components of the claims were widely known: the adjustable pedal, the ability to adjust without changing the pivot point, the use of an electronic sensor, and the mounting of the sensor on the pedal assembly itself. The parties to the case agreed, therefore, that whether the claim was obvious under 35 U.S.C. § 103—and thus the outcome of the

340. Id. at 1321–22.

341. Id. at 1322–23.

342. 127 S.Ct. 1727 (2007).

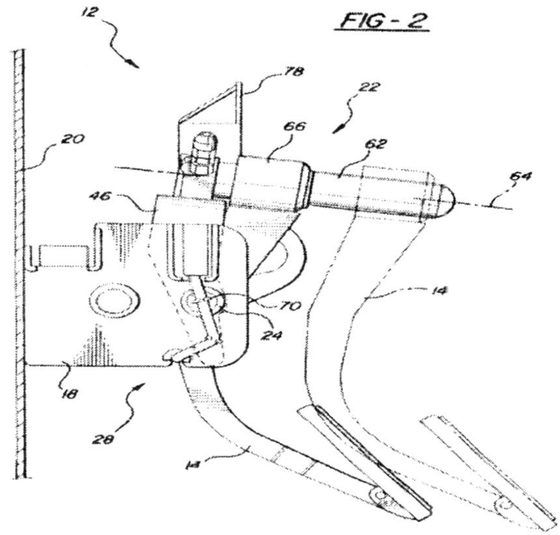

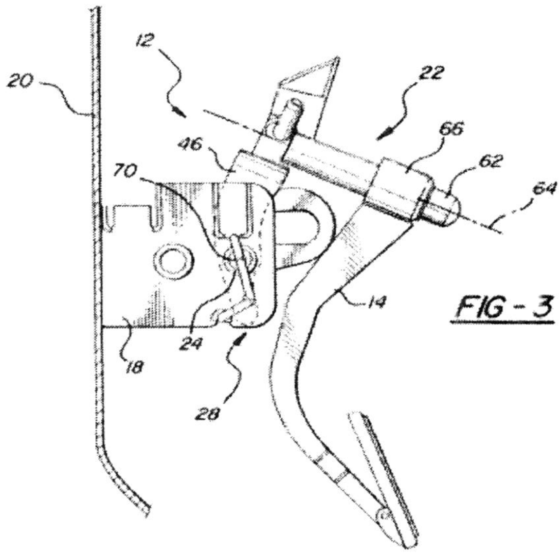

The Invention at Issue in
KSR v. Teleflex

case—turned on whether the prior art (which included pedals with and without electronic sensors, and with and without fixed pivot-points) provided enough detail to render the claim obvious to one of skill in the art.

The district court, on summary judgment, held the Teleflex patent obvious, reasoning that each element of the claim was fully disclosed by the relevant prior art, including the Asano patent, and that (1) the technological advance of the industry would suggest the combination of electronic sensors and adjustable pedals; and (2) certain aspects of the prior art suggested the solutions to the problems solved by the Teleflex patent.[343] Therefore, the district court held that under the Graham framework and the TSM test, the claim was obvious.

The Federal Circuit reversed, holding that although each element of the claim may well have been disclosed in the prior art, the district court's application of the TSM analysis was deficient:

> [T]he district court invalidated claim 4 of the '565 [Engelgau] patent on obviousness grounds without making "finding[s] as to the specific understanding or principle within the knowledge of a skilled artisan that would have motivated one with no knowledge of [the] invention to make the combination in the manner claimed." *Kotzab,* 217 F.3d at 1371. Under our case law, whether based on the nature of the problem to be solved, the express teachings of the prior art, or the knowledge of one of ordinary skill in the art, the district court was required to make specific findings as to whether there was a suggestion or motivation to combine the teachings of Asano with an electronic control in the particular manner claimed by claim 4 of the '565 patent. See *Kotzab*, 217 F.3d at 1371; *Rouffet*, 149 F.3d at 1357. That is, the district court was required to make specific findings as to a suggestion or motivation to attach an electronic control to the support bracket of the Asano assembly.[344]

Thus, the Federal Circuit reasoned, the lack of specific findings linking the teachings of the prior art to one another in the particular manner claimed by the Engelgau patent was fatal to the analysis. The court therefore held that summary judgment was inappropriate, and that further analysis of specific teachings (or lack thereof) was required.

The Supreme Court sided clearly with the district court, describing the Federal Circuit's analysis as "rigid." The Court stated

343. See *Teleflex v. KSR*, 298 F.Supp.2d 581 (E.D.Mich.2003).

344. Teleflex, Inc. v. KSR Intern. Co., 119 Fed.Appx. 282 at 288 (2005).

that the obviousness requirement demanded a flexible, "functional approach," a "broad inquiry." By contrast, noted the Court, the Federal Circuit's demand for specific findings linking the teachings of the prior art together in precisely the way the Teleflex patent claimed them was in conflict with the statute and prior case law, and could not stand.

This aspect of the opinion was widely anticipated; it was clear from the outset that the Court was unhappy with the formality and rigidity of the Federal Circuit's opinion in KSR. Indeed, when the case was argued in November of 2006, the Court expressed contempt for the Federal Circuit's development of the TSM standard. Several justices repeatedly commented that they could not understand it and one justice went so far as to call the standard "gobbledygook."[345] Indeed, the tone of the "colloquy" was so rough and so lopsided that it appeared to foretell a unanimous repudiation of the TSM standard and along with it the last twenty-five years of Federal Circuit jurisprudence.

And yet, this rhetoric is largely belied by the opinion that ultimately emerged in the case. After dispatching the Federal Circuit's analysis in the *KSR* case itself, the Court turned its attention to the TSM test:

> When it first established the requirement of demonstrating a teaching, suggestion, or motivation to combine known elements in order to show that the combination is obvious, the Court of Customs and Patent Appeals captured a helpful insight. As is clear from cases such as *Adams*, a patent composed of several elements is not proved obvious merely by demonstrating that each of its elements was, independently, known in the prior art. Although common sense directs one to look with care at a patent application that claims as innovation the combination of two known devices according to their established functions, it can be important to identify a reason that would have prompted a person of ordinary skill in the relevant field to combine the elements in the way the claimed new invention does. This is so because inventions in most, if not all, instances rely upon building blocks long since uncovered, and claimed discoveries almost of necessity will be combinations of what, in some sense, is already known.
>
> Helpful insights, however, need not become rigid and mandatory formulas; and when it is so applied, the TSM test is incompatible with our precedents. The obviousness analysis

345. See *KSR v. Teleflex*, 127 S.Ct. 1727 (2007), oral arg. transcript, at 41 ("[The TSM analysis] is gobbledygook. It really is, it's irrational.").

> cannot be confined by a formalistic conception of the words teaching, suggestion, and motivation, or by overemphasis on the importance of published articles and the explicit content of issued patents. The diversity of inventive pursuits and of modern technology counsels against limiting the analysis in this way. In many fields it may be that there is little discussion of obvious techniques or combinations, and it often may be the case that market demand, rather than scientific literature, will drive design trends. Granting patent protection to advances that would occur in the ordinary course without real innovation retards progress and may, in the case of patents combining previously known elements, deprive prior inventions of their value or utility. In the years since the Court of Customs and Patent Appeals set forth the essence of the TSM test, the Court of Appeals no doubt has applied the test in accord with these principles in many cases. There is no necessary inconsistency between the idea underlying the TSM test and the *Graham* analysis. But when a court transforms the general principle into a rigid rule that limits the obviousness inquiry, as the Court of Appeals did here, it errs.[346]

Importantly, the legal standard the Court embraces is little different from the TSM standard that the Federal Circuit has traditionally applied.[347] An example is the following language from *In re Dembizcak*:

> We have noted that evidence of a suggestion, teaching, or motivation to combine may flow from the prior art references themselves, the knowledge of one of ordinary skill in the art, or, in some cases, from the nature of the problem to be solved. . . .[348]

In *KSR,* after tracing this "[h]elpful insight[]" back forty-six years to a predecessor court to the Federal Circuit, the Supreme Court affirmed the basic principle of the TSM analysis, holding that predictable (and therefore obvious) extensions of prior art or arrangements of prior art elements are identifiable by considering "whether there was an apparent reason to combine known elements in the fashion claimed by the patent at issue."[349] Likewise, the Federal Circuit had routinely encouraged the broad use of prior

346. See *KSR*, 127 S.Ct. at 1732.

347. See, e.g., Lee Petherbridge and R. Polk Wagner, *The Federal Circuit and Patentability: An Empirical Assessment of the Law of Obviousness*, 85 Tex. L. Rev. 2051, 2059–64 (2007) (canvassing Federal Circuit jurisprudence).

348. *In re Dembiczak*, 175 F.3d 994, 999 (Fed.Cir.1999).

349. *KSR v. Teleflex*, 127 S.Ct. at 1741.

art information to test whether claims are obvious, i.e., from prior art references, the knowledge and skill of the ordinary artisan, or from the nature of the problem to be solved.[350] In its opinion, the Supreme Court embraced this practice, stating that an obviousness inquiry should consider the interrelated teachings of multiple patents, the knowledge and skill of the ordinary artisan, and the demands of the marketplace or design community. Indeed, the Supreme Court emphasized that this flexibility in reviewing the context of an invention was a key element of the obviousness analysis.

As importantly, the Supreme Court affirmed the Federal Circuit's traditional view that a decision maker must provide an explanation for how a combination of the prior art renders the patent claim at issue obvious.[351] Thus, according to the Supreme Court, "[t]o facilitate review, the analysis should be made explicit."[352] Finally, confirming the basic legal standard implemented by the Federal Circuit for more than two decades, the Court expressly rejected the primary argument opponents to the standard have long voiced—that the basis of the TSM analysis is somehow inconsistent with the guidance the Court long ago provided in *Graham v. John Deere*.[353]

While apparently agreeing in principle with the TSM analysis, the Supreme Court did see significant error in the Federal Circuit's opinion as a too-rigorous version of the TSM analysis.

> The first error of the Court of Appeals in this case was . . . [in] holding that courts and patent examiners should look only to the problem the patentee was trying to solve. The Court of Appeals failed to recognize that the problem motivating the patentee may be only one of many addressed by the patent's subject matter. . . .
>
> The second error of the Court of Appeals lay in its assumption that a person of ordinary skill attempting to solve a problem will be led only to those elements of prior art designed to solve the same problem. Ibid. The primary purpose of Asano was solving the constant ratio problem; so, the court concluded, an

350. See Petherbridge and Wagner, *Federal Circuit, supra* note 350, at Figure 8 (empirically demonstrating the Federal Circuit's use of a range of sources).

351. See *Dembiczak*, 175 F.3d at 999. See also, Petherbridge and Wagner, *Federal Circuit, supra* note 350, at 2063–64.

352. 127 S.Ct. at 1741 (citing federal circuit case law for the proposition).

353. Id. ("There is no necessary inconsistency between the idea underlying the TSM test and the *Graham* analysis.").

> inventor considering how to put a sensor on an adjustable pedal would have no reason to consider putting it on the Asano pedal. Ibid. Common sense teaches, however, that familiar items may have obvious uses beyond their primary purposes, and in many cases a person of ordinary skill will be able to fit the teachings of multiple patents together like pieces of a puzzle.... A person of ordinary skill is also a person of ordinary creativity, not an automaton....
>
> The Court of Appeals, finally, drew the wrong conclusion from the risk of courts and patent examiners falling prey to hindsight bias. A factfinder should be aware, of course, of the distortion caused by hindsight bias and must be cautious of arguments reliant upon ex post reasoning. Rigid preventative rules that deny factfinders recourse to common sense, however, are neither necessary under our case law nor consistent with it.[354]

Note that from a jurisprudential perspective the Court's approach in *KSR*—generally upholding the basis of the TSM test, while condemning its application in the instant case—allows the Court to emphasize its most critical advice regarding the law of obviousness. Namely, that when a decision maker examines the content and teachings of the prior art for information or knowledge that shows how and why a claimed combination would have been apparent to a person having ordinary skill in the relevant art, it should remain flexible in its approach. A decision on the question of obviousness, notes the Court, should reflect an effort to maintain a liberal view of sources of information relevant to an obviousness analysis and reflect a searching consideration of how prior art information may be understood and applied by a person of ordinary skill in the art. As stated by the Court, "The obviousness analysis cannot be confined by a formalistic conception of the words teaching, suggestion, and motivation, or by overemphasis on the importance of published articles and the explicit content of issued patents. The diversity of inventive pursuits and of modern technology counsels against limiting the analysis in this way."[355]

The ultimate influence of the Supreme Court's *KSR* opinion on the law of obviousness will need to await future interpretations and applications by the Federal Circuit. On its face, however, the opinion at least preserves the core principle that has driven the Federal Circuit's approach for decades. Moreover, the interim guidance from the Patent Office appears to take the same view.[356] Thus,

354. *KSR*, 127 S.Ct. at 1742–43.

355. Id. at 1731.

356. See USPTO, Memorandum Concerning *KSR v. Teleflex* (May 3, 2007).

while the Court's *KSR* opinion may well muddy the waters of patentability for a time as the early obviousness cases work their way to and through the Federal Circuit, it seems unlikely that the case will upset the settled expectations of the innovation community in the United States.

3. The Person Having Ordinary Skill in the Art

A § 103 obviousness determination is based on whether a person having ordinary skill in the art (sometimes referred to by the acronym "PHOSITA"),[357] to which the claimed invention pertains, would have found the claimed invention obvious. Thus, constructing a PHOSITA is of crucial importance. It is well settled that a PHOSITA is not the inventor or any particular expert or handyman, but rather a *hypothetical* person.[358] The level of skill, of course, is "ordinary," a term that was placed in § 103 to curb those judges who had a penchant for permitting too high of a skill level (e.g., extraordinary skill). The Federal Circuit has set forth several factors that should be considered in determining "ordinary skill," including (1) educational level of inventor and workers in the field, (2) types of problems encountered in the art, (3) prior art solutions to those problems, (4) rapidity with which innovations are made, and (5) sophistication of the technology.[359] Lastly, although the level of skill in the art is ordinary, the breadth of our hypothetical person is perfect. Complete knowledge of all pertinent art is presumed, despite that such a presumption is unrealistic. As Judge Learned Hand stated, "[w]e must suppose the inventor to be endowed, as in fact no inventor is endowed; we are to impute to him knowledge of all that is not only in his immediate field, but in all fields nearly akin to that field."[360]

The hypothetical artisan of ordinary skill pervades patent law. He is fundamental to not only an obviousness determination, but claim interpretation,[361] the disclosure requirements of § 112,[362] and prosecution history estoppel and the doctrine of equivalents.[363]

357. The acronym, PHOSITA, was coined by Cyril A. Soans in his article *Some Absurd Presumptions in Patent Cases*, 10 IDEA 433, 436 (1966). Soans referred to the person having ordinary skill in the art as "Mr. Phosita."

358. See *Kimberly–Clark Corp. v. Johnson & Johnson Co.*, 745 F.2d 1437, 1453–54 (Fed.Cir.1984) (nice discussion of person of ordinary skill in the art).

359. See *Environmental Designs, Ltd. v. Union Oil Co.*, 713 F.2d 693, 696 (Fed.Cir.1983). See also *Custom Accessories, Inc. v. Jeffrey–Allan Industries, Inc.*, 807 F.2d 955, 963 (Fed.Cir.1986) (stating "[n]ot all such factors may be present in every case, and one or more of them may predominate").

360. *International Cellucotton Prod. Co. v. Sterilek Co.*, 94 F.2d 10, 13 (2d Cir.1938).

361. See Chapter 9.

362. See Chapter 5.

363. See Chapter 10.

4. Objective Indicia of Non–Obviousness: Secondary Considerations

The Supreme Court in *Graham* stated that in addition to factual inquiries a court is to undertake in a § 103 analysis, a court may also look to so-called "secondary considerations" such as "commercial success, long-felt but unsolved needs, failure of others . . . to give light to the circumstances surrounding the origin of the subject matter sought to be patented."[364] The Court further noted that these secondary considerations, which are thought to be objective in nature, "focus our attention on economic and motivational rather than technical issues and are, therefore more susceptible of judicial treatment than are the highly technical facts often present in patent litigation."[365]

There are four secondary considerations: (1) commercial success, (2) long-felt, but unresolved needs, (3) failure of others, and (4) licensing/acquiescence.

a. Commercial Success

Commercial success is the most important and most often asserted of the secondary considerations. Commercial success of an invention is relevant to non-obviousness because it assumes that if the invention were obvious, competitors of the inventor would have produced the invention given its significant consumer demand.[366] (At the same time, if an invention does *not* enjoy commercial success, it does not necessarily follow that the invention is obvious.) Of course, commercial success may be due to, and consumer demand may be a result of, factors unrelated to the technical quality of the claimed invention (e.g., clever advertising, aggressive marketing, business acumen, or significant market share). Thus, raw sales data is insufficient to prove commercial success.[367] For evidence of commercial success to be persuasive, the patentee must show a

364. *Graham*, 383 U.S. at 17.

365. Id. at 35–36.

366. See *Merck & Co., Inc. v. Teva Pharmaceuticals USA, Inc.*, 395 F.3d 1364, 1376 (Fed.Cir.2005) ("Commercial success is relevant because the law presumes an idea would successfully have been brought to market sooner, in response to market forces, had the idea been obvious to persons skilled in the art.").

367. See *Vandenberg v. Dairy Equip. Co.*, 740 F.2d 1560, 1567 (Fed.Cir.1984).

nexus between commercial success and the merits of the claimed invention.[368]

Do researchers have the market in mind when they toil away in their laboratories? Can you think of reasons why a firm would not research and develop an invention even if a market existed? Indeed, many commentators have criticized the Federal Circuit's reliance on and treatment of commercial success. For example, Robert Merges offered a thorough criticism of the commercial success doctrine, stating that it "is a poor indicator of patentability because it is indirect; it depends for its effectiveness on a long chain of inferences, and the links in the chain are often subject to doubt."[369] Indeed, the Federal Circuit, once favorably disposed toward secondary considerations,[370] has grown more skeptical of their persuasiveness.[371]

b. Long-Felt Need and Failure of Others

The fact that there is a long-felt need for an invention or a solution to a particular problem in an industry and others in the industry have tried and failed to satisfy that need may imply non-obviousness. As Judge Easterbrook wrote in *In re Mahurkar Patent Litigation*, "if people are clamoring for a solution, and the best minds do not find it for years, that is practical evidence—the kind that can't be bought from a hired expert, the kind that does not depend on fallible memories or doubtful inferences—of the state of knowledge."[372]

368. See *Simmons Fastener Corp. v. Illinois Tool Works, Inc.*, 739 F.2d 1573, 1575 (Fed.Cir.1984) ("A nexus between the merits of the claimed invention and the evidence of secondary considerations is required in order for the evidence to be given substantial weight in an obviousness decision.").

369. Robert P. Merges, *Commercial Success and Patent Standards: Economic Perspectives on Innovation*, 76 CALIF. L. REV. 803, 838–39 (1988).

370. The court's receptivity was particularly pronounced in the early 1980s, soon after the court's creation and its mandate to strengthen patent rights was fresh. See, e.g., *Stratoflex, Inc. v. Aeroquip Corp.*, 713 F.2d 1530, 1538–39 (Fed.Cir.1983) (stating "evidence of secondary considerations may often be the most probative and cogent evidence in the record. It may often establish that an invention appearing to have been obvious in light of the prior art was not. It is to be considered as part of all the evidence, not just when the decision-maker remains in doubt after reviewing the art"); *W.L. Gore & Associates, Inc. v. Garlock, Inc.*, 721 F.2d 1540 (Fed.Cir. 1983) (stating that secondary considerations can "often serve as insurance against the insidious attraction of the siren hindsight when confronted with a difficult task of evaluating the prior art").

371. See, e.g., *Merck & Co.*, 395 F.3d at 1376 (noting "*Graham* relied on the reasoning from a law review note discussing commercial success."); *Syntex v. Apotex* (criticizing district court's commercial success analysis and suggesting district refer to *Merck* for guidance).

372. 831 F.Supp. 1354, 1377–78 (N.D.Ill.1993).

But the fact that there was a failure to achieve the patented solution may simply be the result of a company's complacency towards its existing technology even though such technology is not state of the art. Furthermore, certain firms may not be willing to commit the time and resources to solving identified problems within the industry. That is, economic and business decisions must be considered when one analyzes long-felt need and failure of others.

c. Licensing and Acquiescence

A patentee may assert that the acceptance of a license by the defendant or other competitors is an implicit recognition that the patent is non-obvious. The rationale is that firms would not pay royalties on a patent unless they thought the patent was valid. But there may be reasons to take a license unrelated to the patent's validity. In *EWP Corp. v. Reliance Universal Inc.*,[373] the Federal Circuit noted that licensing programs may be beneficial to the licensed group. For business reasons, licenses might be preferable because "it is cheaper to take licenses than to defend infringement suits, or for other reasons unrelated to the unobviousness of the licensed subject matter."[374] Thus, the court, as in the related commercial success context, requires proof of a "nexus between the license and the merits of the claimed invention."[375]

B. The Importance of Non–Obviousness as a Policy Tool

Within the parameters established by § 103, there resides a significant subjective component. After all of the underlying factual considerations are ascertained, the judge must decide whether the claimed invention is non-obvious. This subjectivity allows a judge to use § 103 as a policy instrument to further the constitutional goal of promoting the progress of the useful arts. In this regard, § 103 can be viewed as serving a "gatekeeper function."[376] Thus, § 103

373. 755 F.2d 898 (Fed.Cir.1985).

374. Id. at 907–08. In response to a question why his company agreed to pay royalties on a patent it thought invalid rather than litigate, a corporate official stated "It was a nuisance lawsuit to us, and it was the most efficient decision to settle it for a minimal amount." *The New York Times* (Business Section, December 25, 2004).

375. See *In re GPAC, Inc.*, 57 F.3d 1573, 1580 (Fed.Cir.1995); *Iron Grip Barbell Co., Inc. v. USA Sports, Inc.*, 392 F.3d 1317, 1324 (Fed.Cir.2004) ("the mere existence of licenses is insufficient to overcome the conclusion of obviousness" when there is a strong prima facie case of obviousness).

376. Robert P. Merges, *Uncertainty and the Standard of Patentability*, 7 Berkeley High Tech. L.J. 1, 2 (1992).

has a policy richness that is absent from § 102 and other Title 35 statutory sections.

Some commentators have seen in § 103 fertile ground to further important functions of the patent system. For instance, in an influential article, Edmund Kitch—concerned about over-rewarding inventive activity—suggested § 103 should reward patents for those innovations that would not have been developed "absent the protection of a patent."[377] Robert Merges, whose work builds on Kitch's insights, has argued that the non-obviousness requirement should act "as a legal rule that influences behavior" and "encourage[] researchers to pursue projects whose success appears highly uncertain at the outset." Thus, Merges views § 103 as a tool to focus on those inventors who need the inducement of the patent system the most—to develop and disclose innovations whose success is rife with early-stage uncertainty. And Dan Burk and Mark Lemley have advocated using the flexibility inherent in constructing the level of skill in the art possessed by a PHOSITA as a "policy lever" to tailor § 103 (and other statutory sections) to the needs of divergent industries.[378]

377. Edmund W. Kitch, *Graham v. John Deere: New Standards for Patents*, 1966 Sup. Ct. Rev. 293, 301.

378. See Dan L. Burk and Mark A. Lemley, *Policy Levers in Patent Law*, 89 Va. L. Rev. 1575, 1648–52 (2003).

Chapter Eight

ELIGIBLE SUBJECT MATTER AND UTILITY

I. Introduction

Section 101 of Title 35 establishes the first rules of patentability. The statutory language establishes at least two separate requirements: the requirement that an invention be "useful"—the "utility requirement"—and the requirement that the invention be within the appropriate subject matter (delineated by the list in the statute)—the "statutory subject matter requirement." (Note that the requirement in § 101 that the invention be "new" is considered subsumed within the scope of §§ 102 and 103, which consider the "newness" of an invention in far more detail rather than the invention's own independent substance.)

Another important aspect of the statutory text in § 101 is how it frames the basic validity inquiry: an invention or discovery meeting the utility and subject matter requirements is eligible for patenting, *unless* it does not meet a later condition or requirement. That is, § 101 suggests that an invention within the scope of its text is in a sense presumed to be patentable, and thus the burden of showing otherwise is on the opposition. (A review of §§ 102 and 103 confirm this presumptive-validity approach.) Conversely, the § 101 text seems to make no such assumption with respect to the utility or statutory subject matter requirements; suggesting that perhaps the inventor herself must bear the burden on these questions—though as we will see below, this turns out not to be the case in the modern application of § 101.

The tale of the modern application of § 101 is one of uncertainty, debate, and (especially) gradually receding importance. Although defining the scope of patentable inventions—and requiring them to be "useful"—are perhaps the most basic requirements of any patent system, the actual application of § 101 in the modern patent law is rather rare.[379] As will be discussed more fully below, there are a variety of reasons for this, but note that perhaps the most important factor is an uneasiness with the blunt instrument of § 101: because the section acts as a screen for particular types of

379. In October Term 2005, the Supreme Court granted *certorari* in *LabCorp v. Metabolite*, a case which might have raised § 101 issues—although the § 101 question was not raised below. Ultimately, the Supreme Court dismissed the *certiorari* as improvidently granted. See *LabCorp v. Metabolite*, 126 S.Ct. 2921 (2006).

inventions or ways of understanding utility, decisions based on § 101 will have potentially far-reaching implications. Consider, for example, the effects of a holding declaring computer software or DNA sequences beyond the scope of § 101—such a decision would have a major impact on innovation, good or ill. From a judicial perspective, then, it might seem far better to use the more tailored tools at hand—the analysis of §§ 102, 103, and 112 for example, which operate at the level of an individual invention rather than an entire technology.

With this introduction, we turn now to a more detailed discussion of the subject matter requirement and the utility requirement.

II. The Subject Matter Requirement

As noted above, the subject matter requirement of § 101 has at its core a simple principle: that patentable inventions must remain within some definable scope of subject matter. In other words, the subject matter requirement tries to define what subjects are in the patent system, and what subjects are out. Although the idea may be simple, the task of drawing any such lines is much more difficult.

We start with first principles—with the list of subject matter that § 101 specifies as eligible for patenting:

- Process
- Machine
- Manufacture
- Composition of matter
- Any improvement thereof

Taken together, this list clearly suggests a statutory intent to sweep the subject matter requirement extremely broadly. This intent has been confirmed by the legislative history of § 101, wherein the committee reports accompanying the 1952 Act state that Congress intended statutory subject matter to "include anything under the sun, made by man."[380]

Given the broad statutory language, and the almost over-the-top legislative history, the interesting questions, then, are these: (1) what things are excluded from the subject matter requirement? and (2) why? The answer to the former is, as a matter of legal doctrine, relatively easy. Historically, courts have made clear that three categories of subject matter are excluded from the scope of § 101:

380. See *Diamond v. Chakrabarty*, 447 U.S. 303 (1980) (discussing the legislative history, and stating that the statutory text was to be given "wide scope").

laws of nature; physical phenomena; and abstract ideas.[381] Unfortunately, what those categories mean has shifted over time, so the precise scope of exclusion is not especially stable. And the answer to the latter question, of course, remains quite open.

Note that one important effect of the interaction among the statutory language, the legislative history, and the judicially-applied gloss of excluded categories on the subject matter requirement is to effectively invert the burden of demonstrating eligibility from that discussed above. The § 101 language, which suggests a (broad) test that a patentable invention must meet, has instead become a (limited) test that a patentable invention cannot fail. Put another way, the doctrinal implementation of the subject matter requirement means that a prospective patentee need only show that her invention does not fall within the categories of laws of nature, physical phenomonena, or abstract ideas to meet the § 101 subject matter requirement.

Another important implication of the judicial interpretation of the subject matter requirement is the fact that the salience of the limitations fall in particular on certain technologies—biotechnology and software. (Though as we noted above, and discuss further below, the modern application of the subject matter requirement doctrine has quite a limited effect even in these areas.) This technological split, then, provides a useful lens by which to trace the contours of the doctrine.

A. The Subject Matter Requirement and Biotechnology

With respect to the § 101 subject matter requirement and biotechnological inventions, there are three key doctrinal pillars upon which the precedent rests. First, the Supreme Court held in *Funk Brothers Seed Co. v. Kalo Inoculant Co.*, that a claim to a naturally occurring (albeit selected and tested) root-nodule bacteria is "the work of nature," and thus beyond the scope of patentability.[382] Second, the Court, in *Diamond v. Chakrabarty*, upheld claims to a non-naturally occurring (i.e., man-made) bacteria, reasoning that it was clearly within the scope of manufacture, and did not fall within the "work of nature" exception.[383] And third, in *Parke–Davis & Co. v. H.K. Mulford & Co.*, Judge Learned Hand held that an

381. See *Chakrabarty*; *Funk Bros. Seed Co. v. Kalo Inoculant Co.*, 333 U.S. 127 (1948); *Parker v. Flook*, 437 U.S. 584, 589 (1978); *Gottschalk v. Benson*, 409 U.S. 63, 67 (1972).

382. 333 U.S. 127 (1948).

383. 447 U.S. 303 (1980).

"isolated and purified" version of a naturally-occurring substance—in that case, adrenalin—was patentable.[384]

Lining up these three datapoints, a relatively clear doctrinal picture emerges: with respect to biotechnology, the subject matter requirement prevents only claims to naturally-occurring products of nature, *in their natural forms*. Living things are not per se unpatentable, nor are natural substances. More complex is the doctrinal reasoning behind this narrow exclusion. In *Funk Brothers*, the court relied on its view that, although the inventor may have carefully selected the bacteria for particular properties, these properties were, in fact, simply the natural properties of the bacteria, rather than properties created through the volition of man. By contrast, in *Chakrabarty*, the Court concluded that the invention at issue there—a non-naturally occurring bacteria—was "a product of human ingenuity having a distinctive, name, character, and use." The Court concluded that because Chakrabarty's invention was "not nature's handiwork, but his own," it was patentable. Further, in *Parke–Davis*, this natural/non-natural line is drawn even more finely: Judge Hand reasoned that although adrenalin was indeed a natural product (in the sense that it was not man-made), the isolated and purified form claimed did not naturally occur. Thus, the remaining doctrinal exclusion in this context: *natural substances, in their natural forms*.

Theoretically, there is some reason to question the sustainability of this remaining subject matter requirement exclusion. First, note again the expansive statutory language and the recognition by the courts of the broad scope of § 101; the *Funk Brothers* exclusion, with little support in the statutory text, seems precarious in this context. At first glance, one might be tempted to suggest that the courts are establishing an invention/discovery distinction, but the statutory text of § 101 appears to explicitly permit discoveries to be patented. (Some have suggested that perhaps there is a constitutional objection to patenting "discoveries," notwithstanding the statute, though this approach has had little apparent impact on the courts' decisions.[385]) What in fact seems to be the driver behind the *Funk Brothers* ruling is the Court's concern about the lack of *inventiveness* inherent in these naturally-occurring substances: that the bacteria in question were newly-discovered, but the patentee

384. 189 F. 95 (S.D.N.Y.1911). Parke–Davis has been followed in most cases, including by the Federal Circuit's predecessor, the CCPA. See *In re Bergstrom*, 427 F.2d 1394 (CCPA 1970); see also *Merck & Co. v. Olin Mathieson Chemical Corp.*, 253 F.2d 156, 161 (4th Cir.1958).

385. See, e.g., Robert Patrick Merges and John F. Duffy, PATENT LAW AND POLICY: CASES AND MATERIALS 124 (3rd ed. 2002) (raising this argument).

merely found their properties rather than created them.[386] This focus on inventiveness, coming from the Court in 1948, suggests that the *Funk Brothers* result could be reached today more easily via other means, perhaps most cleanly by the doctrine of non-obviousness found in § 103.[387] That is, before the advent of the 1952 Patent Act, the doctrine that we today discuss in terms of obviousness was typically referred to as the requirement for *invention*.[388] Thus, one way to think about *Funk Brothers* is to think about it as a case about non-obviousness—the problems with the claim to naturally-occurring bacteria was that their properties were obvious in light of their natural existence.[389]

To be sure, *Funk Brothers* remains good law, and the traditional doctrinal approach to the "natural phenomonena" aspect of the subject matter requirement is that natural substances, in their natural form are excluded from patentability.[390] But a deeper analysis of the question of why this particular exclusion remains valid suggests that the theoretical underpinnings rest more easily on other doctrines of patentability (especially obviousness, and perhaps novelty) than in § 101. This is not to say of course that there aren't a great many important policy reasons to exclude natural substances in their natural form from patentability: real questions about lack of inventiveness, the fairness of allowing discoveries of natural substances to be patented, or even the desire to prevent the exclusive ownership of natural things or traditional knowledge play a real role.[391] The point here is that in the modern patent law, those concerns may be more cleanly met through the application of the standards for inventiveness located in §§ 102 and 103.

The rationale for the prohibition on laws of nature was discussed by Justice Stephen Breyer:

> The justification for the principle does not lie in any claim that "laws of nature" are obvious, or that their discovery is easy, or that they are not useful. To the contrary, research into such

386. 333 U.S. at 132 ("Even though it may have been the product of skill, it certainly was not the product of invention.")

387. 35 U.S.C. § 103.

388. See Edmund W. Kitch, *Graham v. John Deere, Co.: New Standards for Patents*, 1966 Sup. Ct. Rev. 293, 303–327 (1966) (tracing the history of the obviousness doctrine); *Great A&P Tea Co. v. Supermarket Equip. Corp.*, 340 U.S. 147 (1950) (holding that the standard for "invention" is "inherently elusive").

389. A similar point is made in Merges and Duffy, *supra* note 388, at 124.

390. See *Diamond v. Chakrabarty*, 447 U.S. at 310–11 (distinguishing Funk Brothers).

391. See Naomi Roht–Arriaza, *Of Seeds and Shamans: The Appropriation of the Scientific and Technical Knowledge of Indigenous and Local Communities*, 17 MICH. J. INT'L L. 919 (1996) (arguing that patent law is biased against traditional knowledge).

> matters may be costly and time-consuming, monetary incentives may matter; and the fruits of those incentives and that research may prove of great benefit to the human race. Rather, the reason for the exclusion is that sometimes *too much* patent protection can impede rather than "promote the Progress of Science and useful Arts," the constitutional objective of patent and copyright protection.
>
> * * *
>
> Patent law seeks to avoid the dangers of overprotection just as surely as it seeks to avoid the diminished incentive to invent that underprotection can threaten. One way in which patent law seeks to sail between these opposing and risky shoals is through rules that bring certain types of invention and discovery within the scope of patentability while excluding others.[392]

As a matter of public policy, the subject matter requirement in the biotechnology area (or lack thereof) has had enormously important effects in a major area of technological development. The *Chakrabarty* ruling—that biological entities, including living organisms, could be patented—has paved the way towards dramatically increased research in genetic engineering and other biological research. Similarly, the *Parke–Davis* holding (that isolated and purified versions of even natural substances can be patented) supports an enormous research effort in pharmaceuticals, as well as provides the basis for patents on DNA.[393] This expansion of technological development has been controversial, of course. Ethicists and animal rights activists question the wisdom of allowing patents on genetically engineered animals.[394] Many commentators bemoan the apparent race during the 1980s and 1990s to patent as much DNA as possible, noting that because in most cases these patentees have relatively little knowledge about the true uses and functions of such inventions, the possibility that these patents will hinder future research seems high.[395] And the failure of the subject matter requirement to cleanly exclude the patentability of humans or hu-

392. *LabCorp v. Metabolite Laboratories, Inc.*, 126 S.Ct. 2921, 2922 (2006) (dissenting from dismissal of *certiorari*).

393. Enormous numbers of plants or plant-derived substances have utility in the pharmaceutical field. See, e.g., Philip Abelson, *Medicine From Plants* (Editorial), 247 SCI. 513 (2 Feb. 1990), cited in Merges and Duffy, PATENT LAW AND POLICY, *supra* note 388, at 123. On the theory underpinning DNA patents, see Rebecca S. Eisenberg, *Genetics and the Law: Patenting the Human Genome*, 39 EMORY L.J. 721, 727 & n.27 (1990).

394. Rebecca Dresser, *Ethical and Legal Issues in Patenting New Animal Life*, 28 JURIMETRICS J. 399 (1988); Barry Hoffmaster, *The Ethics of Patenting Higher Life Forms*, 4 I. P. J. 1, 14 (1988).

395. Rebecca Eisenberg, *Patents and the Progress of Science: Exclusive Rights and Experimental Use*, 56 U. CHI. L. REV. 1017 (1989).

man-related beings has spurred an ongoing moral and legal debate that seems to have no easy answer: while many would agree that patenting humans or chimeras is extremely problematic, the post-*Chakrabarty* rules on the subject matter requirement make preventing such patents legally difficult.[396]

Finally, no discussion of the limitations or exclusions in patenting in the area of biotechnology would be complete without at least a brief mention of the Plant Patent Act (PPA) and the Plant Variety Protection Act (PVPA), codified at 35 U.S.C. §§ 161–164. The PPA is intended to allow protection for asexually reproduced plants, and was originally enacted in the 1930s, when Congress apparently believed that such plants could not be patented. Patents granted under the PPA have a lower disclosure requirement, are limited to a single claim, and exclude others only from asexual reproduction (e.g., using the seeds or samples from the patentee's plants). The PVPA covers more complex, sexually reproducing plants, and has rules that are even more distinct from the Patent Act. Because of the different treatment, and different rights, patentees will often have an incentive to seek protection under both the PPA or PVPA and a traditional utility patent. In *J.E.M. Ag Supply, Inc. v. Pioneer Hi–Bred Int'l, Inc.*, the Supreme Court in 2001 confirmed the availability of dual-protection—and in doing so reaffirmed the *Chakrabarty* rule that man-made living organisms are fully patentable.[397]

B. The Subject Matter Requirement and Computer Software

The second major technological area affected by the § 101 subject matter requirement is computer software (which in this context encompasses related Internet technologies and inventions). In general, the doctrine in this area follows a similar pattern to that described in connection with biotechnology: a shift in thinking that results in the subject matter requirement play an ever-smaller role in limiting the types of patents that can be granted.

Referring to the traditional list of excluded categories (laws of nature, natural phenomena, and abstract ideas), the Supreme Court in 1972 established in *Gottshalk v. Benson* that "mathematical algorithms" were unpatentable. In *Gottshalk*, the claim was to a

396. See, e.g., *Patent Application is Disallowed as "Embracing" Human Being*, 58 PAT. TRADEMARK & COPYRIGHT J. (BNA) 203 (June 17, 1999) (outlining the PTO's response to a patent application claiming an animal-human chimera); Cynthia M. Ho, *Splicing Morality and Patent Law: Issues Arising From Mixing Mice and Men*, 2 WASH. U. J. L. & POL'Y 247 (2000);

397. 534 U.S. 124 (2001).

process of converting binary-coded-decimal numbers (BCDs) into traditional binary numbers. The Court ruled that such a claim was simply a mathematical process "in the abstract," and thus could not be patented. Although the opinion took pains to disclaim any effort to preclude patenting of computer software, the thrust of the opinion seemed to cast serious doubt on patentability.

A very different answer to the patenting of software was delivered when the Supreme Court returned to the issue in 1981. In *Diamond v. Diehr*, the Court made clear that software was indeed patentable, under the following conditions: first, mathematical algorithms cannot be patented "in the abstract," second, the opinion noted that:

> When a claim containing a mathematical formula implements or applies that formula in a structure or process which, when considered as a whole, is performing a function which the patent laws are designed to protect (e.g., transforming or reducing an article to a different state or thing), then the claim satisfies the requirements of § 101.

While *Diehr* has been the Supreme Court's last word in this context to date, it has been merely the launch-point for what must be understood as a dramatic shift in the doctrine—a shift which has essentially eliminated any serious subject matter requirement for computer-related inventions. The drivers of this change are three-fold. First, the role of software in the national and international economy has radically changed, with software now being understood as a separate (and highly innovative) industry from computer and electronics hardware manufacturing. Because of this economic shift, patent protection for software is tremendously more important than it was in the 1970s, when software was typically provided as part of a large-equipment purchase. This desire for protection has led to an explosion in software patenting activity since the early 1980s.

Hand in hand with the incentives to patent is the role of the patent bar in undermining the 1970s-era attempts to keep software out of the patent system. Prodded by clients, patent attorneys began to draft patent claims strategically, so as to minimize the impact of the prohibition on algorithms. The most important technique was to claim computer software as a machine or apparatus, that is, a "computer capable of performing the following steps. . . ." Because one of the major objections to algorithmic patenting in *Benson* and *Diehr* was the use of broad process claims, this step alone bore substantial fruit in avoiding subject matter requirement problems. Indeed, given the availability of claims under § 112, paragraph 6 (means-plus-function claim format) redrafting process or algorithmic claims into machine or apparatus claims was both relatively easy and provided virtually the same coverage. Note, however, that such claims pose challenges to our understanding of computers—is your computer a different machine depending on which application is being used?—as well as some potential problems with respect to the meaning of infringement—is merely possessing a disk with patented software code an infringement?

The third and perhaps most important driver has clearly been the aggressive approach of the Federal Circuit in this area. In part responding to the economic changes noted above, in part responding to the drafting strategies of the patent community, and in part responding to the unsatisfactory nature of *Diehr* and *Benson*, the Federal Circuit, in a series of major decisions in 1992, 1998, and 1999, provided the doctrinal basis for this effective elimination of the subject matter requirement.

The first of these cases was *In re Alappat*, where the claim was drawn to an anti-aliasing technique for use in oscilloscopes. Although the invention was related to the mathematical formulae that drive the anti-aliasing, the claim was directed to a machine performing the steps, rather than the process or calculations themselves. The Federal Circuit held the claim patentable, even though the claim would, the court acknowledged, read on a general purpose computer implementing the same technique. *Alappat*, then, moved the *Deihr* standard, by holding that where a software program created a "specific machine to produce a useful, concrete, and tangible result," it was easily patentable.

In *State Street Bank & Trust Co. v. Signature Financial Group, Inc.*, the Federal Circuit went a step further, upholding the patentability of a claim to a (computer-implemented) hub-and-spoke accounting system. In *State Street Bank*, the Federal Circuit swept away the last vestiges of the earlier limits on algorithmic inventions, stating that such inventions were patentable, irrespective of claim format, as long as they produced a "useful, concrete, and tangible result." Although the State Street Bank claim was written in section 112 ¶ 6 format (i.e., a machine claim), the court *in dicta* stated that claim format did not determine patentability.

The final, and often overlooked, member of the Federal Circuit's key troika is *AT&T v. Excel Communications* in 1999. In contrast to *Alappat* and *State Street Bank*, the claim in *AT&T* was a simple method claim (generally covering a scheme for billing telephone calls wherein the calls connecting in-network customers are charged a lower rate). In addition, the opinion in *AT&T*, unlike its predecessors, made extensive efforts to reconcile the current case law with the language of *Diehr*. And in a particularly interesting passage—and one that neatly summarizes the court's approach to these questions—the Federal Circuit responded directly to Justice Stevens' powerful dissent in *Diehr* (where he argued that software should be per se unpatentable):

> [Stevens'] first concern, that the rules are not sufficiently clear to enable reasonable prediction of outcomes, should be less of a concern today in light of the refocusing of the § 101 issue that *Alappat* and *State Street* have provided. His second concern, that the ambiguous concept of "algorithm" could be used to make any process unpatentable, can be laid to rest once the focus is understood to be not on whether there is a mathematical algorithm at work, but on whether the algorithm-containing invention, as a whole, produces a tangible, useful, result.

The modern rule of the § 101 subject matter requirement for computer-related inventions is that stated above: the analysis is whether the claim describes an invention that creates a tangible, useful result. As we discuss more fully below, this standard is essentially the same as the modern § 101 utility requirement, meaning that the subject matter requirement in this context has collapsed into the utility inquiry.

The effects of the *Alappat–State Street–AT&T* doctrine have been substantial. In addition to spurring the growth of software patenting, the lowering of the bar to algorithmic inventions generally has resulted in an explosion of patenting in related areas, such as business methods, financial instruments, tax planning, and more. These changes have been deeply controversial;[398] indeed, the consternation over the patenting of business methods was substantial enough to prompt Congress to enact 35 U.S.C. § 273, which shelters "prior users" of business method patents from infringement claims.[399] There are, as with so many issues in patent law, strong arguments on both sides. On the positive side, the recent doctrinal changes have, as the Federal Circuit suggested in *AT&T*, brought a measure of clarity and predictability to this area of the law. Concerns include: the fact that these patents seem to move the patent system away from its traditional roots in technology;[400] serious questions about whether the economic cost-benefit analysis

398. See, e.g., James Gleick, *Patently Absurd*, N.Y. TIMES MAG., Mar. 12, 2000, at 44 (describing Internet business method patents as illustrating "the breakdown of the United States patent system.")

399. See 35 U.S.C. § 273 (2003).

400. The seminal article on this point is John R. Thomas, *The Patenting of the Liberal Professions*, 40 B.C. L. REV. 1139 (1999).

supporting the patent system generally holds as true in these areas, where there may be very strong incentives to innovate aside from those provided by the patent system;[401] and, difficult logistical and administrative problems that result from the PTO becoming overwhelmed by applications in an area where the relevant "prior art" may not be well understood.[402]

Interestingly, in 2004 and 2006, the faintest glimmerings of potential future legal change—perhaps back in the direction of *Diehr*—could be seen. First, in *Ex parte Lundgren*,[403] the PTO's Board of Patent Appeals and Interferences published a long and detailed opinion containing a vigorous debate among members of the board—a debate about whether the subject matter requirement contained an inherent "technological arts" requirement. Lundgren's claim was as "pure" a business method as there can be: a method for compensating a manager. The examiner rejected the claim because it did not fall within what the examiner described as the "technological arts" requirement of § 101. The majority of the board reversed the rejections, citing *AT&T*, but did so over a strong dissent. (Note that the fact that the board both published and designated *Lundgren* as precedential, which are rare moves, might suggest that the board is hoping to stimulate renewed debate within the legal community.)

Second, in late 2005, the Supreme Court granted certiorari in *LabCorp v. Metabolite*, with the following question presented:

> Whether a method patent setting forth an indefinite, undescribed, and non-enabling step directing a party simply to "correlat[e]" test results can validly claim a monopoly over a basic scientific relationship used in medical treatment such that any doctor necessarily infringes the patent merely by thinking about the relationship after looking at a test result.

In June 2006, the Supreme Court dismissed the *certiorari* as improvidently granted (the § 101 issues had not been raised below). Justices Breyer, Souter, and Stevens penned a dissent to the dismissal—one which may foretell further interest at the Court in revisiting these issues:

> Neither does the Federal Circuit's decision in State Street Bank help respondents. That case does say that a process is patentable if it produces a "useful, concrete, and tangible

401. See Merges and Duffy, Patent Law and Policy, *supra* note 388, at 180.

402. See Robert P. Merges, *As Many as Six Impossible Patents Before Breakfast: Property Rights for Business Concepts and Patent System Reform*, 14 Berkeley Tech. L.J. 577 (1999).

403 76 U.S.P.Q.2d 1385 (B.P.A.I. 2005).

result." 149 F.3d, at 1373. But this Court has never made such a statement and, if taken literally, the statement would cover instances where this Court has held the contrary. The Court, for example, has invalidated a claim to the use of electromagnetic current for transmitting messages over long distances even though it produces a result that seems "useful, concrete, and tangible." Morse, *supra*, at 16. Similarly the Court has invalidated a patent setting forth a system for triggering alarm limits in connection with catalytic conversion despite a similar utility, concreteness, and tangibility. Flook, *supra*. And the Court has invalidated a patent setting forth a process that transforms, for computer-programming purposes, decimal figures into binary figures—even though the result would seem useful, concrete, and at least arguably (within the computer's wiring system) tangible. Gottschalk, *supra*.

Despite these rumblings, however, the *Alappat–State Street–AT&T* line of cases remains the key doctrinal framework of the subject matter requirement for software-related inventions. And this doctrinal framework suggests that § 101's primary contribution to the limitation on the scope of patentability is the utility requirement—a subject to which we now turn our attention.

III. The Utility Requirement

As with the subject matter requirement, § 101's utility requirement is founded on a spare bit of statutory language—here, a single word, "useful." Thus the content of the requirement is primarily a function of long-run doctrinal development rather than clearly delineated statutory rules. In broad strokes (to be filled in a bit later), the basic utility requirement has been interpreted to require that patentable inventions have a practical, real-world use or benefit. The screen provided by the utility requirement is modest, but it is a screen nonetheless.

The utility requirement has a rich history, being a part of the patent system from the outset: indeed, given the utilitarian approach that underlies the basic theory of the U.S. patent system, limiting patentability to those inventions that advance society in some way—those that are "useful"—is at the core of the patent system.[404] And yet the modern application of the utility requirement (with its gradually diminishing impact on patenting practices) calls into question the basic policies that support the doctrine.

The basic argument for a robust utility requirement is to effectuate a "policing" of the bargain between patentee and society.

404. William Robinson, *Treatise on the Law of Patents* 462–63 (1890).

That is, without the expectation of a benefit—here, a "useful" innovation—society should not grant valuable proprietary rights to exclude others.[405] And yet there are several possible objections to this approach:

1. First, because the reward of a patent is based on the success of the innovation in the marketplace, the marketplace itself will sort out which inventions are useful, and which are not.[406] Put another way, there is little incentive to patent useless inventions—those that will receive no commercial success. If the market provides an equally-effective (and perhaps more effective) screen for utility, then perhaps there is little need to construct a legal mechanism.
2. Second, even the disclosure of "useless" inventions may benefit society. As part of obtaining a patent, the patentee must disclose extensive detail about her invention.[407] Even if the invention itself fails to have real-world utility, it may be that the information contained in the patent disclosure will, and thus society will benefit.[408]
3. Third, any legal rule for utility will necessarily involve subjective, line-drawing exercises, and thus can be subject to administrative incompetence or political pressure. Plus, where significant subjective decision making is allowed, these decisions may have the effect of suppressing patenting on truly innovative inventions (e.g., great leaps forward).
4. And fourth, there is relatively little demonstrated harm that comes from "useless" patents. "Impossible" patents cannot be infringed. "Useless" patents will not be infringed or enforced. To be sure, they may waste administrative time and effort, but perhaps the imposition of filing fees and other logistical burdens are enough to dissuade frivolous patenting.

405. See *Robinson*, id.; *Brenner v. Manson*, 383 U.S. 519 (1966).

406. *Lowell v. Lewis*, 15 Fed. Cas. 1018 (C.C.D. Mass. 1817) ("Whether [the invention] be more or less useful is a circumstance very material to the interests of the patentee, but of no importance to the public. If it not be extensively useful, it will sink silently into contempt and disregard.").

407. See 35 U.S.C. § 112.

408. See, e.g., *Brenner v. Manson*, 383 U.S. at 537 (Harlan, J, dissenting) ("To encourage one chemist or research facility to invent and disseminate new processes and products may be vital to progress, although the product or process be without 'utility' as the Court defines the term.").

There are good arguments against these concerns, of course. The market is an imperfect mechanism, the disclosures contained in "useless" patents are likely to be less important than the disclosures provided by useful patents, appeals processes and other structures can address incompetence or other administrative problems, and "useless" patents may well harm the system by clogging up the administrative process, by making it more difficult and expensive to find good patents, or by creating vast "thickets" of related patents.[409]

Finally, another argument that is at times invoked in favor of the utility requirement is fraud.[410] That is, many people unfamiliar with the patent system may have an unjustified confidence in the PTO's screening mechanisms, and may thus consider an issued U.S. patent to be a sort of "stamp of approval" on the benefits of a particular invention. Such a belief may lead to cases of fraud, where unknowing members of the public are duped into purchasing products based on their patent status or even buying the worthless patents themselves.

Placing the pros and cons into context, one can understand the policy underlying the § 101 utility requirement as calling for a soft screen: one that attempts at fairly low cost to weed out the truly useless or baseless patents, while allowing patentability for virtually anything else.[411] A higher, more stringent requirement would impose additional costs, including the administration of the requirement on patent applicants themselves, and might run the very real risk of precluding patentability for substantial innovations. Eliminating the requirement, however, would mean losing the benefits—preventing fraud, unclogging the system, etc. So the policy mandate here would seem to be to find a balance where a modest screening function can operate at relatively low cost. As we will see below, for the most part, the modern utility requirement meets this description.

A. Practical Utility

The common-law nature of the utility requirement has resulted in the development of rather distinct utility requirements. The most important among those is what is known as the "practical

409. See, e.g., Carl Shapiro, *Navigating the Patent Thickets: Cross-Licenses, Patent Pools, and Standard-Setting*, in Jaffe, et al., eds., *Innovation Policy and the Economy* (2001); Michael A. Heller and Rebecca S. Eisenberg, *Can Patents Deter Innovation? The Anticommons in Biomedical Research*, 280 Science 698 (1998).

410. See, e.g., Merges and Duffy, *supra* note 388, at 216.

411. See *In re Cortright*, 165 F.3d 1353 (Fed.Cir.1999) (discussed below).

utility" requirement (sometimes referred to as "substantial utility"): a requirement that a patent have a concrete, specific, and real-world use. Although the statement of the general rule is rather simple, the articulation and (more importantly) the procedural application of the standards have varied. In *Brenner v. Manson* (1966), the Supreme Court invalidated claims to a process for making a steroid; the patentee offered no specific use for the product of the process, other than what appeared to be a hopeful intent that the steroid would prove useful in inhibiting tumors. (Related compounds were under investigation at the time.) The Supreme Court held that such a claim lacked utility:

> Whatever weight is attached to the value of encouraging disclosure and of inhibiting secrecy, we believe a more compelling consideration is that a process patent in the chemical field, which has not been developed and pointed to the degree of specific utility, creates a monopoly of knowledge which should be granted only if clearly commanded by the statute. Until the process claim has been reduced to production of a product shown to be useful, the metes and bounds of that monopoly are not capable of precise delineation. It may engross a vast, unknown, and perhaps unknowable area. Such a patent may confer power to block off whole areas of scientific development, without compensating benefit to the public. The basic quid pro quo contemplated by the Constitution and the Congress for granting a patent monopoly is the benefit derived by the public from an invention with substantial utility. Unless and until a process is refined and developed to this point—where specific benefit exists in currently available form—there is insufficient justification for permitting an applicant to engross what may prove to be a broad field.[412]

As articulated by the Court in *Brenner*, the practical utility doctrine rests heavily on the issue of timing; the concern is that granting a patent on a particular compound prior to the identification of a specific, practical, utility, will result in an overbroad patent being allowed.[413] Note, however, that this rule may in some cases result in the unavailability of a product patent: if the knowledge of the product enters the public domain prior to a practical utility being developed, then the product cannot be patented.[414] This does not preclude new patents on various uses of the compound, of course.[415]

412. 383 U.S. 519, 534–53 (1966).

413. See, id.

414. See 35 U.S.C. § 102.

415. See Robert Merges and Richard Nelson, *On the Complex Economics of Patent Scope*, 90 COLUM. L. REV. 839, 903

The other important thing to recognize about the practical utility doctrine is how it is likely to apply differentially across technologies. *Brenner* was a case about chemical compounds, which are notoriously unpredictable in their function; indeed, the Court rejected the patentee's argument about the related compounds for the very reason that the chemistry was so unpredictable that related compounds may in fact have very distinct properties.[416]

In many ways, *Brenner* establishes the high-water mark for the practical utility doctrine, requiring patentees to come forward with a "specific, practical benefit" for their claimed inventions. In the *In re Brana* case in 1995, the Federal Circuit clarified the rules, and in doing so dramatically changed the way the doctrine operates.[417] *Brana* was also a chemical compound claim, which the PTO had rejected on the grounds that the applicant's assertion of utility was insufficient. The Federal Circuit reversed, holding that (a) a general assertion of efficacy in treating a class of identified diseases was specific enough to meet the test, and (b) that the patentee did not bear the burden of showing utility, but instead that the doctrine required a burden-shifting analysis.[418]

> This court's predecessor has stated: [A] specification disclosure which contains a teaching of the manner and process of making and using the invention in terms which correspond in scope to those used in describing and defining the subject matter sought to be patented must be taken as in compliance with the enabling requirement of the first paragraph of § 112 unless there is reason to doubt the objective truth of the statements contained therein which must be relied on for enabling support.
>
> From this it follows that the PTO has the initial burden of challenging a presumptively correct assertion of utility in the disclosure. Only after the PTO provides evidence showing that one of ordinary skill in the art would reasonably doubt the asserted utility does the burden shift to the applicant to provide rebuttal evidence sufficient to convince such a person of the invention's asserted utility.

It is this procedural burden-shifting analysis that is the most significant result of *Brana*. Under the rule, the patentee need only make an assertion of utility, and the PTO (or the challenger) bears the burden of showing evidence of a reasonable doubt about utility.

(1990) (discussing "new use" patents and this importance).

416. 383 U.S. at 532.

417. 51 F.3d 1560 (Fed.Cir.1995).

418. Id. at 1565, 1566.

If such a showing is made, then the applicant/patentee bears the burden of producing evidence to overcome the doubts.[419]

The practical result of the burden-shifting analysis mandated by *Brana* is that it is substantially more difficult to reject patent applications because of lack of utility; because the initial burden rests on the PTO—to prove a negative, no less—the hurdle is relatively high.

Interestingly, in 2001 the PTO issued a set of *Utility Examination Guidelines*, which requires an applicant to make a "credible" assertion of a "specific and substantial utility."[420] A "specific" utility is defined as one that is specific to the claimed invention, rather than generally directed to the "broad class of the invention." A "substantial" utility is "[a] utility that defines a real-world use." Note that, if taken on their face, the 2001 guidelines are at least somewhat more stringent than those discussed in *Brana*, which seemed to suggest that broad, conclusory assertions of utility were sufficient.[421] Because the application of the utility requirement is a question of law, however, the *Brana* rule would seem to be controlling in a legal sense, although the *Guidelines* have important effects in defining how the PTO handles practical utility.

The Federal Circuit's most recent discussion of the practical utility doctrine was in the *In re Fisher* case, wherein a patent applicant was seeking claims to a purified version of genes (specified expressed sequence tags) to maize plants.[422] At the time of application, Fisher was unaware of either the precise structure or function of the genes (or the proteins encoded for by those genes). Nevertheless, Fisher argued that under the *Brana* approach to practical utility, his (seven) assertions for utility were substantial enough to clear the § 101 hurdle: (1) serving as a molecular marker for mapping the entire maize genome, which consists of ten chromosomes that collectively encompass roughly 50,000 genes; (2) measuring the level of mRNA in a tissue sample via microarray technology to provide information about gene expression; (3) providing a source for primers for use in the polymerase chain reaction ("PCR") process to enable rapid and inexpensive duplication of specific genes; (4) identifying the presence or absence of a polymorphism; (5) isolating promoters via chromosome walking; (6) controlling protein expression; and (7) locating genetic molecules of other plants and organisms.

419. Id. at 1566.

420. PTO, Utility Examination Guidelines, 66 Fed. Reg. 1092 (Jan. 5, 2001).

421. 51 F.3d. at 1566.

422. See *In re Fisher*, 421 F.3d 1365 (Fed.Cir.2005).

The Federal Circuit, however, disagreed, describing the inquiry as one requiring the establishment of a "substantial" and "specific" utility:

> Following *Brenner*, our predecessor court, the Court of Customs and Patent Appeals, and this court have required a claimed invention to have a specific and substantial utility to satisfy § 101....
>
> Courts have used the labels "practical utility" and "real world" utility interchangeably in determining whether an invention offers a "substantial" utility. Indeed, the Court of Customs and Patent Appeals stated that " '[p]ractical utility' is a shorthand way of attributing 'real-world' value to claimed subject matter." In other words, one skilled in the art can use a claimed discovery in a manner which provides some immediate benefit to the public. It thus is clear that an application must show that an invention is useful to the public as disclosed in its current form, not that it may prove useful at some future date after further research. Simply put, to satisfy the 'substantial' utility requirement, an asserted use must show that that claimed invention has a significant and presently available benefit to the public.
>
> Turning to the "specific" utility requirement, an application must disclose a use which is not so vague as to be meaningless.... Thus, in addition to providing a "substantial" utility, an asserted use must also show that that claimed invention can be used to provide a well-defined and particular benefit to the public.'"[423]

Under this rubric, a majority of the panel decided that the asserted utilities (the seven noted above) did not meet the standard:

> Regarding the seven uses asserted by Fisher, we observe that each claimed EST uniquely corresponds to the single gene from which it was transcribed ("underlying gene"). As of the filing date of the '643 application, Fisher admits that the underlying genes have no known functions.... Essentially, the claimed ESTs act as no more than research intermediates that may help scientists to isolate the particular underlying protein-encoding genes and conduct further experimentation on those genes.... Accordingly, the claimed ESTs are, in words of the Supreme Court, mere "object[s] of use-testing," to wit, objects upon which scientific research could be performed with no assurance that anything useful will be discovered in the end.

423. 421 F.3d 1365, 1371 (Fed.Cir. 2005).

> Fisher compares the claimed ESTs to certain other patentable research tools, such as a microscope.... As the government points out, a microscope has the specific benefit of optically magnifying an object to immediately reveal its structure.... Accordingly, while a microscope can offer an immediate, real world benefit in a variety of applications, the same cannot be said for the claimed ESTs. Fisher's proposed analogy is thus inapt. Hence, we conclude that Fisher's asserted uses are insufficient to meet the standard for a "substantial" utility under § 101.
>
> Moreover, all of Fisher's asserted uses represent merely hypothetical possibilities, objectives which the claimed ESTs, or any EST for that matter, could possibly achieve, but none for which they have been used in the real world.... Consequently, because Fisher failed to prove that its claimed ESTs can be successfully used in the seven ways disclosed in the '643 application, we have no choice but to conclude that the claimed ESTs do not have a "substantial" utility under § 101.
>
> Furthermore, Fisher's seven asserted uses are plainly not "specific." Any EST transcribed from any gene in the maize genome has the potential to perform any one of the alleged uses.... Nothing about Fisher's seven alleged uses set the five claimed ESTs apart from the more than 32,000 ESTs disclosed in the '643 application or indeed from any EST derived from any organism. Accordingly, we conclude that Fisher has only disclosed general uses for its claimed ESTs, not specific ones that satisfy § 101.[424]

Judge Rader, writing in dissent, argued that the assertion that the ESTs in question could be used as research tools was plainly sufficient, and that the majority was inappropriately discounting the importance of research tools:

> The Board and this court acknowledge that the ESTs perform a function, that they have a utility, but proceed quickly to a value judgment that the utility would not produce enough valuable information. The Board instead complains that the information these ESTs supply is too "insubstantial" to merit protection. Yet this conclusion denies the very nature of scientific advance. Science always advances in small incremental steps.... This court further faults the EST research for lacking any "assurance that anything useful will be discovered in the end." These criticisms would foreclose much scientific research and many vital research tools. Often scientists embark

424. Id. at 1374.

on research with no assurance of success and knowing that even success will demand "significant additional research."

Nonetheless, this court, oblivious to the challenges of complex research, discounts these ESTs because it concludes (without scientific evidence) that they do not supply enough information. This court reasons that a research tool has a "specific" and "substantial" utility only if the studied object is readily understandable using the claimed tool—that no further research is required. Surely this cannot be the law. Otherwise, only the final step of a lengthy incremental research inquiry gets protection.[425]

The *Fisher* case is important not merely for its holding—that ESTs are unpatentable without a disclosure of the function of their related gene—but also for the division it reveals on the court regarding the once-stable practical utility doctrine. It also suggests that as new technologies emerge and are proposed for patenting, the practical utility doctrine may yet indeed provide a substantial hurdle to patentability.

B. Beneficial Utility

The second component of the utility requirement is what is known as "beneficial" utility: a requirement in the law that patentable inventions have "a benefit" to society. The beneficial utility requirement has its origins in the 1800s, when the courts invalidated patents adjudged to be "harmful" to society.[426] Inventions to gambling devices were the primary targets of this doctrine, which persisted in the law until the late 1970s.[427] However, in 1999, the Federal Circuit appeared to essentially put an end to the doctrine of moral utility, in *Juicy Whip, Inc. v. Orange Bang, Inc.*[428] In that case, the claimed invention was a dispenser for juice or other liquids that was constructed in such a way as to make the user of the dispenser believe that the product was dispensed from the large clear container near the spout—when in fact the liquid was piped from below the counter.[429] The District Court had held that the patent was invalid under the beneficial utility doctrine, citing cases from the early 1900s wherein inventions that had "trickery or imitation" as their purpose were declared to be unpatentable. The

425. Id. at 1380.

426. See *Lowell v. Lewis*, *supra* note 408.

427. See, e.g., *Brewer v. Lichtenstein*, 278 F. 512 (7th Cir.1922); *Schultze v. Holtz*, 82 F. 448 (N.D.Cal.1897); *National Automatic Device Co. v. Lloyd*, 40 F. 89 (N.D.Ill.1889). On the end of this line of cases, see *In re Murphy*, 200 USPQ 801 (BPAI 1977).

428. 185 F.3d 1364 (Fed.Cir.1999).

429. Id. at 1365–66.

Federal Circuit quickly disposed of this result: "The fact that one product can be altered to make it look like another is in itself a specific benefit sufficient to satisfy the statutory requirement of utility."[430] Thus, between Juicy Whip and the demise of the anti-gambling cases, there appears to be very little scope of the beneficial utility doctrine remaining.

C. Operable Utility

A third utility doctrine, closely related to the practical utility doctrine, is known as "operable" utility. The operable utility doctrine requires that patentable inventions be "operable"—that is, capable of working as described by the inventor. In practical effect, the operable utility doctrine is used primarily to reject inventions that violate accepted principles of science, for example, perpetual motion machines, cold fusion devices, and methods to prevent aging.[431] (Note that these inventions would also clearly violate the disclosure requirements of § 112, as the patentee would not be able to describe them in a way that those of ordinary skill could practice them.)[432]

One policy concern with respect to the operable utility doctrine is to ensure that the application of the doctrine does not prevent the patentability of genuinely innovative inventions. That is, it may be that the most important inventions to society are *precisely* those which, at first glance, appear to make grand, even "impossible" leaps forward. A too-high hurdle for operability could thus be counterproductive. The Federal Circuit wrestled with this question in *In re Cortright* (1999), wherein the patentee claimed the topical use of a commercially-available compound (Bag–Balm™, typically used to soften cows' udders) to cure baldness.[433] The examiner rejected the claim on the basis of operable utility, noting that the applicant had no clinical evidence to back the method of use claim. Both the PTO Board of Patent Appeals and the Federal Circuit reversed, holding that clinical evidence was not required, and that using a topical solution to treat baldness was not "inherently unbelievable," as the law required.[434] Thus, after *Cortright*, as long as the asserted utility is not "inherently unbelievable" or "involves implausible scientific principles," the operable utility doctrine will not bar patentability.

430. Id. at 1367.

431. See, e.g., *In re Swartz*, 232 F.3d 862 (Fed.Cir.2000).

432. Id. at 863 ("[Q]uestions of whether a specification provides an enabling disclosure under § 112, ¶ 1, and whether an application satisfies the utility requirement of § 101 are closely related.").

433. 165 F.3d 1353 (Fed.Cir.1999).

434. Id. at 1359.

Part III: Enforcing Patents

Chapter Nine

Claim Construction

I. Introduction

It is an oft-cited truism in the patent law that "the name of the game is the claim."[435] Indeed, no single doctrine is more pervasive and more dispositive than claim construction.[436] And intriguingly enough, the doctrine of claim construction is exclusively the province of the courts—there is not a single word concerning claim construction in Title 35. So claim construction, then, is at once an enormously powerful mechanism in the U.S. patent system (perhaps the most powerful), and yet presently, almost completely out of the control of the legislative or executive branches.

Patent claims are, put simply, the textual description of what a patentee "claims" as her patented invention.[437] They establish the basic boundaries of the patentee's right to exclude others from the marketplace, as well as establish whether the patentee receives a patent at all. In an ideal world claims would be clear, specific, and unambiguous, delineating subject matter much like a deed to a piece of real property defines neighbors' lot lines. Of course, the reality is far more complex. The words in patent claims describe the margins of *technology*, not land—a far more malleable and elusive target. Further, in some technological areas, words may simply not adequately describe the concepts desired, if at all. And yet they must be used: without a clear understanding of what is and is not covered by a particular patent, the costs of the patent system rise dramatically.

Claim "construction" or "interpretation," then, is the process of placing the language found in patent claims into a meaningful context, given the circumstances involved. Sometimes claim lan-

435. See Giles Sutherland Rich, *Extent of Protection and Interpretation of Claims—American Perspectives*, 21 Int'l Rev. Indus. Prop. & Copyright L. 497, 499 (1990) ("The U.S. is strictly an examination country and the main purpose of the examination, to which every application is subjected, is to try to make sure that what each claim defines is patentable. To coin a phrase, the name of the game is the claim.").

436. See, e.g., *Markman v. Westview Inst., Inc.*, 52 F.3d 967, 991–92 (Fed.Cir. 1995) (*Markman I*) (Mayer, J. concurring) (asserting that claim construction typically determines the outcome of the entire patent case).

437. 35 U.S.C. § 112.

guage will be unexpectedly vague—does the term "coupled" require a physical connection?[438] On other occasions, the language is intentionally difficult—how flat is "generally flat"?[439] In either case, the patent law's system of claim construction analysis guides the inquiry. Virtually every player in the U.S. patent system undertakes claim construction. For example, the U.S. Patent and Trademark Office necessarily interprets claim language when evaluating the patentability of an invention.[440] Private parties are constantly interpreting patent claim language, of course, either to evaluate potential infringement risk, to gauge patentability, to determine the value of a licensing agreement, or to consider an investment decision. But the really important claim interpretations are those conducted by the courts, usually during infringement proceedings.[441]

Note as well the complex incentives on the part of the patentee who actually writes the claims. First, a patentee has incentives to claim *broadly*, so as to encompass as much subject matter as possible within the patent grant. Second, and conversely, a patentee has an incentive to claim *narrowly*: a narrow claim will more easily comply with the disclosure requirements of 35 U.S.C. § 112, and will avoid more potentially invalidating prior art under §§ 102 and 103. Thus a strategic claim drafter must walk the narrow line between claiming too broadly—which could result in an invalid claim (either because it ensnares the prior art, or because it violates § 112)—and claiming too narrowly—which could result in a valid, but economically and practically worthless patent.

From a strategic perspective, one way to finesse the above-noted dilemma is to exploit the fact that different parties will be interpreting the claim language, and at different times. That is, during the prosecution process in front of the PTO (call this Time 1), the claims will be construed for purposes of evaluating their compliance with the validity requirements. At some point later (often years later), the claims will be construed with an eye towards

438. No. At least not in U.S. Patent No. 5,202,835 (issued Apr. 13, 1993), entitled "Trolling Motor with Heading Lock." See *Johnson Worldwide Assocs. v. Zebco Corp.*, 175 F.3d 985 (Fed.Cir. 1999).

439. Not 12° of rise in U.S. Patent No. 5,456,202 (issued Oct. 10, 1995), entitled "Planing Boat Hull." See *Schoell v. Regal Marine Indus.*, 247 F.3d 1202 (Fed.Cir.2001).

440. The standard used by the PTO is the "broadest reasonable interpretation," which is not a standard present in the non-PTO context.

441. Some commentators, notably John Duffy, suggest that the PTO's constructions should be given increased deference, due to the PTO's technical competence and lower operating cost. See John F. Duffy, *On Improving the Legal Process of Claim Interpretation: Administrative Alternatives,* 2 WASH. U. J.L. & POL'Y 109, 125–35 (2000).

infringement litigation (call this Time 2). In general, the strategic patentee will want to have narrow claims at Time 1, and broader claims at Time 2. (Validity is still at issue at Time 2, of course, but the statutory presumption of validity—as well as the cost of litigation—tilt the balance in Time 2 towards the patentee.) By claiming "flexibly" (or, to choose another word, "vaguely"), the patentee can attempt to, in essence, have two distinct meanings imparted—a narrow meaning at Time 1, and a broader meaning at Time 2. This form of strategic behavior—known as the "nose of wax" problem—imparts substantial costs on the patent system, and addressing it is (or should be) the primary goal of claim construction principles.

Thus, the process of claim construction can be understood in context as not merely an exercise in translation—from the technological to the textual and back again—but also as an exercise in managing uncertainty and allocating its costs. So while the doctrinal framework—how claim construction is to be done—is critically important, so too is the allocation of authority: who makes the decision. We turn next to these questions.

II. The Institutional Design of Claim Construction

Starting with broad strokes, the important institutional design features of the current claim construction scheme are:

1. The meaning of claim language is determined solely by judges, typically well prior to trial during what are known (tellingly) as *Markman* hearings.[442]
2. A district court's claim construction is reviewed *de novo* on appeal to the Federal Circuit. No formal deference is given to the district court (or, for that matter, the PTO).[443] At this point the Federal Circuit has never accepted any interlocutory appeals on issues of claim construction.[444]

We start with point 1 above. In *Markman II*, the Supreme Court set into place the basic structural design of the claim construction process. Holding that the Seventh Amendment's guarantee of a jury trial did not apply to the interpretation of the patent document, the Court made quite clear that the question was

442. See *Markman v. Westview Inst., Inc.*, 517 U.S. 370 (1996) (*Markman II*)

443. See *Cybor Corp. v. FAS Techs., Inc.*, 138 F.3d 1448 (Fed.Cir.1998) (en banc).

444. See, e.g., Craig Allen Nard, *Process Considerations in the Age of Markman and Mantras*, 2001 U. Ill. L. Rev. 355, 372 (decrying the denial of interlocutory appeals). Many district court judges, however, simply enter summary judgment for one of the parties after construing the claims, creating a de facto interlocutory appeal.

"exclusively within the province of the court." More important than the holding, however, was the reasoning. Justice Souter, writing for a unanimous Court, initially framed the issue in traditional (and traditionally narrow) Seventh Amendment terms: whether the right to a trial by jury existed under the English common law in the late 18th Century.[445] Here the Court noted that while patent infringement actions were unquestionably tried to juries during the relevant time period, the historical record was far less clear regarding the locus of decision making on interpretation. The Court's historical analysis—as one might imagine—was substantially complicated on this point due to the fact that patent claims (at least as we understand them now) did not exist until the 1820s,[446] did not receive formal legal recognition until 1836,[447] and were not required of patentees until 1870.[448] Thus the Court turned to the body of the patent document itself—the specification[449]—as a contemporaneous analogue. Surveying what it described as the "mere smattering" of relevant evidence,[450] the Court concluded that there was no evidence that juries had interpreted patent documents, and found it telling that "as soon as the English courts did begin to describe the construction of patent documents" in the early 1800s, they indicated that the judge was the interpreter, not the jury.[451] Thus, the Court rejected the argument that the Seventh Amendment guaranteed the role of the jury in claim construction.[452]

Significantly, *Markman II* here turns from description to prescription. That is, having found no constitutional reason to task the jury with claim construction, the Court—after noting that longstanding precedent at least weakly supported an exclusive judicial role[453]—ultimately rested its decision on purely "functional considerations."[454] These factors took two forms. The first was the Court's expectation that judges—by virtue of their special skills and experience, as well as the "highly technical" nature of patent claim construction and the "special doctrines" developed by the courts

445. *Markman II, supra* note 444, at 383.

446. See William Woodward, *Definiteness and Particularity in Patent Claims*, 46 MICH. L. REV. 755, 758 (1948).

447. Act of July 4, 1836, ch. 357, § 6, 5 Stat. 119.

448. Act of July 8, 1870, ch. 230, § 26, 16 Stat. 201.

449. In patent parlance, the "specification" is the document itself, which includes a written description, the claims, and, often, drawings or diagrams.

450. *Markman II, supra* note 444, at 381.

451. *Id.* at 382.

452. *Id.* at 383–84.

453. See id. at 384–88. See also id. at 387 (noting the "fine" line drawn between questions of interpretation and infringement, and the roles thereof, in 19th-century Supreme Court patent cases), id. at 388 (suggesting such precedent provided "no clear answers").

454. Id. at 388.

for their interpretation[455]—were simply more likely to be better at the task than "jurors unburdened by training in exegesis."[456] Second, the allocation of interpretive authority to judges was, the court suggested, likely to promote the goals of intrajurisdictional certainty and uniformity.[457] Whether the Court got it "right" when analyzing these factors is obviously a matter of some debate, and has been widely discussed and debated in the literature.[458] However, from the perspective of institutional design, the importance of the Court's discussion is not the detailed analysis as much as the underlying assumptions (and, indeed, requirements) concerning the framework of the claim construction process. As an initial point, the Court was fairly explicit about the criteria by which it was measuring the goodness of competing systems; to wit, correctness,[459] uniformity,[460] and certainty.[461] Second, and perhaps more significantly, both functional factors identified by the court shared a unifying underlying principle: the existence of specific legal rules guiding the interpretation of patent claims. For example, in suggesting that judges were likely to be better at construing claims, the Court cited "special doctrines" relating to construction embedded in the law.[462] Further, *stare decisis*—that is, the existence (and development) of legal rules—anchored the Court's argument that judicial decision making

455. Id. at 389. The Court downplayed the influence of credibility determinations (which it described as "the jury's forte") in claim construction analyses, reasoning that credibility determinations would rarely be a deciding factor, and that to the extent they existed, they would be "subsumed within a necessarily sophisticated analysis of the whole document."

456. Id. at 388.

457. The Court's discussion noted that it was especially concerned with uniformity of treatment concerning a particular patent—one that presumably might be litigated nearly contemporaneously in multiple jurisdictions. By designating the interpretive issue as a matter of law, *Markman II* suggested that principles of *stare decisis* might serve to maintain intrajurisdictional uniformity prior to appellate review. See *id.* at 391 (noting that issue preclusion would be unavailable against new and independent infringement defendants). On this ground, however, the Court's concerns seem overstated; the district courts have used their discretionary case management tools to largely avoid any potential intrajurisdictional conflicts concerning the same patent.

458. For example, the court makes an explicitly empirical assumption about the prevalence of conflicting expert testimony on claim construction. See id. at 389.

459. Id. at 388 (noting "judges often do and are likely to do better" at interpreting written instruments).

460. Id. at 390–91 (discussing the benefits of uniform treatment of patents, and citing the creation of the Federal Circuit as an example of the push for such uniformity).

461. Id. (discussing certainty).

462. Id. at 389 (citing Woodward, *supra*). This reasoning, of course, has the flavor of circularity about it: citing the existence and strength of judicially-created doctrine as a reason to allocate interpretive authority to judges. Clearly the Court here was assuming a stronger baseline in favor of judicial interpretation than it seemed to have acknowledged earlier in the opinion.

in this context would enhance uniformity and certainty.[463] Thus, in both cases, *Markman II*'s functionalist approach was largely based on the theory that allocating the interpretive task to judges would extend and enhance the development of legal rules guiding the construction of patent claims.

And yet the logic of *Markman II* clearly encompasses a prescriptive aspect as well. If the Court made its decision to assign claim construction to judges on the theory that this would result in the continued use and development of legal rules for the process, then it follows that such legal rules (and their development) are not simply hortatory—but instead a mandatory aspect of the institutional arrangements surrounding claim construction. In essence, the *Markman II* decision granted the judges the power to construe patent claims, but this grant was clearly conditioned on the use and development of legal-doctrinal "rules and tools" to provide clarity and uniformity in the treatment of interpretive issues. Absent a uniform legal framework, the basic premise of the Court's functionalist analysis is absent.

We move now to the second major aspect of the institutional design of the claim construction system: the issue of appellate review. Importantly, in this regard, the Federal Circuit amplified the effect of the Supreme Court's prescription in *Markman II.* In *Cybor Corp. v. FAS Technologies*, the court responded to the challenge laid down by the Supreme Court two years earlier.[464] In *Cybor*, a majority of the Federal Circuit declared that claim construction was a pure issue of law, and thus no deference was due to district courts on the question.[465] As commentators have noted, though the *Cybor* court purported to be following the edicts of *Markman II*, it is difficult to reconcile the majority opinion in *Cybor* with the actual statements made with respect to the fact/law distinction by the Supreme Court.[466] In that sense, *Cybor* is a disappointing decision.

But the importance of Cybor extends well beyond the reasoning surrounding the fact/law distinction. Indeed, as the Supreme Court itself noted, divining the fact/law distinction is considerably less satisfactory than an analysis grounded in historical analogues and functional considerations.[467] By declaring the interpretation of pat-

463. Id. at 391.

464. See *Cybor Corp. v. FAS Techs.*, Inc., 138 F.3d 1448 (Fed.Cir.1998) (en banc).

465. Id. at 1456.

466. See generally Nard, *supra* note 446; Duffy, *supra* note 443; William H. Burgess, *Simplicity at the Cost of Clarity: Appellate Review of Claim Construction and the Failed Promise of Cybor*, 153 U. PA. L. REV. 763 (2004).

467. *Markman II*, *supra* note 344, at 378, 384. See also Duffy, *supra* note 443, at 122–123 and nn. 51–53 (suggesting

ent claims as "purely legal," the *Cybor* majority held that no deference was due a district court's claim construction, and that appellate review was to be conducted de novo.[468] From an institutional design perspective, this decision (though perhaps not the reasoning) merges well with the theory of *Markman II* noted above: that by allocating legal authority to a centralized body (the Federal Circuit), the legal framework for claim construction can best be developed. It is unfortunate, then, that the *Cybor* majority did not base its argument on institutional design considerations—the instrumentally appropriate location of this decision making authority—but the opinion can really only be viewed as implicitly reinforcing the Federal Circuit as the superlative administrative player in the claim construction process.[469] Thus, the Federal Circuit has not merely embraced the special mandate underlying the *Markman II* decision, it has reinforced it.

There is a rich debate regarding whether this set of institutional arrangements—judicial interpretations, and *de novo* appellate review—has been beneficial. Some commentators argue that the arrangements (especially *de novo* appellate review) damage the opportunity for uniformity by undermining district court decision making.[470] Other commentators, notably including Judge Mayer of the Federal Circuit, describe the various machinations surrounding current allocation of authority as "akin to rearranging the deck chairs on the Titanic," for their failure to address the factual underpinnings of the claim construction process.[471] These points are important: the present scheme has clear problems associated with it.[472] And yet it is not necessarily the case that a *de novo* standard of

that *Cybor*'s choice between standards of review "cannot be made on the basis of metaphysical distinctions between fact and law."). See also Gary Lawson, *Proving Law*, 86 Nw. U.L. Rev. 859, 863 (1992) (describing the historical convention of the fact/law distinction); *United States v. McKinney*, 919 F.2d 405, 418–19 (7th Cir.1990) (Posner, J. concurring) (determining standard of review on the basis of facts versus law would be "absurd"). *Cooter & Gell v. Hartmarx Corp.*, 496 U.S. 384, 401 (1990) (observing the problems in distinguishing between legal and factual issues);

468. *Cybor Corp.*, 138 F.3d at 1456 ("[W]e therefore reaffirm that, as a purely legal question, we review claim construction de novo on appeal....").

469. Duffy, *supra* note 443, at 123 ("The majority's holding in favor of de novo review must be viewed as an implicit determination [regarding institutional design]. ") Duffy (and others) have argued that the choice of de novo review in *Cybor* undermined the goal of uniformity, perhaps in an effort to increase procedural efficiency. See *id.* See also *Cybor Corp.*, 138 F.3d at 1476 (Judge Rader discussing Federal Circuit's reversal rate of district courts).

470. See, e.g., Duffy, *supra* note 443.

471. See *Phillips v. AWH Corp.*, 415 F.3d 1303, 1335 (Fed.Cir.2005) (Mayer, J., dissenting).

472. See, e.g., Christian A. Chu, *Empirical Analysis of the Federal Circuit's Claim Construction Trends*, 16 Berkeley Tech. L.J. 1075, 1078–79 (2001) (suggesting the Federal Circuit has failed to achieve greater predictability); Nard,

review will either undermine certainty or reduce the efficiency of the system. If the framework established in *Markman II–Cybor* enabled the Federal Circuit to establish clear guidelines for the interpretation of patent claims, certainty and efficiency would be enhanced, not diminished. Clear rules would allow district court judges to implement claim constructions with greater confidence, allow the parties to better evaluate their chances of success (both post-judgment and pre-litigation), and, perhaps most significantly, result in patentees drafting clearer claims even prior to a patent's issue. But this debate continues—and which of these views is correct largely depends upon how well one understands the Federal Circuit to have implemented the *Markman II–Cybor* mandate to establish clear and uniform rules for the interpretation of patent claims. It is to this issue that we turn next.

III. Interpreting Patent Claims

The legal doctrine establishing the process of claim construction took a sharp step back into the past in 2005, with the Federal Circuit's (unanimous) opinion in *Phillips v. AWH*.[473] In *Phillips*, the court stated that it was reaffirming the principles of claim construction set forth in 1996 in *Vitronics Corp. v. Conceptronics, Inc.*[474] In doing so, the court was attempting to end a ten-year struggle over how the court should address, as a matter of legal doctrine, the way

Process Considerations, supra note 344, at 357 (calling for the Federal Circuit to accept interlocutory appeals of district court claim interpretations in order to promote certainty). The views of the bar are noted by various authors, e.g., Luke L. Dauchot, *The Federal Circuit's De Novo Review of Patent Claim Construction: A Need for a More Balanced Approach*, 18 INTELL. PROP. L. NEWSL. (Am. Bar. Ass'n Sec. on Intell. Prop., Chicago, Ill.), Fall 1999, at 1, 1 (arguing for the Federal Circuit to give greater deference to trial court interpretations); Ted D. Lee and Michelle Evans, *The Charade: Trying a Patent Case to All "Three" Juries*, 8 TEX. INTELL. PROP. L.J. 1, 11–20 (1999) (characterizing the Federal Circuit as a "second jury" in patent cases); Paul R. Michel, *The Court of Appeals for the Federal Circuit Must Evolve to Meet the Challenges Ahead*, 48 AM. U. L. REV. 1177, 1186–1200 (1999) (addressing oft-cited practitioner concerns); Douglas D. Salyers, *The Paper Side of Jury Litigation in Patent Cases—Don't Become Just Another Statistic in The Federal Circuit*, in PATENT LITIGATION 1999, at 557, 566–88 (PLI Intell. Prop. Course, Handbook Series No. G–572, 1999). The reported opinions of judges have been largely negative on this issue. One district judge has stated publicly that the Federal Circuit is full of "little green men who don't know Tuesday from Philadelphia." Victoria Slind–Flor, *The Markman Prophecies*, IP WORLDWIDE, March 13, 2002, at 28, 30 (quoting Judge Samuel Kent of the Southern District of Texas); see also id. (" 'Frankly, I don't know why I'm so excited about bringing this [patent case] to closure. It goes to the Federal Circuit afterwards. You know, it's hard to deal with things that are ultimately resolved by people wearing propeller hats.' " (quoting Judge Kent in *O.I. Corp. v. Tekmar Co.*, No. 95–CV–113 (S.D. Tex. June 17, 1996))).

473. 415 F.3d 1303 (Fed.Cir.2005) (en banc).

474. 90 F.3d 1576 (Fed.Cir.1996).

to interpret patent claims.[475] This struggle emerged soon after the Supreme Court spoke in *Markman II*; once judges (and especially the Federal Circuit) were tasked with developing legal principles for claim construction, the effort to define those principles began.

It is useful to note that there is relatively little disagreement or debate about the fundamental framework at issue here. That is, the patent law has for some time held that claim language should be interpreted though the lens of a person having ordinary skill in the art at the time of the patent's filing.[476] The struggle surrounds how to determine what information should be used—and how—to answer this question.

Note as well that there are a number of oft-cited "canons of construction" that purport to guide the analysis. As has been noted by the Federal Circuit itself, many, if not all of these canons are contradictory and are not especially useful.[477] Indeed, it is the efforts to resolve the tension between a pair of these canons—(a) that claims are to be interpreted in light of the specification and prosecution history, and (b) that claims may not be modified beyond their actual language by reference to the specification or prosecution history—that illustrates the basic doctrinal struggle the court has been seeking to resolve.

Vitronics, noted above, represents an early effort. There, the court developed a key evidentiary distinction; one between what it called *intrinsic evidence*—information found within the public record of the patent, and what it called *extrinsic evidence*—information not within the public record, but still potentially relevant to the inquiry.[478] In *Vitronics*, the court held that intrinsic evidence was to be given precedence, and that the use of extrinsic evidence was improper if the intrinsic evidence could answer the interpretive questions.[479] However, *Vitronics* left much to be desired as a governing framework. First, it said too little: although it established an

475. For an empirical analysis of this struggle, see R. Polk Wagner and Lee Petherbridge, *Is the Federal Circuit Succeeding: An Empirical Assessment of Judicial Performance*, 152 U. Penn L. Rev. 1105 (2004).

476. See *Phillips*, 415 F.3d at 1313.

477. Indeed, the patent law features canons to avoid the use of canons. *Autogiro Co. of Am. v. United States*, 181 Ct.Cl. 55, 384 F.2d 391, 397, 155 U.S.P.Q. (BNA) 697, 702 (Ct.Cl.1967) ("In utilizing all the patent documents, one should not sacrifice the value of these references by the 'unimaginative adherence to well-worn professional phrases.' " (quoting Frankfurter, *Some Reflections on the Reading of Statutes*, 47 Col. L. Rev. 527, 528 (1947))). See also *Renishaw PLC v. Marposs Societa' Per Azioni*, 158 F.3d 1243, 1248 n.2 (Fed.Cir.1998) (citing Karl N. Llewellyn, *Remarks on the Theory of Appellate Decision and the Rules or Canons About How Statutes Are to be Construed*, 3 VAND. L. REV. 395, 401–06 (1950)).

478. 90 F.3d at 1582–83.

479. Id.

understandable hierarchy of evidence, the opinion gave little guidance about when extrinsic evidence was justified. Second, it said too much: the intrinsic/extrinsic distinction—which was made on the basis of the reliability and objectivity of the evidence—failed to adequately grapple with the fact that certain "extrinsic" sources, most especially dictionaries and other objective references, were often the single most important sources of relevant information. Thus, *Vitronics*, while usefully establishing certain evidentiary guideposts, did not establish a particularly reliable framework.

Out of the confusion of *Vitronics* developed two classes of claim construction opinions. These two lines of cases were distinct enough as to be empirically verified in leading to distinct results, and were strongly associated with different groups of judges on the Federal Circuit.[480]

1. The first approach established an evidentiary presumption in favor of the "ordinary meaning" of claim language, and required good reason to deviate from such a meaning. Because an ordinary meaning is often derived from a contemporaneous technical or general purpose dictionary, this approach is conventionally associated with an extensive use of dictionaries. This has been called the "procedural" approach.[481]
2. The second approach took a broader view, and eschewed any presumptive default rule or procedural guidelines. Instead, this approach sought to find the meaning of claim language by carefully examining its context, most especially by a close reading of the disclosures contained in the public record of the patent. This has been called the "holistic" approach.[482]

From *Markman II* until the 2005 decision in *Phillips*, the Federal Circuit alternated between holistic and procedural approaches, with the procedural approach slowly gaining a majority (about 65 percent) of the decisions.[483] (As alluded to above, the approach used appears to have been largely determined by the judges assigned to the case.[484]) It is important to understand that although the distinction is often framed as one concerning the role of dictionaries,[485] in reality the choice of approach has more to do with one's theory about the institutional role of the Federal Circuit

480. See *Wagner* and *Petherbridge*, *supra* note 477, at 1163–69.

481. Id. at 1130–36.

482. Id.

483. Id. at 1150–52.

484. Id. at 1163–66.

485. See *Phillips*, 415 F.3d at 1319 (suggesting that a "greater emphasis to dictionary definitions" is a hallmark of the procedural line of cases).

than with the use of any particular source of information. That is, adherence to the more rule-like procedural approach suggests a managerial role for the Federal Circuit in claim construction: establishing a (rule-like) legal framework, even if results in particular cases seem "incorrect." Conversely, using an approach like the holistic approach, with its emphasis on context and sensitivity to getting the best possible results given available information, suggests a decision maker role for the Federal Circuit: a focus on getting the right results, with a secondary goal of setting forth a clear and consistent legal approach to claim construction.

In *Phillips v. AWH*, the Federal Circuit addressed what it described as the "role of dictionaries" in claim construction analyses. Concluding that dictionaries were unreliable and often lacked the context provided by a close reading of the public record of the patent, the Phillips opinion held that the procedural approach noted above "place[s] too much reliance on extrinsic sources such as dictionaries, treatises, and encyclopedias, and too little on intrinsic sources, in particular the specification and prosecution history."[486] Interestingly, while the court extensively outlined what it described as the principles of claim construction, it offered very little that was not firmly settled law (under either of the dueling approaches), and almost nothing in the way of guidance. Among the principles the *Phillips* court articulates:

- Claim construction is conducted through the lens of one of skilled in the art at the time of filing;
- Claims are to be read and understood within the context of the entire patent;
- The context provided by the claim language may often be helpful;
- The context provided by the written description or specification may often be helpful;
- The context provided by the prosecution history may often be helpful;
- Extrinsic evidence, such as dictionaries, treatises, and expert testimony, can often be helpful, if understood in the context of the intrinsic evidence.

With respect to the core issue that the Federal Circuit itself had been wresting with for nearly ten years—*when should particular types of information be credited over others*—the *Phillips* court offered very little guidance, stating merely that:

486. Id. at 1320.

1. "[T]he court should keep in mind the flaws inherent in each type of evidence and assess that evidence accordingly,"[487] and that

2. "The sequence of steps used by the judge in consulting various sources is not important; what matters is for the court to attach the appropriate weight to be assigned to those sources in light of the statutes and policies that inform patent law."[488]

Indeed, apparently overlooking the recent doctrinal struggles, the court even suggested that this problem was not especially difficult: "the line between construing terms and importing limitations can be discerned with reasonable certainty and predictability if the court's focus remains on understanding how a person of ordinary skill in the art would understand the claim terms."[489]

Under the *Phillips* doctrine, it is difficult to see what is *not* allowed with respect to claim construction analyses: other than a rigid adherence to dictionaries without context, anything goes. In particular, note that dictionaries and other forms of extrinsic evidence are fully authorized, as long as the court, in its discretion, considers their role in the context of the rest of the patent.[490] Indeed, the obvious avoidance of any language that could be construed as a rule in the *Phillips* opinion suggests that the case is best understood as assertion of a distinct institutional role for the court as the ultimate decision maker on these questions. (Note that the *Phillips* court refused to reconsider the *Cybor* standard of review issue, so the *de novo* review standard remains.[491])

In mid–2007, it remains early to draw any firm conclusions about the effects of *Phillips*. According to one scorecard, however, the effects of *Phillips* are quite modest; the overall distribution of procedural versus holistic analyses has changed little since the *Phillips* opinion.

487. Id. at 1319.

488. Id. at. 1324.

489. Id. at 1323.

490. Id. at 1322 ("as we have noted above, however, we do not intend to preclude the appropriate use of dictionaries.")

491. The Federal Circuit requested briefing on the standard of review question in the order granting en banc treatment in *Phillips*. See *Phillips v. AWH Corp.*, 376 F.3d 1382, at 3 (Order, 2004). The en banc court, however, declined to address the question. See *Phillips*, 415 F.3d at 1328.

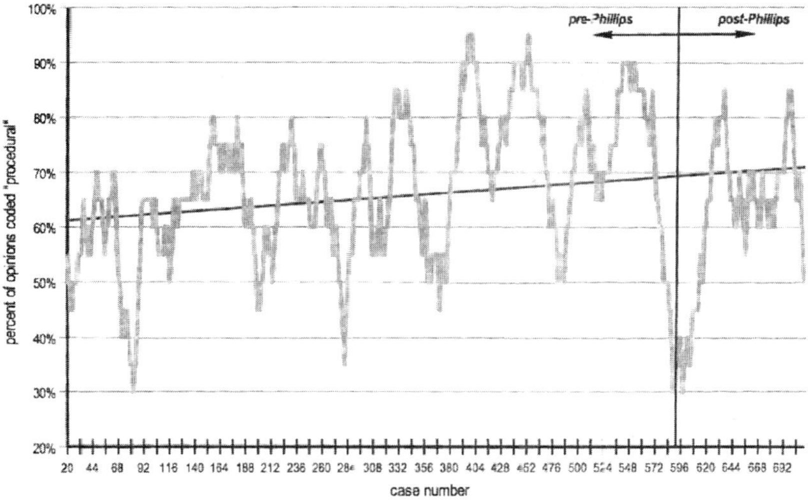

Figure 9–2. Federal Circuit Claim Construction Methodologies, 1995–2007[492]

[20–case lagged average, court opinions only, n = 714]

A few things to watch, however:

- The effects of *Phillips* might be quite modest indeed, because of its no-rules approach. Under this view, the judges of the Federal Circuit will be essentially free to pursue whatever methodological approach they like, with little guidance or restraints; we might, then, expect the pre-*Phillips* methodological split to persist, at least in some form.
- *Phillips* might shift even greater institutional power to the Federal Circuit, as noted above.
- Especially if no further guidance emerges from the post-*Phillips* claim construction case law, one might expect *Phillips* to at least modestly increase the numbers of disputes and litigation. That is, with more uncertainty about the scope of patents (the real scope won't be decided until the *de novo* review of the Federal Circuit), we can expect more litigation.
- Most troubling, the *Phillips* court's repeated emphasis on the context provided by the patent specification might have the perverse effect of reducing the amount of disclosure in patents. The reason is simple: if *Phillips* suggests that claim language can be easily altered (especially narrowed) via

492. Data through April 15, 2007. Data and additional analysis available at http://www.claimconstruction.com/.

information provided in the specification, then savvy patent attorneys will simply provide less relevant information (subject, as always, to the statutory validity requirements). This "minimal disclosure" approach has a second major advantage in light of *Phillips*: because of the lack of guidance provided about how information—especially non-patent information—is to be regarded and weighted in the analysis, a patent with a very thin disclosure is far more likely to gain one interpretation (a narrow one, to enhance the chance of issuance) from the PTO and another for later litigation (a broader one, to expand scope). As noted above, this "nose of wax" problem is of serious import.

- Finally, the way the *Phillips* court discussed the process of claim construction—a context-specific, fact-driven, discretionary-weighing process—makes it very difficult to reconcile with the assertion in *Cybor* that claim construction is a "pure issue of law." It seems likely that the question of standard of review (or fact/law) will have to be revisited in the future, or at least informally adjusted. It seems difficult to sustain a *de novo* review of district court decision making when the Federal Circuit so pointedly refuses to constrain itself to any rules.

In any event—and by any measure—the struggle to create a coherent legal framework for claim construction continues.

Chapter Ten

INFRINGEMENT

I. Introduction

Patent law is exclusively federal, and therefore, a patentee wishing to enforce his patent rights must proceed in federal district court.[493] In a patent infringement suit, a patentee asserts that the patent *claims* are infringed, not the commercial embodiment of the claimed invention or what is set forth in the specification.[494] Patent claims are the touchstone of patent protection, and it is the claims that set forth the patentee's proprietary boundaries. Thus, as explored in Chapter 9, a crucial and oftentimes determinative aspect of patent litigation is determining what the claims mean. Construing the claims is always the first step in an infringement (and validity) analysis. The second step is determining whether the accused product infringes the patent claim(s) at issue.

A determination of infringement requires a two-step analysis. First, the claims are to be construed as a matter of law. The second step is a factual determination that examines whether the construed claims "read on" or cover the accused device. In other words, every limitation of the claimed invention is found in the accused product, either literally or an equivalent.[495] The causes of action for patent infringement can be divided into two broad categories: (1) *direct infringement*; and (2) *indirect infringement.* Under the theory of direct infringement, the patentee may bring an action against a defendant who himself is committing acts (e.g., making a product or practicing a process) that infringe one or more patent claims. Direct patent infringement comprises both (1) *literal* infringement; and (2) infringement under the *doctrine of equivalents* (or "DOE"). Indirect infringement relates to a third party facilitating or aiding and abetting direct infringement by, for example, providing instructions to infringe or manufacturing a particular component of the claimed invention where the component, for practical purposes, can only be used to infringe the patent directly. Both direct and indirect infringement will be explored below, as

493. See 28 U.S.C. § 1338 (2007).

494. See *ACCO Brands, Inc. v. Micro Sec. Devices, Inc.*, 346 F.3d 1075, 1081–82 (Fed.Cir.2003) ("The language of the claim, not the patent owner's commercial product, is the measure of infringement.").

495. See *SmithKline Diagnostics v. Helena Laboratories Corp.*, 859 F.2d 878, 889 (Fed.Cir 1988).

well as important limitations on the DOE, namely prosecution history estoppel, public dedication rule, and the all-elements rule.

Recent empirical scholarship on patent litigation suggests that only about 1% of patents are ever litigated.[496] Of this small percentage, 5% of the cases go to trial,[497] an additional 6–9% are resolved on the merits through summary judgment,[498] and the remaining are resolved through some form of settlement.[499] One of the more prominent incentives driving settlement is the high cost of patent litigation. One survey showed that for litigation with less than $1 million at risk, litigation fees, inclusive of all costs, were $767,000; with $1–25 million at risk, the fees rose to $2,645,000 million; and when more than $25 million is at stake, litigation expenses approached $5.5 million.[500] Moreover, patent litigation has risen dramatically over the past 20 years,[501] with patents in some industries

496. See Mark A. Lemley, *Rational Ignorance at the Patent Office*, 95 Nw. L. Rev. 1495, 1501 (2001). Some scholars have suggested that the small number of patents being litigated is because "[m]any patents are not worth enforcing—either because the inventions they cover turn out to be worthless, or because even if the invention has economic value the patent does not." John R. Allison, Mark A. Lemley, Kimberly A. Moore and R. Derek Trunkey, *Valuable Patents*, 92 Geo. L.J. 435, 436 (2004). Of course, many patents are licensed (or subject to cross-licensing agreements), can be used to intimidate competitors, or be useful in attractive capital investment. See Shubha Ghosh and Jay Kesan, *What Do Patents Purchase? In Search of Optimal Ignorance in the Patent Office*, 40 Hous. L. Rev. 1219 (2004). But see Lemley, *Rational Ignorance*, *supra* (estimating only 3.5% of patents are licensed for a royalty).

497. Jean O. Lanjouw and Mark Schankerman, *Protecting Intellectual Property Rights: Are Small Firms Handicapped?* 47 J. L. Econ. 45 (2004); Jay P. Kesan and Gwendolyn G. Ball, *How Art Patent Case Resolved? An Empirical Examination of the Adjudication and Settlement of Patent Disputes*, 84 Wash. U. L. Rev. 237 (2006). Paul Janicke's empirical work on patent litigation shows that in 2006, 3.1% of patent cases went to trial (2.2% jury trial and 0.9% bench trial). Paul Janicke, *Patent Litigation Remedies: Some Statistical Observations* (2007) at http://www.patstats.org/editors_page.rev6.html.

498. See Janicke, *Patent Litigation Remedies, supra* note 499 (in 2006, 7% of patent cases were resolved through summary judgment).

499. See Kesan and Ball, *How Are Patent Cases Resolved, supra* note 499; Janicke, *Patent Litigation Remedies*, *supra* note 499 (showing in 2006, 86.5% of patent cases were settled, which includes consent judgments, voluntary dismissals, and dismissals stating settlement or "other dismissals"). These figures, of course, only tell part of the picture. In testimony on patent reform before the House Subcommittee on Courts, the Internet, and Intellectual Property, an Apple Computer representative stated: "[F]or every lawsuit that goes to final judgment, there is 25 more that don't go to final judgment, that get adjudicated or settled ahead of time, and for every one of those, there's 25 [cease and desist] letters that were written that never made it to a lawsuit at all." H.R. Rep. 109–11, pt. 1, at 122 (2005).

500. American Intellectual Property Law Association, Report of the Economic Survey I–90–1 (2007).

501. See Jean O. Lanjouw and Mark Schankerman, *Protecting Intellectual Property Rights: Are Small Firms Handicapped?* 47 J.L. & Econ. 45 (2004) (noting an "almost 10–fold" increase in pat-

much more likely to be litigated than in other industries.[502]

II. Literal Infringement

Literal infringement of a patent is straightforward and occurs when every limitation recited in the claim is found in the accused device.[503] An example of literal infringement is found in *Transmatic, Inc. v. Gulton Industries, Inc.*[504] Transmatic owned the '415 patent directed to a unitary (single-piece) cornice lighting fixture for public transit vehicles, such as buses. The patented lighting fixture was capable of supporting and illuminating an advertising card, while also illuminating the interior of the transit vehicle. Claim 1 required, among other things, "a light housing that defines one longitudinal margin of the fixture." The light housing is set forth below in Figure 10–1:

ent litigation over the past two decades); Joseph P. Cook, *On Understanding the Increase in Patent Litigation*, 9 AM. L. & ECON. REV. 48, 48 (2007) (stating "[f]or the last 20 years, patent litigation in the United States has been steadily increasing. In the last 10 years, the number of patent cases filed in US federal courts has approximately doubled"). But a recent study conducted by PricewaterhouseCoopers found that after increasing from 07 1991 (1,171 patent cases filed) to 2004 (3,074 cases), patent litigation filings decreased from 2004 to 2005, when 2,720 cases were filed. This decrease represents the first decline in 16 years. The report suggests that several factors influenced the reduction in patent cases, including greater use of ADR, high litigation fees, recent Supreme Court rulings, and reduced damage awards.

502. See John R. Allison, Mark A. Lemley, Kimberly A. Moore and R. Derek Trunkey, *Valuable Patents*, 92 GEO. L.J. 435, 471–75 (2004) (finding "patents on medical devices, computer-related inventions, software, electronics, and mechanics are significantly more likely to be litigated than the average of all patents. By contrast, chemistry, automotive, and semiconductor patents are significantly less likely to be litigated."). See also Josh Lerner, *Patenting in the Shadow of Competitors*, 38 J.L. & ECON. 463 (1995) (finding biotechnology patents more likely to be litigated than other forms of technology).

503. See *Mannesmann Demag Corp. v. Engineered Metal Prod. Co.*, 793 F.2d 1279, 1282 (Fed.Cir.1986); *Mas–Hamilton Group v. LaGard, Inc.*, 156 F.3d 1206, 1211 (Fed.Cir.1998) (stating that literal infringement does not exist if one limitation is missing in the accused product).

504. 53 F.3d 1270 (Fed.Cir.1995).

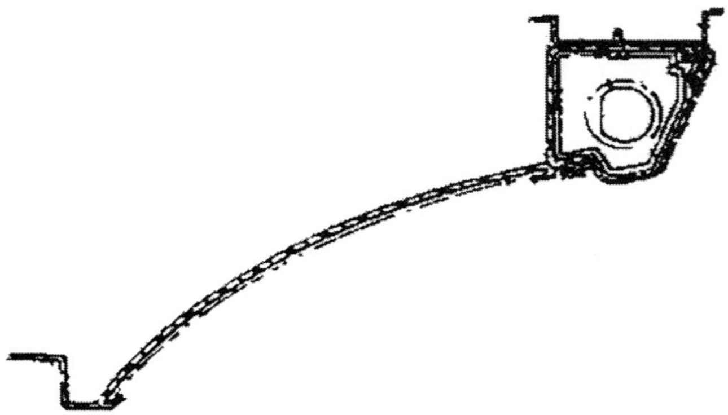

Figure 10–1. '415 Patent (the "light housing" is located at the upper right and looks like a fishing reel)

The accused infringer, Gulton, manufactured a unitary cornice lighting fixture. The district court found that the Gulton device possessed each and every limitation of the '415 patent, except Gulton's device includes an approximately three and one-half inch extension or flange that extends the light housing to a point beyond a light cover associated with the light housing. The Gulton device is depicted in Figure 10–2, below:

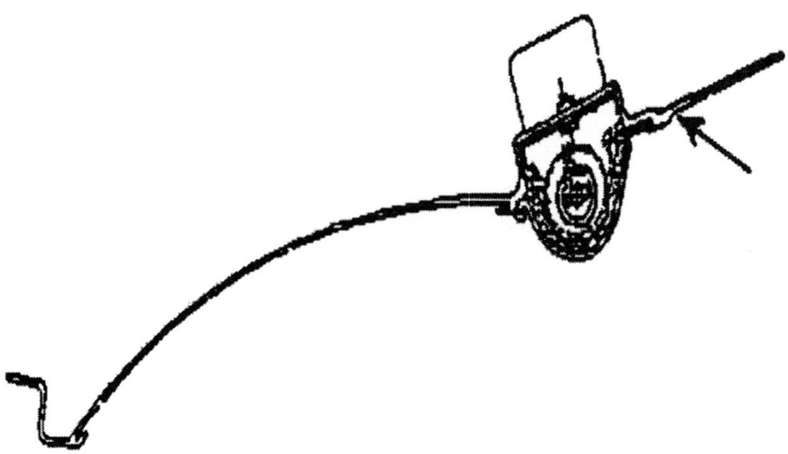

Figure 10–2: Gulton's Accused Product

According to the district court, Gulton's device meets every limitation of claim 1 except for "a light housing that defines one longitudinal margin of the fixture." The court viewed the flange as a separate component from the light housing itself, and therefore, did not find literal infringement because the flange, not the light housing, defined a longitudinal margin of the lighting fixture. The Federal Circuit reversed, stating it was "persuaded that the flange in Gulton's device is simply an extension of the light housing and thus part of it." As such, Gulton's device literally infringes claim 1 of the '415 patent because Gulton's light housing (with flange) "clearly defines a longitudinal margin of the lighting fixture."[505]

III. The Doctrine of Equivalents

The doctrine of equivalents (DOE) is a common law doctrine that comes into play when there is no literal infringement. The DOE allows for a finding of infringement when an accused infringing device (or process) is "equivalent" to that claimed in the patent. Returning to the chair example, let's say Inventor still claims a chair having a seat portion, a back portion and four legs. But now Competitor makes a chair having a seat portion, a back portion, and *three* legs. There is no literal infringement because Competitor's product does not have each and every limitation of Inventor's claim, but Competitor may still infringe under the DOE if it is determined that three legs are equivalent to four legs.

Unlike literal infringement, which is straightforward, the DOE is controversial and thorny, and thus deserving of more attention. The DOE is one of the oldest and more controversial common law doctrines in American patent law. What makes the DOE controversial is its inherent tension with patent law's clear claiming requirement (see § 112, ¶ 2) and the importance of certainty in a property rights regime. Indeed, it is frequently quite difficult to discern *ex ante* what is or is not an "equivalent"—how does Competitor know in advance that four legs is or is not equivalent to three legs? As such, a degree of uncertainty hangs over the patentee's competitors and their decision making process regarding investment in the manufacture or sale of competing products. On the other hand, strict and literal adherence to the written claim in determining the scope of protection can invite unfair subversion of a valuable right, which would substantially diminish the economic value of patents.

In recent years, the Federal Circuit has erred on the side of certainty and clear claiming, which has invited numerous challenges to the DOE, two of which made their way to the United States Supreme Court. The DOE survived these challenges, although, as explored in Section C, *infra*, the reach of the doctrine

505. Id. at 1278.

has been curtailed. The two cases nicely capture the arguments for and against the DOE, *Graver Tank v. Linde Air Prods. Co.* and *Warner–Jenkinson Company, Inc. v. Hilton Davis Chemical, Inc.*

A. Foundational Cases

1. *Graver Tank v. Linde Air Prods. Co*

In *Graver Tank*,[506] Linde Air Products owned a patent for certain electric welding compositions known as fluxes, which facilitated the fusing of metals. Two sets of claims were involved. One set of claims described a major element as any "silicate." The other set of claims, which was narrower, described "a combination of alkaline earth metal silicate and calcium fluoride." The Supreme Court held the first set of claims invalid for undue breadth. The narrower claims were held not invalid and the question became whether these claims were infringed.

The patent disclosed silicates of calcium and magnesium, two alkaline earth metal silicates, but the accused product, known as Lincolnweld 660, comprised silicates of calcium and manganese. The issue was whether manganese, which is not an alkaline earth metal, is equivalent to magnesium. A majority of five justices held that manganese was indeed an equivalent. Justice Jackson, who wrote for the majority, viewed the DOE as protection for the patentee against the "unscrupulous copyist" who without the DOE as a deterrent, would be inclined "to make unimportant and insubstantial changes and substitutions in the patent which, though adding nothing, would be enough to take the copied matter outside the claim."[507] For Justice Jackson and the majority, a patent system that permitted such activity would "convert the protection of the patent grant into a hollow and useless thing."[508] With these equitable principles in mind, the court explained that equivalence "is not the prisoner of a formula," but "must be determined against the context of the patent, the prior art, and the particular circumstances of the case."[509] The Court adopted the following linguistic test for determining equivalents: the accused device is equivalent to the claimed invention if the accused device " 'performs substantially the same function in substantially the same way to obtain the same result.' "[510] This test has come to be

506. 339 U.S. 605 (1950).

507. Id. at 607.

508. Id.

509. Id. at 609.

510. Id. at 608 (quoting *Sanitary Refrigerator Co. v. Winters*, 280 U.S. 30, 42 (1929)). The Court noted that the theory on which this test is founded is that " 'if two devices do the same work in sub-

known as the tripartite test or the function-way-result test.[511] The majority thought the evidence was clear, including the prior art and expert testimony, that manganese was substantially equivalent to magnesium.[512]

Whereas the majority justified application of the DOE on largely equitable principles, the four-person dissent took a more rule-oriented approach that emphasized separation of powers and the importance of certainty in a property rights regime such as patent law. Regarding certainty, the dissent, authored by Justice Black, argued that applicants are required to particularly point out and distinctly claim what their invention is, and "[w]hat is not specifically claimed is dedicated to the public."[513] The majority, in Justice Black's view, ignores this principle and impermissibly treats the patentee's claim "like a nose of wax, which may be turned and twisted in any direction, by merely referring to the specification."[514] As for separation of powers, the dissent asserted the majority ignored administrative remedies for patentees who claimed too narrowly. For instance, a patentee may return to the PTO and seek reissue of its patent with broader claims. Unlike the majority opinion, argued the dissent, the reissue proceeding "protects business men from retroactive infringement suits and judicial expansion of a monopoly sphere beyond that which a patent expressly authorizes."[515]

Graver Tank became a key judicial precedent, perhaps because the Supreme Court did not address the subject again for almost 50 years, but also because the majority and dissent set forth the arguments for and against DOE that are still asserted and debated today.

2. *Warner–Jenkinson Company, Inc. v. Hilton Davis Chemical, Inc.*

As intellectual property, particularly patent, became increasingly more important in the 1980s and '90s, questions relating to the role of jury and the need for greater certainty and predictability

stantially the same way, and accomplish substantially the same result, they are the same, even though they differ in name, form or shape.' " *Id.* at 608 (quoting *Union Paper–Bag Machine Co. v. Murphy*, 97 U.S. 120, 125 (1877)).

511. See, e.g., *Caterpillar Inc. v. Deere & Co.*, 224 F.3d 1374, 1379 (Fed. Cir.2000) (referring to the "well-known tripartite test"); *Oak Technology, Inc. v. International Trade Comm'n*, 248 F.3d 1316, 1321 (Fed.Cir.2001) (referring to the "familiar three-part function/way/result test").

512. Id. at 610–11.

513. Id. at 613–14.

514. Id. at 614.

515. Id. at 615.

occupied patent policy makers, attorneys, the Federal Circuit, and eventually the Supreme Court. The DOE was at center stage in this debate, and after nearly five decades of silence on the DOE, the Supreme Court granted *certiorari* in *Warner–Jenkinson Company v. Hilton Davis Chemical, Inc.*[516]

The patent at issue in *Warner–Jenkinson* involved a filtration process for purifying dyes such as F, D & C (food, drug and cosmetic) Red Dye #6 and Yellow Dye #6. (Impurities must be removed from these dyes to meet food and drug regulations.) In particular, the patented process filters impure dye through a porous membrane at certain pressures and pH levels, resulting in a high-purity dye product. When prosecuting the patent, Hilton Davis originally claimed a pH above nine. The PTO issued a rejection citing the Booth patent, which disclosed a comparable filtration process but with a pH of above 9. In response, Hilton Davis amended its claim and introduced a pH range of between 6 and 9. The issued claim read:

> In a process for the purification of a dye . . . the improvement which comprises: subjecting an aqueous solution . . . to ultrafiltration through a membrane having a nominal pore diameter of 5–15 Angstroms under a hydrostatic pressure of approximately 200 to 400 p.s.i.g., at *a pH from approximately 6.0 to 9.0*, to thereby cause separation of said impurities from said dye. . . .[517]

Warner–Jenkinson employed a similar filtration process, but used a pH of 5. The issue was whether the Warner–Jenkinson process infringed the Hilton Davis patent under the DOE.

The Supreme Court, to the dismay of those who advocated a more limited role for what they considered an unwieldy doctrine, "decline[d] the invitation" from Warner–Jenkinson to overrule *Graver Tank* or to restrain the DOE in a significant way. The Court refused to revisit the arguments against DOE that were made by Justice Black in his *Graver* dissent, but noted that application of *Graver Tank* "is not free from confusion" and the DOE "as it has come to be applied since *Graver Tank*, has taken on a life of its own, unbounded by the patent claims."[518]

With an understanding of the certainty/equity issue surrounding the DOE, the Court, early on in the opinion, adopted the all-elements test for determining equivalency. The all-elements rule, advocated by Judge Helen Nies in her dissent below, holds that to

516. 520 U.S. 17 (1997).

517. Id. at 22 (emphasis added).

518. Id. at 28–9.

find infringement under the DOE, the doctrine must be applied to each element of the patent claim rather than to the invention as a whole. That is, each claim element must have a matching equivalent in the accused device. The Court cited approvingly Judge Nies' statement that "[t]he [patent] 'scope' is not enlarged if courts do not go beyond the substitution of equivalent elements." (The all-elements rule is discussed in Section C.3 of this chapter.)

Warner–Jenkinson made several arguments designed to limit the reach of the DOE. First, with an eye towards minimizing the DOE's tension with the notice function of the patent claim, the DOE "should be limited to equivalents that are disclosed within the patent itself"[519] or "limited to equivalents that were known at the time the patent was issued, and should not extend to after-arising equivalents."[520] The Court rejected both of these arguments because the proper time for measuring equivalency, wrote the Court, "is at the time of infringement, not at the time the patent was issued."[521] Therefore, the DOE can capture after-arising technology that was neither set forth in the patent itself, nor known at the time the patent issued. (The DOE and after-arising technologies are discussed in Section B.3, *infra*).

Warner–Jenkinson's second argument was that "any surrender of subject matter during patent prosecution, regardless of the reason for such surrender, precludes recapturing any part of that subject matter, even if it is equivalent to the matter expressly claimed."[522] In other words, the reason behind the surrender or narrowing of claim scope is irrelevant. The Court rejected this argument, viewing it as advocating a very aggressive form of prosecution history estoppel (discussed in Section C.1 of this chapter). The Court stated that it always probed the reason behind a change in claim language during prosecution, and noted further prosecution history estoppel applied only for a limited set of reasons.[523]

But the facts of *Warner–Jenkinson* presented the Court with a dilemma, namely the record did not reveal the reason behind Hilton

519. This argument is a milder version of the Public Dedication Rule, a doctrine adopted by the Federal Circuit subsequent to *Warner–Jenkinson*. The Public Dedication Rule is discussed in Section C.2 of this chapter.

520. Id. at 37.

521. Id.

522. Id. at 30.

523. Id. at 31–2. The Court was concerned, in part, about usurping the role of PTO, stating "if the PTO has been requesting changes in claim language without the intent to limit equivalents or, indeed, with the expectation that language it required would in many cases allow for a range of equivalents, we should be extremely reluctant to upset the basic assumptions of the PTO without substantial reason for doing so."

Davis' amendment to include a lower pH of 6. In this situation, the Court placed the burden on the patentee to provide a reason for the amended language. But if the reason given were insufficient in the judgment of a court or if no reason were provided, a "court should presume that the PTO had a substantial reason related to patentability for including the limiting" claim language and prosecution history estoppel would act as a complete bar to application of the DOE. By constructing this rebuttable presumption, the Court sought to further the policy goals of the definitional and notice function of the patent claim as well as the "primacy of the PTO in ensuring that the claims allowed cover only subject matter that is properly patentable in a proffered patent application."

A few more comments about *Warner–Jenkinson* are in order. First, the Federal Circuit devoted a great deal of text to the proper linguistic framework for the DOE and the role of the jury in deciding equivalence infringement. Regarding the former, the debate at the Federal Circuit centered on the respective benefits and drawbacks between *Graver Tank*'s tripartite test and the "insubstantial differences" test. The Federal Circuit adopted "insubstantial differences" as the "ultimate test," retaining the tripartite function-way-result test as a permissible formulation in particular cases. The Supreme Court expressed concern with each linguistic test, stating "[t]here seems to be substantial agreement that, while the triple identity test may be suitable for analyzing mechanical devices, it often provides a poor framework for analyzing other products or processes." On the other hand, the insubstantial differences test offers little additional guidance as to what might render any given difference "insubstantial." The Court neither adopted a new linguistic framework, not endorsed the two existing frameworks. Rather, the Court thought that focusing on individual claim elements during an equivalency determination and assuring against vitiation of claim elements would "reduce considerably the imprecision of whatever language is used."[524] In the end, the Court left to the Federal Circuit to "refine the formulation of the test for equivalence in the orderly course of case-by-case determinations."[525]

524. Id. at 40.

525. Id. Indeed, the Federal Circuit continues to use both linguistic tests, and, at times, conflates the two. See, e.g., *Searfoss v. Pioneer Consol. Corp.*, 374 F.3d 1142, 1150 (Fed.Cir.2004) (" 'An element in the accused product is equivalent to a claim limitation if the differences between the two are 'insubstantial' to one of ordinary skill in the art.' In determining whether the differences between the accused product and the claim limitation are 'insubstantial,' it is axiomatic that we may determine whether the accused product performs the same function, in the same way with the same result.").

With respect to whether a jury should or must decide infringement under the DOE, as the Federal Circuit held, the Supreme Court thought that it could decide the issues relating to application of the DOE without deciding the jury question. The Court upheld the Federal Circuit's decision and said there is ample supporting precedent, but, interestingly, closed this section of the opinion by noting that "[w]hether, if the issue were squarely presented to us, we would reach a different conclusion than did the Federal Circuit is not a question we need decide today."[526]

B. The DOE and After–Arising Technologies

Why measure equivalency at the "time of infringement" as opposed to time of issuance? To answer this question it is important to first understand that the infringement inquiry is an objective one: does the accused product or process contain each and every element of the claimed invention or an equivalent thereof? Other subjective or time-variable issues, such as when or how the accused infringer developed the accused product or process, are not determinative. Once the state of mind of the accused infringer is out of the way, it becomes easier to understand that the DOE is applied at the time of infringement because of the cumulative and unforeseeable nature of complex and ramified technologies, whereby one inventor opens a door for a subsequent inventor, a door which was perhaps not foreseeable at the time the first inventor filed for a patent, yet was eventually made possible because of the first inventor's patent disclosure. An illustrative case is *Hughes Aircraft Co. v. United States*.[527] Williams, an employee of Hughes, invented a means of controlling the attitude of a synchronous communications satellite. The claim specified that the satellite have means for receiving and directly executing control signals from a ground control station on earth. After the patent issued, satellites were developed that did not respond directly to control signals, as required by the claim, because they utilized on-board microprocessors that received control signals and then executed them after processing. Such microprocessors were unknown at the time the patent application was filed. The court found there was infringement, noting that "partial variation in technique, an embellishment made possible by post-Williams technology, does not allow the accused spacecraft to escape the web of infringement."[528] In other

526. *Id.* at 39.

527. 717 F.2d 1351 (Fed.Cir.1983).

528. *Id.* at 1365. See also *Chiuminatta Concrete Concepts, Inc. v. Cardinal Industries*, 145 F.3d 1303, 1310 (Fed. Cir.1998) ("The doctrine of equivalents is necessary because one cannot predict the future Due to technological ad-

words, the inventor is not required to predict all future developments that enable the practice of his invention in substantially the same way.

Another example of capturing after-arising technology was provided by an amicus brief filed by the United States in *Warner–Jenkinson*. The brief, in a footnote, stated:

> Of course, when an accused equivalent (meeting the objective standard of insubstantiality) could not have been known because it was developed or discovered only after the patent issued, the case for application of the doctrine of equivalents becomes especially clear. For example, a claim to a chemical composition might include an inactive filler as a minor, unimportant ingredient. After the patent issues, a competitor of the patentee might manufacture a composition exactly as claimed but use a different, inactive filler, unknown in the art at the time the patent application was filed, that performs exactly as those literally covered by the claim. Such a substitution, once it became available, might be known to persons of skill in the relevant art to be interchangeable with the claimed filler, and yet it would not have been possible to include the accused element in the patent because it did not exist at the time of issue.[529]

One could rightly ask if measuring equivalency at the time of infringement conflicts with patent law's disclosure requirements in § 112. Recall that compliance with the enablement requirement is measured at the time of filing. Moreover, enablement is properly viewed as a claim-limiting tool—the claims and specification must be commensurate. By measuring equivalency at the time of infringement, a patentee can capture subject matter that is not enabled. Also, claim terms are to be construed as one with ordinary skill in the art at the time of the invention would have understood the term to mean.[530]

IV. Limitations on the Doctrine of Equivalents

There are three important limitations on the DOE: (1) prosecution history estoppel; (2) public dedication rule; and (3) the all-elements rule. The first two limitations focus on actions by the

vances, a variant of an invention may be developed after the patent is granted, and that variant may constitute so insubstantial a change from what is claimed in the patent that it should be held to be an infringement. Such a variant, based on after-developed technology, could not have been disclosed in the patent.").

529. 1996 WL 172221, *23 n.8.

530. See *Markman v. Westview Instruments, Inc.*, 52 F.3d 967, 968 (Fed. Cir.1995) (en banc), aff'd 517 U.S. 370 (1996).

patentee during prosecution of the patent and whether the patentee surrendered or dedicated subject matter to the public. These two rules, when successfully invoked, bar application of the DOE and essentially say to the dismayed patentee, "You have no one to blame but yourself."

A. Prosecution History Estoppel

Prosecution history estoppel ("PHE") precludes a patent owner in an infringement proceeding from recapturing claim scope that was surrendered (through, for example, amendment or cancellation) during the prosecution of the patent application before the PTO; thus the name *prosecution* history estoppel. When applicable, PHE supersedes the doctrine of equivalents. PHE's rationale is based on the notice function of the claim and on third-party detrimental reliance. As the Supreme Court noted in *Warner–Jenkinson,* PHE is linked to both "the role of claims in defining an invention and providing public notice," and to the "primacy of the PTO in ensuring that the claims allowed cover only subject matter that is properly patentable in a proffered patent application."[531]

But *Warner–Jenkinson* created ambiguity regarding two issues: (1) What types of amendments give rise to PHE? and (2) if PHE is invoked, what effect does it have on the scope of the Doctrine of Equivalents; that is, does PHE completely bar application of DOE or simply limit the range of DOE? With respect to types of amendments, the Court referred alternatively to amendments not relating "to the prior art" and amendments not relating to "patentability." It did not indicate whether "patentability" referred solely to prior art-based reasons (novelty and non-obviousness under §§ 102 and 103), or extended to other statutory grounds, such as non-enablement or lack of written description (§ 112, first paragraph) or indefiniteness (§ 112, second paragraph). On the issue of the *effect* of PHE on the doctrine of equivalents, the Court created a rebuttable presumption that DOE does not apply if no reason is given for an amendment. But there remained some uncertainty regarding effect when the reason for amendment is known.

This uncertainty prompted the Federal Circuit to sit en banc in *Festo Corporation v. Shoketsu Kinzoku Kogyo Kabushiki Co., Ltd.*[532]

1. The *Festo* Doctrine

In *Festo*, the patentee owned two patents—known as the Stoll and Carroll patents—for an improved magnetic rodless cylinder,

531. *Warner–Jenkinson*, 520 U.S. at 33–34.

532. 234 F.3d 558 (Fed.Cir.2000).

which was a piston-driven device that relied on magnets to move objects in a conveying system. During prosecution, both patents were amended by adding a new limitation, namely that each invention contained two one-way sealing rings with a lip on one side. The Stoll patent also added the limitation that the sleeve, the outer shell of the device, be made of a magnetizable material. The accused infringer, SMC, began making a similar device, but included a single sealing ring with a two-way lip rather than two one-way sealing rings. Additionally, the sleeve made by SMC contained a non-magnetizable allow. Thus, SMC argued that under the doctrine of prosecution history estoppel, Festo is prevented from capturing a single sealing ring and a sleeve made of a non-magnetizable allow.

The district court disagreed with SMC and held that because Festo's amendment was not made to avoid the prior art, PHE did not apply. The Federal Circuit affirmed. But the Supreme Court granted *certiorari*, vacated, and remanded in light of its intervening decision in *Warner–Jenkinson*. The Federal Circuit decided to sit en banc to address several questions, most notably the following two:

1. *Substantial Reason Related to Patentability*. For the purposes of determining whether an amendment to a claim creates prosecution history estoppel, the court asks if the amendment was for "a substantial reason related to patentability," *Warner–Jenkinson Co.*, limited to those amendments made to overcome prior art under § 102 and § 103, or does "patentability" mean any reason affecting the issuance of a patent?
2. *Range of Equivalents*. If a claim amendment creates prosecution history estoppel, under *Warner–Jenkinson* what range of equivalents, if any, is available under the doctrine of equivalents for the claim element so amended?

The Federal Circuit held that a "substantial reason related to patentability" is not limited to overcoming or avoiding prior art, as the district court held. Rather, a narrowing amendment made for any reason that relates to the statutory requirements for a patent—including §§ 101–103 and 112—will give rise to prosecution history estoppel with respect to the amended claim element. Note that the amendment narrowed the scope of the claim and PHE only applies to the narrowed claim limitation, not the entire claim.

With respect to "range of equivalents," the court held that when PHE is created with regard to a claim limitation, the patentee is completely barred from invoking the DOE. In other words, there is no range of equivalents available to the patentee. In the Federal Circuit's opinion, the flexible bar engendered too much uncertainty and was inconsistent with the notice function of patent claims. The Federal Circuit's adoption of a "complete bar" was particularly controversial, and prompted the Supreme Court to grant *certiorari*. The Court addressed both the types of amendments that give rise to PHE and the range of equivalents issue.[533]

The Supreme Court affirmed the Federal Circuit's holding regarding the types of amendments that may give rise to PHE, noting that § 112 was to be satisfied to obtain a patent just as §§ 101–103 must be met. In response to petitioner's argument that § 112 amendments relate to the form of the application and not subject matter, the Court stated "[i]f a § 112 amendment is truly cosmetic, then it would not narrow the patent's scope or raise an estoppel." But if a § 112 amendment "is necessary and narrows the patent's scope—even if only for the purpose of better description—estoppel may apply."[534]

While the Court saw eye to eye with the Federal Circuit regarding types of amendments that may give rise to PHE, it was unmistakably troubled by the Federal Circuit's adoption of the complete bar approach. The Court rebuked the Federal Circuit for not learning the lessons of *Warner–Jenkinson*, which held that the DOE and PHE are established law and fundamental changes thereto "risk destroying the legitimate expectations of inventors in their property." As for the uncertainty caused by a flexible bar approach, the Court noted that this argument has been repeatedly made and rejected. Uncertainty is tolerated, stated the Court candidly, "as a price of ensuring the appropriate incentives for innovation."

Nonetheless, as in *Warner–Jenkinson*, the Court sought to cabin what could be characterized as needless uncertainty—that which is not needed to ensure "appropriate levels for innovation." A central theme of the opinion was that the DOE is "premised on language's inability to capture the essence of innovation." This premise is supported by PHE, in the Court's opinion, because PHE prevents a patentee who surrendered subject matter during prosecution from asserting he lacked the words to describe the surrendered subject matter. With the inherent limitations of language as a premise, the Court proceeded to build on *Warner–Jenkinson's* rebuttable presumption by creating another rebuttable presumption. The Court believed that a "patentee, as the author of the claim language, may be expected to draft claims encompassing readily known equivalents." Therefore, a narrowing amendment is "presumed to be a general disclaimer of the territory between the

533. 535 U.S. 722 (2002).

534. Id. at 724.

original claim and the amended claim." Once this presumption kicks in, the patentee has the burden to show "that at the time of the amendment one skilled in the art could not reasonably be expected to have drafted a claim that would have literally encompassed the alleged equivalent." In other words, the patentee must show why he was unable to come up with language to describe literally what he is currently trying to capture under the DOE. The patentee is completely barred from invoking the DOE if he is unable to meet his burden.

The Court provided three reasons why a PHOSITA "could not reasonably be expected" to capture alleged equivalent: "[1] the equivalent may have been unforeseeable at the time of the amendment; [2] the rationale underlying the amendment may bear no more than a tangential relation to the equivalent in question; or [3] there may be some other reason suggesting that the patentee could not reasonably be expected to have described the insubstantial substitute in question." A successful rebuttal does not necessarily lead to a finding of equivalency. Rather, it only provides the patentee with an opportunity to prove the accused product is equivalent to the claimed invention.

Because a patentee is given an opportunity to rebut the presumption, the Court did not view the presumption as a "complete bar by another name." For the Court, the presumption reflected "the fact that the interpretation of the patent must begin with its literal claims, and the prosecution history is relevant to construing those claims. When the patentee has chosen to narrow a claim, courts may presume the amended text was composed with awareness of this rule and that the territory surrendered is not an equivalent of the territory claimed."

Festo and *Warner–Jenkinson* create a series of presumptions and burdens that seek to strike a balance between the notice function of the patent claim and appropriate incentives to innovate. The incentives created by these cases could be profound. Certainly, pre-*Festo*/*Warner–Jenkinson*, amendment practice was quite common because original patent applications are usually met with rejections of one sort or another. As you could imagine, in a post-*Festo*/*Warner–Jenkinson* world, patent applicants may file more claims in their original applications, hoping to avoid filing amendments; and make increased use of continuation applications, which entitle applicants to file new claims while retaining an earlier filing date. And applicants who must inevitably file amendments will be motivated to detail the reason behind the amendment. Some applicants may also be inclined to perform more thorough prior art searches to make themselves aware of "foreseeable" equivalents.

The following flowchart may be helpful in understanding these presumptions and burdens.

Warner-Jenkinson / Festo Flowchart

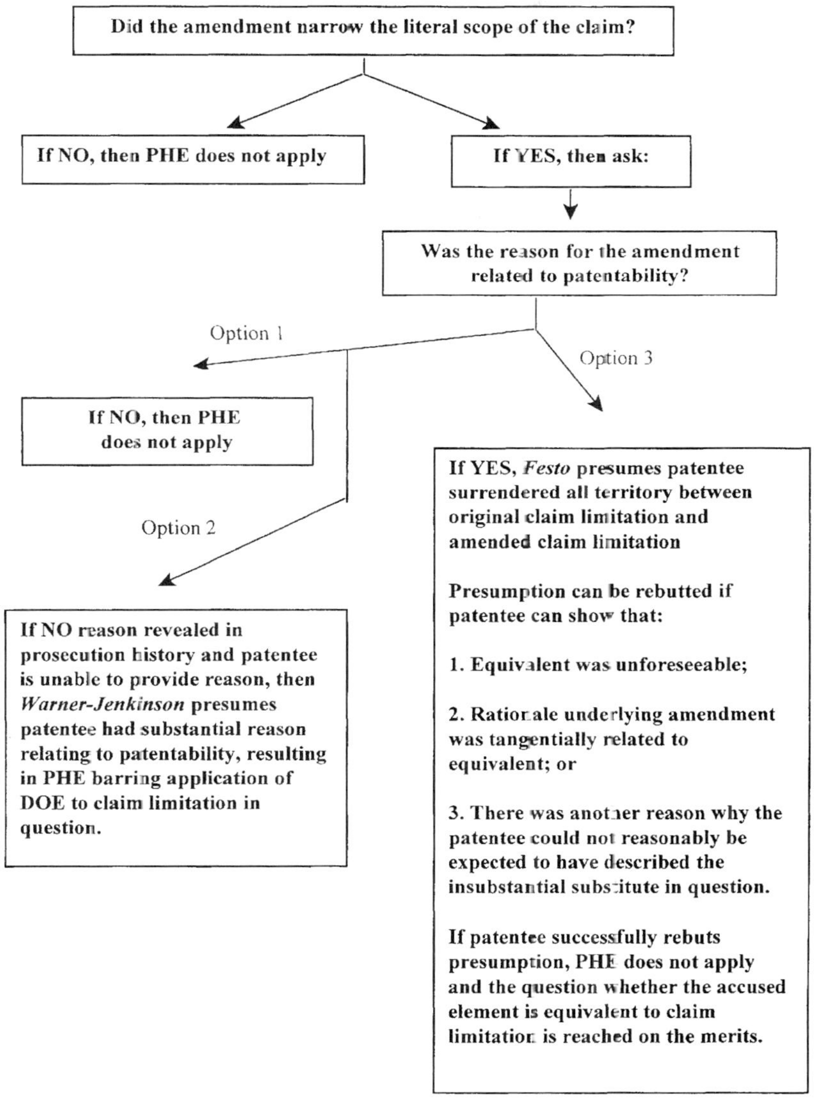

2. Rebutting *Festo's* Presumption

The Federal Circuit has had several opportunities to decide whether *Festo's* presumption applies and whether it has been rebutted. For example, in *SmithKline Beecham Corp. v. Excel Pharmaceuticals, Inc.*,[535] the patent related to antidepressant "controlled sustained release tablets" containing bupropion hydrochloride, which were developed to avoid multiple dosages. The key ingredient for obtaining sustained release was hydroxypropyl methylcellulose (HPMC). But the claims in question did not originally recite HPMC. Rather, HPMC was added through a narrowing amendment in response to a § 112 enablement rejection. The accused product, made by Excel, did not literally infringe the patent because the accused product used polyvinyl alcohol or PVA (not HPMC) as its release agent. And Excel argued that the patentee is precluded from arguing that PVA is equivalent to HPMC because the patentee narrowed its claim to add HPMC. The patentee argued that it could not have claimed PVA because its patent disclosure only recited HPMC, and therefore, asserted (correctly) that there was no support in the specification as required by § 112 for PVA. The Federal Circuit rejected this argument because it did not fit into one of the three *Festo* exceptions. PVA was not an unforeseeable equivalent at the time of amendment, and the rationale underlying the amendment was germane to the equivalent in question—in other words, not tangentially related. As the court stated, "the Supreme Court in *Festo* neither excuses an applicant from failing to claim 'readily known equivalents' at the time of application nor allows a patentee to rebut the *Festo* presumption by invoking its own failure to include a known equivalent in its original disclosure."

But in another significant opinion, the Federal Circuit held that the patentee successfully rebutted the *Festo* presumption. In *Insituform Technologies, Inc. v. CAT Contracting, Inc.*,[536] the patent related to a process for repairing cracks and structural defects of underground pipes (e.g., sewer pipes) without having to dig up the pipe. The repair was accomplished by installing a liner into the pipe. The liner had an impermeable film on the outside and a resin-absorbent, felt layer on the inside. A vacuum is applied to the inside of the liner by cutting a window into the outer, impermeable film, applying a single "vacuum cup" to the outside of the window, and connecting the other end of the cup to a vacuum source. Using the

535. 356 F.3d 1357 (Fed.Cir.2004).

536. 385 F.3d 1360 (Fed.Cir.2004).

created vacuum, a section of the inside of the liner is impregnated with resin, which is drawn through the liner. The vacuum cup is then moved to another section of the liner while the previously used window is sealed. This process for impregnating the liner with resin allows for impregnation at the jobsite, eliminating the need to transport a heavier, already impregnated liner to the site. The originally filed claim covered a process using single or multiple cups at any location downstream of the resin front. The claim was rejected for reasons related to the location of the cups at the far end of the line. The patentee narrowed the claim to address the placement issue, but also narrowed the claim to include only a single cup. The defendant used multiple cups to create a vacuum. In response to the defendant's *Festo* argument, the patentee argued that the reason for the amendment was to overcome the prior art teaching of the *location* of a single vacuum source (i.e., cup) at the far end of the tube liner, and did not relate to the number of cups. Therefore, argued the patentee, the amendment was tangentially related to the equivalent, a multiple cup method. The Federal Circuit agreed.

B. Public Dedication Rule

The "Public Dedication Rule" or "Disclosure–Dedication Rule" has its basis in the 19th century Supreme Court case of *Miller v. Bridgeport Brass Co.*[537] The *Miller* court held that subject matter disclosed in the patent specification, but not claimed, is dedicated to the public.[538] The dedication theory, which acts as a complete bar to the DOE, relies in part on the view that equivalency subverts the claiming, examination, and reissue provisions of the patent. But for much of the 20th century, the rule was in a state of desuetude. Recall, the *Miller* case was cited by Justice Black in his *Graver* dissent,[539] but all but ignored by the majority. And in *Warner–Jenkinson*, the Supreme Court rejected what it characterized as a "milder" version of the public dedication rule, namely equivalents should be limited to that which is disclosed in the patent.

In *Johnson & Johnston Associates, Inc. v. R.E. Service Co.*,[540] however, the Federal Circuit breathed new life into the doctrine. The court sat en banc in *Johnson & Johnston* to settle an intra-circuit conflict on the viability of the public dedication rule stem-

537. 104 U.S. 350 (1881).

538. See id. at 352 (stating "the claim of a specific device or combination, an omission to claim other devices or combinations apparent on the face of the patent are, in law, a dedication to the public of that which is not claimed").

539. 339 U.S. at 613–4.

540. 285 F.3d 1046 (Fed.Cir.2002).

ming from two disparate panel opinions, *Maxwell v. J. Baker, Inc.*[541] and *YBM Magnex, Inc. v. ITC.*[542] In *Johnson & Johnston*, the '050 patent related to the manufacture of printed circuit boards, which are composed of "thin sheets of conductive copper foil joined to sheets of a dielectric (nonconductive) resin-impregnated material called 'prepreg.'" During the process of making multi-layered circuit boards, stacks of copper foil and prepreg sheets are put in place and heated to bond the layers. During the layering process, the delicate copper foil sheets are handled manually, and there is a significant risk that the foils will be damaged. The '050 patent claims an assembly that prevents damage to the copper foil during manual handling by adhering the copper foil to a durable substrate sheet made of aluminum.

Claim 1 of the '050 patent read:

> A component for use in manufacturing articles such as printed circuit boards comprising: a laminate constructed of a sheet of copper foil which, in a finished printed circuit board, constitutes a functional element and a sheet of *aluminum* which constitutes a discardable element ... (emphasis added).

The specification stated that "[w]hile aluminum is currently the preferred material for the substrate, other metals, such as stainless steel or nickel alloys, may be used. In some instances ... polypropelene [sic] can be used."

The accused infringer, RES, joined copper foil with steel (instead of aluminum) when making laminates for manufacture of printed circuit boards. Steel was expressly recited in the '050 patent specification, but not claimed. The Federal Circuit, relying on *Maxwell*, held that Johnson & Johnston dedicated steel to the public. Allowing Johnson & Johnston to invoke the DOE to recapture what was "deliberately left unclaimed would 'conflict with the primacy of the claims in defining the scope of the patentee's

541. 86 F.3d 1098 (Fed.Cir.1996) (applying a theory of dedication by unclaimed disclosure to bar a finding of equivalency). See also *Moore U.S.A., Inc. v. Standard Register Co.*, 229 F.3d 1091, 1107 (Fed.Cir.2000) ("In *Maxwell* we explained the contrary principle that subject matter disclosed in the specification, but not claimed, is dedicated to the public in determining infringement under the doctrine of equivalents. Having fully disclosed two distinct embodiments, one in which the first and second longitudinal strips extend a majority of the length of the longitudinal marginal portions, and one in which they do not, Moore is not entitled to 'enforce the unclaimed embodiment as an equivalent of the one that was claimed.' ").

542. 145 F.3d 1317, 1320 (Fed.Cir. 1998) (stating the "Supreme Court's guidance in *Warner–Jenkinson* and *Graver Tank* does not permit the blanket rule that everything disclosed but not claimed is barred from access to the doctrine of equivalents, whatever the facts, circumstances, and evidence").

exclusive right.' "[543] The court was also motivated to construct a rule that would discourage or prevent patentees from claiming narrowly to obtain a patent, but thereafter use the DOE to prove infringement based on the specification's recitation of equivalents. Without the public dedication rule, the court believed patent applicants needed "to present a broad disclosure in the specification of the application and file narrow claims, avoiding examination of broader claims that the applicant could have filed consistent with the specification."[544] Also, to prevent a patentee from successfully asserting that he failed to claim subject mistakenly or without intent, the court stated (although in a footnote) the "patentee's subjective intent is irrelevant to determining whether unclaimed subject matter has been disclosed and therefore dedicated to the public."[545]

The Federal Circuit also had to reconcile *Graver Tank*. In his dissent, Justice Black relied on *Miller* and stated "[w]hat is not specifically claimed is dedicated to the public." Of course, this argument was rejected by the majority. In *Graver Tank*, the alleged equivalent element (manganese silicate) was disclosed in the specification and the patent contained both a broad claim that included manganese silicates generically and a narrower claim that was limited to alkaline earth silicates, which excluded manganese silicates. The Supreme Court held that the broader claim was invalid but that the narrower claim was valid and infringed under the doctrine of equivalents. Thus, according to the Federal Circuit, the disclosed equivalent was in fact claimed and could not be said to have been dedicated by the patentee, "even if the Court eventually held the relevant claims too broad."[546]

Application of the public dedication rule naturally prompts the question of sufficiency of the disclosure. That is, how sufficient must the disclosure be to dedicate subject matter to the public? Does the disclosure have to be enabling or simply mention the equivalent? The Federal Circuit addressed this issue in *PSC Computer Products, Inc. v. Foxconn Intern., Inc.*[547] According to the court, a mere "generic reference in a written specification" does not "necessarily dedicate[] all members of that particular genus to the public."[548] Rather, for subject matter to be deemed dedicated to the public, a PHOSITA must be able to "understand the unclaimed

543. 285 F.3d at 1054.

544. Id. at 1055.

545. 285 F.3d at 1053 n.1. See also *Toro Co. v. White Consolidated Industries, Inc.*, 383 F.3d 1326, 1333 (Fed.Cir. 2004) (holding intent irrelevant to determination of whether public-dedication rule applies).

546. Id. at 1060

547. 355 F.3d 1353 (Fed.Cir.2004).

548. Id. at 1360

disclosed teaching upon reading the written description." But the court then stated, arguably inconsistently, the "disclosure must be of such specificity that one of ordinary skill in the art could identify the subject matter that had been disclosed and not claimed."[549] What is the difference, if any, between the terms "understand the unclaimed disclosed teaching" and "identify" the disclosed subject matter? Although the word "teaching," unlike "identify," suggests an enablement-like standard, the Federal Circuit held in *Toro Co. v. White Consolidated Industries, Inc.*,[550] that the public dedication rule "does not impose a § 112 requirement on the disclosed but unclaimed subject matter."[551] The court reaffirmed the test set forth in *PSC*, and added that "[i]ndeed, disclosures implicating the disclosure-dedication rule need not directly relate to the description of the claimed invention or be contained in the 'Detailed Description of the Invention' section of the patent, but may appear merely in the portion of the patent describing the 'Background of the Invention.' "[552]

C. All–Limitations and Specific Exclusion Rule

In *Warner–Jenkinson* the Court, relying on the late Judge Nies' dissent below, adopted an all-limitations rule (or all-elements rule)[553] when applying the DOE. According to the Court, this rule

549. Id. at 1360.

550. 383 F.3d 1326 (Fed.Cir.2004).

551. Id. at 1334.

552. Id.

553. The Federal Circuit has expressed a preference for the word "limitation" (instead of "element") when referring to claim language, and "element" when referring to the accused device. See *Festo Corp. v. Shoketsu Kinzoku Kogyo Kabushiki Co., Inc.,* 234 F.3d 558, 563 n.1 (Fed.Cir.2000) () ("In our prior cases, we have used both the term 'element' and the term 'limitation' to refer to words in a claim. It is preferable to use the term 'limitation' when referring to claim language and the term 'element' when referring to the accused device."). To this end, the court has also noted that the "All Elements rule might better be called the All Limitations rule." *Ethicon Endo–Surgery, Inc. v. U.S. Surgical Corp.*, 149 F.3d 1309, 1317 n.* (Fed.Cir.1998). See also Raj S. Davé, *A Mathematical Approach to Claim Elements and the Doctrine of Equivalents*, 16 HARV. J.L. & TECH. 507, 532 n.133, quoting Judge Paul Michel as follows:

> I like to call it [referring to the "all-elements rule"] the "all-limitations rule," because I don't know what an element is. And every time I've had to debate with someone, it's clear that they have a slightly different idea of what an element is than what I think it is. Once you get past atomic elements, I don't think it's a useful word.

See, e.g., *Allen Engineering Corp. v. Bartell Industries, Inc.*, 299 F.3d 1336, 1345 (Fed.Cir.2002) ("Equivalents are assessed on a limitation-by-limitation basis."). See also Philip M. Nelson, *Definition for "Limitation" in the Context of Prosecution History Estoppel and the All Elements Rule: A Proposed Solution to the Troubling Dictum in Kustom Signals v. Applied Concepts*, 2003 B.Y.U. L. REV. 353, 373 (2003) (arguing "all-limitations" is a better name than "all-elements" because the word element refers to both a claim limitation and a component of a device).

"reconcile[s] the prohibition against enlarging the scope of claims and the doctrine of equivalents by applying the doctrine to each element of a claim, rather than to the accused product or process 'overall.' "[554] Under this rule, each limitation of a patent claim is material to defining the scope of the patented invention and must not be vitiated or rendered meaningless.[555] Thus, for there to be infringement under the DOE, an equivalent of each claim limitation must be found in the accused device. The Federal Circuit addressed the implications of the all-limitations rule in *Freedman Seating Co. v. American Seating Co.*[556] According to the court,

> First, the all-limitations rule requires that equivalence be assessed on a limitation-by-limitation basis, as opposed to from a perspective of the invention as a whole. Second, an element of an accused product or process is not, as a matter of law, equivalent to a limitation of the claimed invention if such as finding would entirely vitiate that limitation.[557]

The all-limitations approach to equivalency was part of the Federal Circuit's DOE jurisprudence prior to *Warner–Jenkinson*.[558] But identifying exactly what constitutes a limitation, and when a claim limitation is vitiated are questions that are sometimes difficult to answer. For example, in *Corning Glass Works v. Sumitomo Electric U.S.A.*,[559] the court recognized that the all-limitations rule has led to "confusion . . . because of misunderstanding or misleading uses of the term 'element' in discussing claims." According to the court, " '[e]lement' may be used to mean a single limitation, but it has also been used to mean a series of limitations which, taken together, make up a component of the claimed invention."[560] The court continued, stating that under the all-limitations rule, "[a]n equivalent must be found for every limitation of the claim somewhere in an accused device, but not necessarily in a corresponding component, although that is generally the case."[561] This

554. *Warner–Jenkinson*, 517 U.S. at 25.

555. See *Bell Atlantic Network Services, Inc. v. Covad Communications Group, Inc.*, 262 F.3d 1258, 1279–80 (Fed.Cir.2001) (stating "if a court determines that a finding of infringement under the doctrine of equivalents 'would entirely vitiate a particular claim element,' then the court should rule that there is no infringement under the doctrine of equivalents.") (citing *Warner–Jenkinson Co., Inc. v. Hilton Davis Chemical Co.*, 520 U.S. 17, 39 n.8 (1997)).

556. 420 F.3d 1350 (Fed.Cir.2005).

557. Id. at 1358.

558. See *Pennwalt Corp. v. Durand–Wayland*, 833 F.2d 931 (Fed.Cir.1987) (en banc). Judge Nies concurred with the majority, but filed "additional views," which provides a wonderful discussion of 19th and 20th century precedent relating to infringement under the DOE. See *Pennwalt*, 833 F.2d at 949–55.

559. 868 F.2d 1251 (Fed.Cir.1989).

560. Id. at 1259.

561. Id.

language suggests the all-limitations rule is more flexible than a one-to-one correspondence that demands each claim limitation have a corresponding equivalent in the accused device.

But subsequent decisions sought to clarify *Corning Glass.* In *Dolly, Inc. v. Spalding & Evenflo Companies, Inc.*,[562] for instance, the Federal Circuit, referring to the *Corning Glass* language noted above, stated the "language in *Corning Glass* did not substitute a broader limitation-by-limitation comparison for the doctrine of equivalents than the element-by-element comparison in *Pennwalt.* Rather, ... *Corning Glass* reaffirmed that the rule requires an equivalent for every limitation of the claim, even though the equivalent may not be present in the corresponding component of the accused device."[563] Thus, the court remarked that equivalency will result "when two components of the accused device perform a single function of the patented invention" or "when separate claim limitations are combined into a single component of the accused device."[564] A recent example of the latter can be found in *Eagle Comtronics, Inc. v. Arrow Communication Laboratories, Inc.*[565] In *Eagle*, the invention related to an improved cable filter structure used to decode or unscramble protected television signals. Claim 1, the only independent claim, recited several limitations, three of which included (1) a front cap, (2) a rear insert body including a rear end portion, and (3) a seal located between the front cap and the rear insert body. The accused products did not have separate elements corresponding to the front cap and rear insert body limitations, but did have a seal located along the periphery of the accused products. The patentee conceded there was no literal infringement, but argued infringement under the DOE. The accused infringer asserted that the accused devices did not possess a corresponding element to the aforementioned claim limitations, therefore, applying of the DOE would impermissibly vitiate these limitations. The Federal Circuit disagreed, stating:

> While a claim limitation cannot be totally missing from an accused device, whether or not a limitation is deemed to be vitiated must take into account that when two elements of the accused device perform a single function of the patented invention, or when separate claim limitations are combined into a single element of the accused device, a claim limitation is not

562. 16 F.3d 394 (Fed.Cir.1994).

563. Id. at 399. See also *Forest Labs v. Abbott Labs*, 239 F.3d 1305, 1313 (Fed.Cir.2001) (noting *Corning Glass* "did not dispense with the need for one-to-one correspondence of limitations and elements").

564. *Dolly*, 16 F.3d at 398. See also *Eagle Comtronics, Inc. v. Arrow Communication Laboratories, Inc.*, 305 F.3d 1303, 1317 (Fed.Cir.2002) (same).

565. 305 F.3d 1303 (Fed.Cir.2002).

necessarily vitiated, and the doctrine of equivalents may still apply if the differences are insubstantial.[566]

In *Sage Prods. v. Devon Indus.*,[567] however, vitiation was a concern and led to a finding of no infringement under the DOE. In *Sage*, the invention was a container for disposing of hazardous medical waste. The relevant claim language stated the invention comprised a container body with "an elongated slot at the top of the container body" . . . .[568] The defendant made a similar container, but the slot for disposing the waste was within the container body.[569] Both containers featured two constrictions that kept the waste securely within the container. The plaintiff argued "having two constrictions below the top of the container is the same, for purposes of infringement, as having one constriction above and one constriction below."[570] The court found no literal infringement and ruled the all-limitations rule would be violated if the patentee were allowed to show the slot within the container was equivalent to a slot at the top of the container.

V. Indirect Infringement

Indirect infringement focuses on the acts of parties who, while not directly infringing themselves, are facilitating or aiding and abetting direct infringement. There can be no indirect infringement without direct infringement.[571] Indirect infringement can be a very important enforcement tool for patent owners because it may be infeasible to sue direct infringers, who may either be too numerous, difficult to locate, or not lend themselves to a particular jurisdictional framework.

There are two types of indirect infringement: active inducements found in 35 U.S.C. § 271(b) and contributory infringement found in 35 U.S.C. § 271(c).

A. Active Inducement

Two elements must be established to show inducement of infringement: direct infringement and intent to cause the acts that

566. Id. at 1317.

567. 126 F 3d 1420 (Fed.Cir.1997).

568. Id. at 1422.

569. Id. at 1423.

570. Id. at 1424.

571. See *Aro Manufacturing Co., Inc. v. Convertible Top Replacement Co., Inc.*, 365 U.S. 336, 341–42 (1961) ("It is plain that § 271(c)—a part of the Patent Code enacted in 1952—made no change in the fundamental precept that there can be no contributory infringement in the absence of a direct infringement."); *Joy Techs., Inc. v. Flakt, Inc.*, 6 F.3d 770, 774 (Fed.Cir.1993) ("Liability for either active inducement of infringement or for contributory infringement is dependent upon the existence of direct infringement.").

constitute the infringement. Unlike § 271(c), which codifies contributory infringement, § 271(b) does not use the word "knowing;" rather, the statute merely states that "whoever actively induces infringement of a patent shall be liable as an infringer." Nonetheless, the cases have held, correctly so, that there is a knowledge or intent requirement,[572] which can be proved through circumstantial evidence.[573] But the nature of this requirement remains unclear. As the Federal Circuit stated, "there is a 'lack of clarity concerning whether the required intent must be merely to induce the specific acts [of infringement] or additionally to cause an infringement.' "[574] At the very least, what is required is intent to induce specific acts.[575]

Whether the intent requirement was satisfied was at issue in *Fuji Photo Film Co., Ltd. v. Jazz Photo Corp.*[576] In this case, a jury found Jazz Photo liable for direct infringement of Fuji's patents on disposable cameras by refurbishing Fuji's used cameras. The same jury also found Jack Benun, the former CEO and consultant to Jazz Photo, liable for active inducement. Jazz Photo and Benun asserted that Benun lacked the requisite intent for active inducement. The Federal Circuit disagreed, stating that:

> A patentee may prove intent through circumstantial evidence. Although Mr. Benun took the position that he did not believe refurbishing LFFPs had any effect on Fuji's patent rights, the record shows he was aware of Fuji's infringement contentions. In fact, the record shows that Mr. Benun twice sought a license from Fuji. This court has acknowledged the relevance of that kind of evidence supporting proof of intent for inducement. Moreover, under Mr. Benun's leadership, Jazz continued to sell refurbished LFFPs even after the ITC found infringement.... Fuji also demonstrated that Mr. Benun's acts of selecting the foreign refurbisher supply factories and his overall acts of directing Jazz's business model caused the infringement.[577]

572. Reading an intent component into § 271(b) makes sense, given the fact that § 271(b) and (c) were intended to be complementary provisions, together codifying the basic common law pre–1952 principle of contributory infringement.

573. *See Water Techs. v. Calco, Ltd.*, 850 F.2d 660, 668 (Fed.Cir.1988) (noting that "circumstantial evidence may suffice" to prove intent).

574. *MercExchange, LLC v. eBay, Inc.*, 401 F.3d 1323, 1332 (Fed.Cir.2005) (quoting *Insituform Techs., Inc. v. CAT Contracting, Inc.*, 385 F.3d 1360, 1378 (Fed.Cir.2004)).

575. *MercExchange*, 401 F.3d at 1332. But in *Manville Sales Corp. v. Paramount Sys., Inc.*, 917 F.2d 544, 552 (Fed.Cir.1990), the court stated that the patentee must also show that the accused inducer "knew or should have known his actions would induce actual infringements."

576. 394 F.3d 1368 (Fed.Cir.2005).

577. *Id.* at 1377–78.

In proving the intent requirement, "[t]he plaintiff has the burden of showing that the alleged infringer's actions induced infringing acts and that he knew or should have known his actions would induce actual infringements."[578] The requirement that the alleged infringer knew or should have known his actions would induce actual infringement necessarily includes the requirement that he or she knew of the patent. But "knowledge of the acts alleged to constitute infringement" is not enough.[579] The "mere knowledge of possible infringement by others does not amount to inducement; specific intent and action to induce infringement must be proven."[580]

B. Contributory Infringement

Section 271(c) pertains to contributory infringement, and concerns itself with the third-party sale of a component of a patented device or the sale of a component for use in practicing a patented process.[581] The component must be a non-staple item that is not "suitable for substantial non-infringing use."[582] Also, a seller under § 271(c) must have knowledge that the component is "especially made or especially adapted for use in an infringement of" a patent. Assuming the non-staple and knowledge requirements are met, contributory infringement acts to prevent a third party from successfully arguing that he is not infringing the patent because he is merely making or selling only a part of what is claimed.[583]

The substantial non-infringing use requirement was at play in *C. R. Bard, Inc. v. Advanced Cardiovascular Systems, Inc.*[584] *In*

578. *DSU Medical Corp. v. JMS Co. Ltd.*, 471 F.3d 1293 (Fed.Cir.2006) (quoting *Manville Sales Corp. v. Paramount Systems, Inc.*, 917 F.2d 544, 554 (Fed.Cir.1990)).

579. *Warner–Lambert Co. v. Apotex Corp.*, 316 F.3d 1348, 1363 (Fed Cir. 2003).

580. *Id.* at 1364.

581. Contributory infringement is also featured prominently in copyright law, particularly in cases relating to peer-to-peer filing sharing. See *A & M Records v. Napster, Inc.*, 239 F.3d 1004 (9th Cir.2001); *Metro–Goldwyn–Mayer Studios, Inc. v. Grokster Ltd.*, 380 F.3d 1154 (9th Cir.2004). Indeed, in the seminal *Sony Corp. v. Universal City Studios, Inc.* case, 464 U.S. 417 (1984), which is central to the peer-to-peer cases, the Supreme Court expressly looked to patent law for guidance on contributory infringement.

582. See *Dawson Chemical Co. v. Rohm & Haas Co.*, 448 U.S. 176 (1980).

583. The rationale for contributory infringement was recognized as early as the late 19th century. See *Wallace v. Holmes*, 29 F.Cas. 74, 80 (C.C.D.1871) ("It cannot be, that, where a useful machine is patented as a combination of parts, two or more can engage in its construction and sale, and protect themselves by showing that, though united in an effort to produce the same machine, and sell it, and bring it into extensive use, each makes and sells one part only, which is useless without the others, and still another person, in precise conformity with the purpose in view, puts them together for use.").

584. 911 F.2d 670 (Fed.Cir.1990).

Bard, the claimed invention related to a method for using a catheter in coronary angioplasty. The accused infringer, ACS, was marketing and selling a catheter for use in coronary angioplasty. The ACS catheter had a series of ten openings. Bard asserted that ACS was a contributory infringer because ACS sold catheters to surgeons, who would then use the catheter in a way that directly infringed Bard's method patent. (Note that Bard could also sue the surgeons for direct infringement.) ACS argued that the catheters it sells have substantial non-infringing uses, and therefore, ACS cannot be a contributory infringer under § 271(c).

The court noted that there are three possible ways to use the catheter. The first way to use the ACS catheter would be to locate all of the catheter openings within the coronary artery. This method is claimed by Bard's patent. But the two other methods of using the ACS catheter qualified, stated the court, as substantial non-infringing uses. For instance, one method was to position the catheter such that all of the side openings of the catheter were located only in the aorta. This method of using the ACS catheter was disclosed in the prior art, and thus, constituted a substantial non-infringing use.

In addition to the non-staple requirement, § 271(c) has a knowledge requirement. Under § 271(c), the alleged contributory infringer must sell his component "*knowing* the same adapted for use in an infringement of such patent."[585] (Recall, "knowing" is absent in § 271(b).) Prior to 1952, it was unclear whether the knowledge element meant knowledge of the use to which the component would be put, or knowledge of both the character of the use and the existence of a patent and a claim of infringement. The legislative history of § 271(c) is equally unclear as to the intended meaning of "knowing." But in *Aro Mfg. Co. v. Convertible Top Replacement Co.*, (*Aro II*),[586] the Supreme Court stated that "§ 271(c) does require a showing that the alleged contributory infringer knew that the combination for which his component was specially designed was both patented and infringing."[587] The Federal Circuit has followed suit.[588]

585. Emphasis added.

586. 377 U.S. 476 (1964).

587. Id. at 488–90.

588. See, e.g., *Preemption Devices, Inc. v. Minnesota Mining & Mfg., Co.*, 803 F.2d 1170, 1174 (Fed.Cir.1986) (stating patentee must show that alleged contributory infringer "knew that the combination for which its components were especially made was both patented and infringing").

Chapter Eleven

DEFENSES TO PATENT INFRINGEMENT

I. Introduction: The High Stakes of Patent Litigation

The patent law is relatively unique among civil causes of action in that a typical plaintiff (e.g., a patentee) can—by seeking to enforce rights or receive remedies for past damages—end up in a significantly worse position than where she started. This is because of the powerful array of defenses and counterclaims that accused infringers can deploy. Indeed 35 U.S.C. § 282, which establishes the "presumption of validity" in favor of patentees, also specifies a series of defenses to patent infringement, including:

- Non-infringement;
- absence of liability for infringement;
- unenforceability of the patent;
- the invalidity of the patent; and
- other defenses (such as, patent misuse, prosecution laches, etc.)

Many defenses to patent infringement can result in the permanent elimination or restriction of the patentee's rights. For example, a judicial declaration of the invalidity of patent claims is preclusive of all future litigation on the subject. Similarly, a finding that the patentee committed inequitable conduct during the prosecution of the patent will render the entire patent permanently unenforceable.

At the same time, of course, patent enforcement is a powerful tool in the marketplace, enabling a successful patentee to seek a permanent injunction and full compensatory damages. (See Chapter 12 for more on remedies.) Further, the presumption of validity means that in most cases the accused infringer will bear the burden of proving any defects in the patent. It is this juxtaposition—powerful remedies countered by powerful defenses—that makes modern patent litigation an extremely high-stakes affair. Patents can shape the future of an industry; their invalidation can similarly have tremendous consequences. Many patent lawsuits will have a "bet the company" flavor, with the risks felt on both sides of the case.

Because of the very high—but relatively symmetric—stakes in patent enforcement, a provision of federal law allows what are known as "declaratory judgments," which enable prospective defendants to file suits to determine their liability. In the patent context, declaratory judgments can allow defendant-infringers several advantages, including the ability to dictate the timing of the litigation, choose a district court, as well as the ability to challenge the validity of the patent prior to any infringement.

II. Inequitable Conduct

Patents, of course, are by their nature "affected with a public interest."[589] Thus, it is important to protect and enforce the relationship between a patent applicant, and the public—represented during patent prosecution by the USPTO. The law's interest in this enforcement gives rise to one of the most important counterclaims against a patent-holder: a charge that the patent was obtained via "inequitable conduct" during prosecution before the USPTO. Inequitable conduct is a judicially-created doctrine, based on historical principles of fraud against the public.[590] Inequitable conduct seeks to provide a remedy for abuses that can occur during prosecution, which (as noted above in Chapter 4) is an ex parte process. This remedy is important because much of the integrity of the prosecution phase depends upon the prospective patentee's actions—correctly following the various rules and regulations of prosecution, especially those relating to the disclosure of known prior art. A finding that a patent was obtained via inequitable conduct will result in the patent being held permanently "unenforceable"—an extraordinarily harsh penalty that, because it applies to all claims, is often worse than a declaration of invalidity.

A. The Doctrine of Inequitable Conduct

The doctrinal analysis for inequitable conduct is fairly straightforward. The violation includes material misrepresentations to the USPTO, or (more typically) material failures to disclose. As an equitable doctrine, the imposition of the remedy is ultimately at the discretion of the court. However, the Federal Circuit has established relatively strict guidelines for the analysis under inequitable conduct, which proceeds in two steps: one factual in nature, and one discretionary. Factually, at least some evidence of two distinct elements is necessary: (1) materiality of the breach, and (2) intent

589. *Precision Instrument Mfg. Co. v. Automotive Maintenance Machinery Co.,* 324 U.S. 806 (1945).

590. *J.P. Stevens & Co. v. Lex Tex Ltd.*, 747 F.2d 1553 (Fed.Cir.1984). See also *Precision Instrument, supra.*

to deceive. *Materiality* refers to the importance or magnitude of the violation; *intent to deceive* reflects the required mental state of the applicant. If minimal ("baseline levels") of each of the factual elements are present, then the judge must balance the quantum materiality and intent to determine whether the remedy of unenforceability is justified in the particular case. This is a form of sliding scale analysis: the greater the materiality, the less intent is necessary to support inequitable conduct, and vice-versa.

The critical issues in inequitable conduct revolve around the following two questions: First, what does "materiality" mean in this context? And second, what is the minimal level of intent required to support a finding of inequitable conduct?

Materiality. The level of materiality, of course, determines the scope of the inequitable conduct remedy. A high threshold for materiality will allow some misbehavior to go unpunished, while setting the threshold too low will result in even very minor transgressions that didn't affect the outcome of the prosecution to destroy the value of otherwise valid patents. The general principle here is that the transgression must have the potential for affecting the course of the prosecution of the patent. In practice, the Federal Circuit cites the USPTO's regulations on whether a nondisclosure or misrepresentation is "material." Under 37 CFR 1.56 ("Rule 56"), information is material when:

> [1] It is not cumulative to information already in the prosecution record; and
>
> [2a] It establishes (or helps establish) the prima facie invalidity of a claim; or
>
> [2b] It refutes or is inconsistent with a position the applicant takes with respect to patentability during the course of prosecution.

A prima facie case of invalidity is made when the information "compels a conclusion that a claim is unpatentable under the preponderance-of-evidence . . . standard." Note that all parties involved in prosecution—the applicants, the attorneys or agents, and "any other person who is substantively involved"—are required to disclose material information known to them. Note also that the Federal Circuit has stated that although Rule 56 provides an important definition of *materiality*, especially of prior art references, it does not encompass all possible cases of inequitable conduct.[591] For example, a failure to disclose activities that might

591. See, e.g., *Critikon, Inc. v. Becton Dickinson Vascular Access, Inc.*, 120 F.3d 1253 (Fed.Cir.1997).

trigger a bar under § 102(b), or falsehoods relating to dates of invention, results of testing data, and the like are all candidates for a finding of inequitable conduct.

Intent. The key questions with respect to intent are whether such a mental state may be inferred from circumstances, and whether gross negligence is sufficient, where the level of materiality is very high, to support a finding of inequitable conduct. The answers to those questions appear to be yes and no, respectively. Recognizing the difficulty (if not impossibility) of producing direct evidence of intent to deceive, the courts have allowed circumstantial evidence (including a highly material omission and a lack of evidence of good faith) of bad intent.[592] On the other hand, the courts have been firm in holding that gross negligence cannot substitute for an intent to deceive—to hold otherwise would result in mistakes and oversights potentially triggering unenforceability.[593]

B. The Policy of Inequitable Conduct

The theory underlying inequitable conduct is reasonably straightforward: by providing a defense to accused infringers based on improper behavior during prosecution, the law harnesses the private incentives to investigate and police such conduct—and thus provides a significant deterrent against being less than fully candid with the USPTO. Note, however, that this arrangement comes at a cost. First, because a charge of inequitable conduct is an enormously powerful remedy, implemented at the discretion of the courts, it has become a typical feature of many patent lawsuits—almost certainly in far more cases than warranted. Indeed, the Federal Circuit has described the incidence of claims of inequitable conduct to be "an absolute plague."[594] This raises the cost of patent enforcement, and thus the patent system more generally. Second, the prevalence of arguments concerning inequitable conduct can have perverse incentives, such as an incentive among patent applicants to avoid searching for relevant prior art, for fear that a later-discovered nondisclosure—whether because the applicant or her representatives believed the information to be immaterial, or because of some mistake or oversight—will provide an opening for (at minimum) extensive litigation on inequitable conduct. It may well be that the chilling effect on prior art searches, and the resulting lower quality of patent applications, means that the costs of the inequitable conduct doctrine might outweigh its benefits, especially

592. See id.

593. See *Kingsdown Medical Consultants, Ltd. v. Hollister Inc.*, 863 F.2d 867 (Fed.Cir.1988).

594. See *Burlington Industries v. Dayco Corp.*, 849 F.2d 1418 (Fed.Cir. 1988).

when one considers the possible alternatives, such as the validity requirements, USPTO disciplinary proceedings against attorneys or agents, and even criminal statutes prohibiting lying to federal agencies.[595]

C. Prosecution Laches

The defense of "prosecution laches" is intended to address a form of strategic behavior among patentees: the unreasonable delay during patent prosecution that affects the rights and expectations of the public. This counterclaim is based on the ability of patentees—at least until recently—to use the secrecy of the prosecution process and the ability to alter claim language at will during prosecution to gain an advantage in the marketplace. The idea is that in some cases patentees could extend the prosecution of their patent applications for an extremely long time—perhaps for decades—and, either simply by the passage of time, or by altering claim language as technology develops, such "submarine" patents can become valuable.

Although recent changes to the patent statute—keying the expiration date of a patent to its filing date rather than issue date, and the publication of most patent applications after eighteen months—have made a so-called "submarine" strategy much less viable (though perhaps not completely infeasible), there are still thousands of patents subject to the former rules. Thus, the doctrine of prosecution laches, which originated in Supreme Court cases of the 1920s and 1930s, has recently re-emerged as a viable counterclaim.[596]

Prosecution laches is an equitable doctrine, and is defined by "an unreasonable and unexplained delay in prosecution, even though the applicant complied with pertinent statutes and rules."[597] A finding of laches will render the affected claims permanently unenforceable. The content of a laches analysis has not been fleshed out by the Federal Circuit in great detail, though the court has noted that "there are no strict time limitations for determining whether continued refiling of patent applications is a legitimate utilization of statutory provisions or an abuse of those provisions," and that the doctrine should be applied "only in egregious cases of misuse of the patent system."[598] The District Courts have, thus far, varied in their application of the doctrine.

595. See 18 U.S.C. § 1001 (2005).

596. See, e.g., *Woodbridge v. United States*, 263 U.S. 50 (1923); *Webster Electric Co. v. Splitdorf Electrical Co.*, 264 U.S. 463 (1924). See *Symbol Techs. v. Lemelson Medical, Education, and Research Foundation*, 277 F.3d 1361 (Fed. Cir.2002).

597. See, e.g., *Symbol Techs., supra.*

598. See, e.g. *Symbol Technologies v. Lemelson Medical, Education, and Research Foundation*, 422 F.3d 1378 (Fed. Cir.2005).

III. Patent Misuse and Antitrust Violations

One general rule is that patents are an exception (a government-granted exception) to general principles against anticompetitive behavior in the marketplace. This, however, does not mean that patentees are immune from all challenges to their behavior on these grounds; the patent law itself provides a doctrine, known as "patent misuse," which seeks to address activities that run counter to patent policy. In addition, in some cases a patentee can be found guilty of antitrust violations based on activities related to patents. Thus, both patent misuse and antitrust regulations provide important potential defenses for accused infringers.

A. The Complexities of Patents and Competition Policy

Policing the boundary between the right to exclude given by a patent on the one hand, and principles of fair and free marketplace competition on the other is an enormously difficult enterprise, for several reasons. First, at a conceptual level, the United States has traditionally been understood to be a country that dislikes monopolies, and has long had vigorous antitrust laws in place. At the same time, the U.S. values innovation and technological development; a robust patent system has long been an important feature of our economic regulation. The patent-antitrust divide, then, exposes a real conflict between two deeply held theories: first, that free and unfettered markets are the best way to sustain economic development, and, second, that invention is essential to development and must be encouraged.

A second major challenge to the law in this area is that understanding the dynamics of the marketplace in areas of significant technological change—e.g., where patents are most likely to be in play—is exceedingly complex. These markets change quickly, and have complex structures. Even defining a relevant market for analysis can be very difficult. For example, consider a company that has a patent on a device ("A"); during the term of the patent, of course, the company can exclude others from the scope of the patent, and thus—by definition—has "market power" in the market for this device. However, the market for device A may not be relevant for antitrust purposes—there may be several close substitutes for the device, which means that there is little chance for consumer harm. Further, even if the existence of the patent on device A leads to supra-competitive prices, the net effect on consumers is unclear, since this will serve to encourage innovation (both in substitutes for device A, as well as more generally encouraging inventive behavior). Thus, in both cases, the existence of a patent may—or may not—confer market power of the sort that would implicate laws protecting competition, and even if market power existed, it might—or might not—have a positive net effect on overall consumer welfare. This obviously stylized, simplistic example illustrates the serious technical complexities at the patent-antitrust border.

Finally, a third major challenge is related to the historical developments of patent and antitrust law. The major trend of the past several decades in antitrust and competition law has been an increasingly sophisticated economic understanding of the marketplace—the net result of which means that many commercial arrangements that were once thought to be illegal are now either upheld or subject to more nuanced analysis. These same principles, of course, should apply to antitrust analysis where patents are involved. However, because many of the important cases (especially Supreme Court cases) regarding the relationship between patents and competition laws are from an earlier era, with different understandings, in some ways this law has lagged well behind both current economic standing and modern antitrust principles. Thus, the patent-antitrust line is one that is both difficult to apply, as well as subject to significant doctrinal uncertainty. Indeed, in 2006, the Supreme Court in *Illinois Tool Works Inc. v. Independent Ink, Inc.* formally abrogated the longstanding (and much criticized) rule that the existence of a patent conferred with it a presumption of market power.[599]

B. Analyzing Market Power and the Scope of the Claims

Patents confer rights to their holders, and those rights, by law, can be sold, licensed, or otherwise transacted in various ways. Thus, most arrangements, business combinations, and other licensing schemes are perfectly legal. For example, territorial or field-of-use restrictions on patent licenses are permissible (even though such restrictions are likely antitrust violations where patents are not involved). Where antitrust and patent misuse applies, then, is in those circumstances where the patent right has been abused or overextended in some way. As noted above, the line between a legal use of the patent grant and an abuse of the patent grant is not crystal clear. However, at least two dimensions of analysis drive most of these cases. The first is the distinction between activities that occur *within* the scope of the patent claims, and those that

599. See 547 U.S. 28 (2006).

extend *outside* the scope of the claims. Activities within the claims will generally be permissible, while those that expand beyond the claims will be viewed with substantially more suspicion. The second key dimension of the analysis is to evaluate whether the patentee has "market power" in the market for the patented good or service. Market power refers to a situation where the lack of economically relevant substitutes confers the ability to act without primary regard for competitive pressures. As in general principles of antitrust law, where market power exists, there are significant competitive concerns, and thus a stronger case for illegality. Where market power does not exist, however, the law generally understands most arrangements to have relatively minor competitive effects. Thus, in the patent context, the following table illustrates (in a very simplified fashion) some of the ways these two factors impact a range of cases:

	Market power in patented product	**No market power in patented product**
Activities within the scope of the claims	Liability rare, but depends on specific circumstances. Refusals to deal, territorial or field of use restrictions.	Unlikely to be liability in most cases. Refusals to deal, territorial or field of use restrictions.
Activities outside the scope of the claims	Highest risk for liability under either misuse or antitrust theories. Examples: Tying arrangements, grant-backs.	Liability rare, but depends on specific circumstances. [examples: temporal extensions, tying arrangements, grant-back provisions]

Finally, given the number and diversity of business arrangements that can be made with patents, an exhaustive treatment is impossible here. Instead, we address a few of the important limitations on the use of patents in the marketplace.

1. Tying Arrangements

Tying arrangements involve situations where an unpatented good or service is "tied" to the sale or license of a patented good. These scenarios raise concerns because they might, in some cases, allow a patentee to "leverage" her patent rights into areas beyond the subject matter of the patent, and thus in effect extend the patent rights to cover unpatented goods.

Historically, tying arrangements were viewed as clear cases of patent misuse and perhaps antitrust violations. This understanding came under serious criticism in the late 20th century, however. For one thing, many tying arrangements were in fact a more economically efficient way of selling patented goods, allowing pricing to be based on use of the good rather than a single lump-sum payment.[600] For another, many economists viewed the possibility that the patentee could in fact "force" a tying arrangement on its customers as implausible except in limited circumstances—where the patentee had market power in the market for the patented good. The modern law of tying arrangements reflects this understanding. Under 35 U.S.C. § 271(d)(5), it is not patent misuse to enter into a tying arrangement, "unless, in view of the circumstances, the patent owner has market power in the relevant market for the patent or patented product on which the license or sale is conditioned." Antitrust principles reflect a similar analysis: tying arrangements are illegal only when market power exists in the tying product.[601] And since the 2006 *Illinois Tool Works* case, no presumption of market power attaches to patents—thus harmonizing the misuse and antitrust analyses.[602]

2. Refusals to License

In the patent misuse context, refusals to license a patent are expressly allowed under § 271(d)(4) of the Patent Act: "No patent owner otherwise entitled to relief for infringement or contributory infringement of a patent shall be denied relief or deemed guilty of misuse or illegal extension of the patent right by reason of his having . . . (4) refused to license or use any rights to the patent."

In the antitrust context, however, the issue is more complicated. In *In re Independent Service Organizations Antitrust Litigation*, the Federal Circuit held that Xerox could refuse to sell patented parts and supplies to "independent service organizations," even though this meant that Xerox controlled the market for service of its copiers:

> [A] patent owner who brings suit to enforce the statutory right to exclude others from making, using, or selling the claimed invention is exempt from the antitrust laws, even though such a suit may have an anticompetitive effect, unless the infringement defendant proves one of two conditions. First, he may

600. See, e.g., *Morton Salt v. G.S. Suppiger*, 314 U.S. 488 (1942), where the patentee required purchasers of its patented canning equipment to purchase its salt tablets for use in the equipment. Thus the patentee was able to price-discriminate: lower-quantity users paid less, and higher-volume users paid more.

601. See, e.g., *Jefferson Parish Hosp. Dist. No. 2 v. Hyde*, 466 U.S. 2 (1984)

602. See 547 U.S. 28 (2006).

> prove that the asserted patent was obtained through knowing and willful fraud within the meaning of *Walker Process Equipment, Inc. v. Food Machinery & Chemical Corp.* Or he may demonstrate that the infringement suit was a mere sham to cover what is actually no more than an attempt to interfere directly with the business relationships of a competitor. Here, CSU makes no claim that Xerox obtained its patents through fraud in the Patent and Trademark Office; the *Walker Process* analysis is not implicated ... CSU has alleged that Xerox misused its patents but has not claimed that Xerox's patent infringement counterclaims were shams.[603]

Significantly, in *In re ISOs*, the Federal Circuit expressly declined to follow the Ninth Circuit's approach in *Kodak v. Image Technical Services*, wherein the court suggested that an analysis of the validity of the business justification for such an exclusion was necessary. Instead, the Federal Circuit held that there was no need to inquire into the motivations of a patentee's efforts to enforce a patent unless the suit is objectively baseless.[604]

As noted above, a similar case in the Ninth Circuit produced at least a slightly different legal analysis. In Kodak, the Ninth Circuit held that refusals to deal were to be analyzed using a rebuttable presumption: "while exclusionary conduct can include a monopolist's unilateral refusal to license a patent or copyright, or to sell its patented or copyrighted work, a monopolist's desire to exclude others from its protected work is a presumptively valid business justification for any immediate harm to consumers."[605]

Thus, under the Federal Circuit rule, patentees needn't justify their refusals to license their patents, as long as they were not procured by fraud or involved in objectively baseless legal claims. Under the Ninth Circuit rule, patentees must also show that their business justification for the refusal is legitimate under the antitrust laws—or at least show that the antitrust plaintiff cannot prove otherwise.

3. Temporal Limitations

While granting time-limited patent licenses is perfectly legal, the current law makes it impermissible to license patents beyond their expiration date. *In Brulotte v. Thys Co.*, 379 U.S. 29 (1964),

603. *In re Independent Service Organizations Antitrust Litigation*, 203 F.3d 1322 (Fed.Cir.2000).

604. 203 F.3d at 1327–28.

605. *Image Technical Services, Inc. v. Eastman Kodak Co.*, 125 F.3d 1195 (9th Cir.1997).

the Supreme Court held that an agreement that obligated the licensee to pay royalties on a patented invention beyond the expiration date of the patent was per se unlawful. This has been an unpopular rule among modern antitrust and patent thinkers. As the Seventh Circuit noted in 2002:

> The [*Brulotte*] decision has, it is true, been severely, and as it seems to us, with all due respect, justly, criticized, beginning with Justice Harlan's dissent, and continuing with our opinion in *USM Corp. v. SPS Technologies, Inc.* The Supreme Court's majority opinion reasoned that by extracting a promise to continue paying royalties after expiration of the patent, the patentee extends the patent beyond the term fixed in the patent statute and therefore in violation of the law. That is not true. After the patent expires, anyone can make the patented process or product without being guilty of patent infringement. The patent can no longer be used to exclude anybody from such production. Expiration thus accomplishes what it is supposed to accomplish. For a licensee in accordance with a provision in the license agreement to go on paying royalties after the patent expires does not extend the duration of the patent either technically or practically, because, as this case demonstrates, if the licensee agrees to continue paying royalties after the patent expires the royalty rate will be lower. The duration of the patent fixes the limit of the patentee's power to extract royalties; it is a detail whether he extracts them at a higher rate over a shorter period of time or a lower rate over a longer period of time.

But despite the widespread scorn heaped upon the *Brulotte* opinion, the Supreme Court has never taken up the question, and as the Seventh Circuit noted, "However, we have no authority to overrule a Supreme Court decision no matter how dubious its reasoning strikes us, or even how out of touch with the Supreme Court's current thinking the decision seems." Thus, the rule of *Brulotte*—that patent licenses which provide for payments beyond the expiration date of the patent—remains the law of the land.

4. Patent Pools

"Patent pools" describe scenarios where multiple patentees agree to jointly license their patents. This typically occurs when several patents held by multiple parties are related to a particular technology; aggregating the patentee rights for uniform licensing terms can result in efficiency gains. For example, modern DVD technology is licensed via a pool of related patents. However, because patent pools can often represent agreements between competitors, and can involve important grants of rights, they do raise concerns. The current law takes a case-by-case approach to the legality of patent pools, evaluating, for example, whether the pools are exclusionary, offer verifiable gains in efficiency, and so forth.[606]

5. Reverse Payments

One relatively recent form of agreement that has attracted the attention of antitrust regulators of late is "reverse payments," in which the patentee pays an accused infringer to stay off the market. These arrangements have been especially visible in the pharmaceutical drug context, where there are enormous advantages to being an exclusive provider of an approved therapy, and where aspects of the law might encourage the extension of litigation. At present, the courts are divided on the treatment of these cases. Some courts, and the Federal Trade Commission, have held them to be *per se* or presumptively illegal.[607] Others subject the arrangements to more nuanced analysis.[608] And still others have held such arrangements to be almost always legal.[609] Many observers suggest that this issue will have to be resolved at the Supreme Court in the near future.

6. Grant–Back Licenses

A "grant-back" license is one where the patentee conditions the sale or license of a patented good on the licensee's licensing of improvements back to the patentee. In other words, the "grant back" of future patent rights. Like many other arrangements, in some cases these licenses could raise anticompetitive concerns. The courts have refused, however, to treat them as *per se* illegal, and instead the modern understanding is that a case-by-case analysis is required, focusing especially on whether the patentee has market power in the patented product.[610]

606. For more on the competitive implications of such arrangements, see Robert P. Merges, *Institutions for Intellectual Property Exchange: The Case of Patent Pools, in Intellectual Products: Novel Claims to Protection and their Boundaries* (Rochelle Dreyfuss, ed. 2001), and Carl Shapiro, *Navigating the Patent Thicket: Cross Licenses, Patent Pools and Standard Setting, in Innovation Policy and the Economy*, Vol. 1 (Adam Jaffee et al., eds., 2001).

607. See *In re Cardizem CD Antitrust Litig.*, 332 F.3d 896 (6th Cir.2003); *In re Schering Plough Corp.*, No. 9297 (F.T.C. Dec. 18, 2003).

608. See *Valley Drug Co. v. Geneva Pharmaceuticals, Inc.*, 344 F.3d 1294 (11th Cir.2003).

609. See *In re Tamoxifen Citrate Antitrust Litigation*, 466 F.3d 187, 212 (2d Cir.2006).

610. See *Transparent–Wrap Machine Corp. v. Stokes & Smith Co.*, 329 U.S.

C. Exhaustion of Patent Rights: First Sale and Repair

Even within the scope of the claims, patent rights are not unlimited. One key example is the doctrine of "exhaustion," which prevents patentees from receiving rewards from their patent in ways that expand beyond the initial sale of a patented good. Thus, under this theory, a patentee who sold a patented product into the stream of commerce could not exclude others from that product—though she could, obviously, exclude others from making copies. This basic case is known as the "first sale" doctrine, and essentially enforces an implied right to use a patented invention that attaches to the sale of that invention. Under this rule, unless there is some clear agreement to the contrary, a patentee cannot claim infringement for sales of those goods that were originally sold with her authorization.[611]

A more complex form of the first sale rule arises when a purchaser of a patented product alters that product in some way. In this case, is the user merely using the invention within the scope of the first sale rule, or has she created a new product, thus subjecting herself to claims of infringement? For these cases the courts have developed what is known as the "repair versus reconstruction" doctrine. Under this doctrine, "repair" is within the scope of the first sale, and thus not infringing; "reconstruction" is not, and thus is potential infringement.

The line between repair and reconstruction is, as one would expect, rather indistinct.[612] The Federal Circuit has identified three primary situations implicating a repair-versus-reconstruction analysis:[613]

1. First, where the entire patented item is spent, and the alleged infringer reconstructs it to make it useable again. This has been held to be infringement of the patent.[614]
2. Second, where a spent part is replaced. In *Aro Manufacturing Co. v. Convertible Top Replacement Co.*, the Supreme Court established that replacement of a spent part of a

637 (1947). See also U.S. Department of Justice, DOJ/FTC Antitrust Guidelines for the Licensing of Intellectual Property § 5.6 (1996) (focusing on market power).

611. See *Virginia Panel Corp. v. MAC Panel Co.*, 133 F.3d 860 (Fed.Cir. 1997).

612. See Donald S. Chisum, *Chisum on Patents*, § 16.03[3], at 16–159 (1997) ("The line between permissible 'repair' and impermissible 'reconstruction' is a difficult one to draw and is the subject of numerous cases.")

613. See *Husky Injection Molding Systems Ltd. v. R & D Tool Engineering Co.*, 291 F.3d 780, 785 (Fed.Cir.2002).

614. See *American Cotton–Tie Co. v. Simmons*, 106 U.S. (16 Otto) 89(1882); *Morgan Envelope Co. v. Albany Perforated Wrapping Paper Co.*, 152 U.S. 425(1894).

combination patent, which is not separately patented, is not impermissible reconstruction no matter how "essential it may be to the patented combination and no matter how costly or difficult replacement may be."[615] Further, the Federal Circuit has clarified that even the replacement of all of the parts of the patented invention successively, or the same part repeatedly does not constitute infringement, but instead "is no more than the lawful right of the owner to repair his property."[616]

3. And third, where a part is not spent but is replaced to enable the machine to perform a different function. In *Wilbur–Ellis Co. v. Kuther*, the Supreme Court held that changing the size of cans in fish-canning machines constituted "adapting the old machine to a related use" and "were doing more than repair in the customary sense; but what they did was kin to repair for it bore on the useful capacity of the old combination...."[617] This form of adaptation was within the scope of the purchased patent rights (and thus not infringement) because the size of the cans was not "part of the invention."[618]

Notwithstanding the reasonably clear distinctions between these sets of cases, discerning the line between repair and reconstruction can be elusive. In close cases the Federal Circuit has held that:

> There are a number of factors to consider in determining whether a defendant has made a new article, after the device has become spent, including the nature of the actions by the defendant, the nature of the device and how it is designed (namely, whether one of the components of the patented combination has a shorter useful life than the whole), whether a market has developed to manufacture or service the part at issue and objective evidence of the intent of the patentee.[619]

Further, the Federal Circuit has also held that a form of "safe harbor" exists, wherein if a part is readily replaceable, then replacing that part will constitute repair rather than reconstruction.[620] However, the Federal Circuit has expressly declined to offer a "test" for analyzing repair versus reconstruction, suggesting that the question "should be determined less by definitions or technical

615. 365 U.S. 336, 345 (1961).

616. See *Surfco Hawaii v. Fin Control Sys. Pty, Ltd.*, 264 F.3d 1062, 1065 (Fed.Cir.2001)

617. 377 U.S. 422, 425 (1964).

618. *Id.* at 424.

619. *Sandvik Aktiebolag v. E.J. Co.*, 121 F.3d 669 (Fed.Cir.1997).

620. See *Husky Injection Molding Systems*, 291 F.3d at 787.

rules than by the exercise of sound common sense and intelligent judgment."[621]

D. The Reverse Doctrine of Equivalents

Where an accused infringer literally infringes the claims of a patent, and yet can demonstrate that the infringing good or service is sufficiently distinct from the patented invention so as to be substantially non-equivalent, then the doctrine of the reverse doctrine of equivalents may come into play. That is, the reverse doctrine of equivalents provides an accused infringer with a defense based on the technological advance represented by the infringing good or service; where the advance is sufficiently large, the doctrine will step in to prevent what might otherwise be an unjust situation. At least in theory—the reverse doctrine of equivalents garners far more mention in academic work than it does in contemporary judicial proceedings. Indeed, the Federal Circuit has never affirmed a decision on this ground.[622] On the other hand, the doctrine has never been overruled, though some commentators suggest that it is merely a vestige of the practice of "central claiming," rather than the "peripheral claiming" used in the modern patent law. The argument here is that where patentees expressly stake out claims to defined subject matter (a "periphery") as opposed to stating an example of the claimed invention (a "central claim"), there is no need to impose an analysis of equivalency in cases of literal infringement.[623] Further, the Federal Circuit itself has noted that the enactment of 35 U.S.C. § 112, and its requirement that the patentee provide a full disclosure of the scope of her claims, may have essentially codified the reverse doctrine of equivalents, by preventing the scope of patent claims from expanding beyond the actual invention.[624]

On the other hand, academic commentators have made strong arguments that the existence—even if unused—of the reverse doctrine of equivalents forms an important part of the framework for negotiation between patentees and later improvers. Under this view, the reverse DOE serves to temper the ability of earlier patentees to claim ownership over later-developed technologies, especially where the later-developed technology provides most of the value.[625] Without the doctrine, the argument goes, the earlier

621. See, e.g., *FMC Corp. v. Up-Right, Inc.*, 21 F.3d 1073 (Fed.Cir.1994).

622. See, e.g., *Tate Access Floors, Inc. v. Interface Architectural Res. Inc.*, 279 F.3d 1357, 1368 (Fed.Cir.2002).

623. See, e.g., *Hobbs v. Beach*, 180 U.S. 383 (1901).

624. See *Tate Access Floors*, *supra*.

625. See Robert Merges and Richard Nelson, *On the Complex Economics of Patent Scope*, 90 Colum. L. Rev. 839 (1990).

patentee might be able to extract too much of the value of later innovations, thus potentially limiting improvements in patented technologies.

Irrespective of the theoretical viability of the reverse doctrine of equivalents, it remains at least a potential defense to patent infringement—one that may just be awaiting a particular set of circumstances to reassert its role.[626]

E. Inventorship and Ownership

It is important to distinguish the issue of *inventorship* for patent law purposes from the issue of *ownership* of patent rights in an invention. Patent law requires that the true and original inventor or inventors be named in the application for a patent, and United States patent law requires that a patent issue to the correct inventive entity, that is, the individual(s) who actually invented the claimed subject matter, not the entity who owns the patent right. Failure to satisfy this requirement may lead to the invalidation of the patent. Because of this potential sanction, the patent law provides for the correction of non-deceptive misjoinder and nonjoinder of inventors.[627]

Inventorship provides the starting point for determining ownership of patent rights. Absent some effective transfer or other obligation to assign patent rights, the individual inventor owns the right to apply for and obtain a patent. There can be either a sole inventor or joint inventors, and joint inventors jointly own the patent right. To be sure, invention is often driven by collaborative efforts that are, based on principles of contract, owned by a common employer. Indeed, assignment of patent rights is quite common. Federal law explicitly provides that patents have the attributes of personal property, and that both patents and applications for patents are assignable. And, importantly, there is a recording statute for patents; so the chain of title should be searched before any assignment is executed.[628]

1. Attributes of an Inventor

American patent law places a great deal of formal emphasis on the "inventor," perhaps because the United States is a first-to-invent country or perhaps this emphasis is a vestige of the 19th

626. See, e.g., *Scripps Clinic & Research Foundation v. Genentech, Inc.*, 927 F.2d 1565 (Fed.Cir.1991) (reversing a summary judgment that the reverse doctrine of equivalents did not apply).

627. *See* 35 U.S.C. §§ 116 and 256.

628. See 35 U.S.C. § 261.

century romanticized inventor.[629] Thus, a patent can be invalidated if the named inventor on the issued patent, who is presumed to be the true and only inventor,[630] is not the actual or only inventor of the claimed invention.[631]

To qualify as a legal inventor, one does not have to be of a particular age or citizenship. Rather, an inventor is one who contributes to the conception of the claimed subject matter.[632] Conception, as discussed in Chapter 6, is defined as the "formation in the mind of the inventor, of a definite and permanent idea of the complete and operative invention, as it is hereafter to be applied in practice."[633] An idea is definite and permanent when "only ordinary skill would be necessary to reduce the invention to practice, without extensive research or experimentation."[634]

This requirement does not mean that joint inventors must make equal contributions or that each inventor must contribute to the subject matter in each and every claim. In fact, § 116 of Title 35 states that inventors may jointly apply for a patent "even though (1) they did not physically work together or at the same time, (2) each did not make the same type or amount of contribution, or (3) each did not make a contribution to the subject matter of every claim of the patent." In *Pannu v. Iolab Corp.*,[635] the Federal Circuit interpreted § 116 to mean that a joint inventor must "(1) contribute in some significant manner to the conception or reduction to practice of the invention, (2) make a contribution to the claimed invention that is not insignificant in quality, when that contribution is measured against the dimension of the full invention, and (3) do more than merely explain to the real inventors well-known concepts and/or the current state of the art."[636] But a joint inventor does not have to contribute significantly to every claim; indeed, a "contribution to one claim is enough."[637]

An additional important implication of a decision on inventorship is that joint inventors are also joint owners, and under 35

629. See Mark Janis, *Patent Abolitionism*,17 BERKELEY HIGH TECH. L.J. 899 (2002).

630. See *Hess v. Advanced Cardiovascular Sys., Inc.*, 106 F.3d 976, 980 (Fed.Cir.1997).

631. 35 U.S.C. § 116.

632. See *Ethicon, Inc. v. United States Surgical Corp.*, 135 F.3d 1456, 1460 (Fed.Cir.1998).

633. *Hybritech Inc. v. Monoclonal Antibodies, Inc.*, 802 F.2d 1367, 1376 (Fed.Cir.1986).

634. *Burroughs Wellcome,* 40 F.3d at 1228.

635. 155 F.3d 1344 (Fed.Cir.1998).

636. Id. at 1351. See also *Fina Oil & Chem. Co. v. Ewen*, 123 F.3d 1466, 1473 (Fed.Cir.1997); *Ethicon, Inc. v. United States Surgical Corp.*, 135 F.3d 1456, 1460 (Fed.Cir.1998).

637. *Ethicon*, 135 F.3d at 1456.

U.S.C. § 262 in the absence of any agreement to the contrary, each joint owner of a patent can practice the claimed invention or license others to do so without the consent of and even without accounting to the other owners. Thus, anyone interested in owning a patent must be very careful to get an assignment from each and every individual who contributed to the conception of any claim in that patent.

Because of the severe sanction for improperly naming the correct inventor, §§ 116 and 256 allow correction of pending applications and issued patents. The third paragraph of § 116 allows correction of an inventorship error, which "arose without any deceptive intention," by misjoinder or nonjoinder in a pending application by amendment. Section 256 allows correction of an inventorship error committed without "deceptive intention" after the patent issues.

2. Inventorship, Ownership and Rights of the Employee

Although inventorship and ownership are separate concerns, determining who is the inventor of the claimed subject matter has implications not only for drafting and filing the patent application, but also for determining who owns the patent rights in the subject matter. This determination is important because ownership of the patent right vests in the inventor.[638]

The inventor owns his invention even if he conceived or reduced to practice in the course of his employment.[639] But most employees agree to assign ownership rights in the invention to their employer as part of an express contract; or, absent an express contract, the employer may own the invention under an implied-in-fact contract if the employee was "hired to invent something or solve a particular problem."[640] This latter scenario is known as the "employed to invent" exception. Under this exception, "a court must examine the employment relationship at the time of the inventive work to determine if the parties entered an implied-in-fact contract to assign patent rights."[641] Furthermore, an employer may obtain a "shop right" in the employee's invention where the employer contributed to the development of the invention. A "shop right" is a common law doctrine that allows an employer to use an invention patented by one or more of its employees without liability

638. See *Teets v. Chromalloy Gas Turbine* Corp., 83 F.3d 403, 407 (Fed. Cir.1996); *Beech Aircraft Corp. v. EDO Corp.*, 990 F.2d 1237, 1248 (Fed.Cir. 1993).

639. *Teets*, 83 F.3d at 407; *Banks v. Unisys Corp.*, 228 F.3d 1357 (Fed.Cir. 2000).

640. *Banks*, 228 F.3d at 1359.

641. *Id.*; *Teets*, 83 F.3d at 407.

for infringement.[642] Some of the factors endorsed by the Federal Circuit in determining whether a "shop right" exists are (1) the contractual nature of the relationship between employer and employee, (2) whether the employee consented to the employer's use of the invention, and (3) whether the employee induced, acquiesced in, or assisted the employer in the use of the invention. The employer usually has a strong case for shop rights if he financed the employee's invention whether by providing wages, tools, or a work place.[643]

642. See *McElmurry v. Arkansas Power & Light Co.*, 995 F.2d 1576, 1580 (Fed.Cir.1993).

643. *Id.* at 1581. For more on the issue of employer/employee inventions, see Robert P. Merges, *The Law and Economics of Employee Inventions*, 13 HARV. J. L & TECH. 1 (1999), and Ann Bartow, *Inventors of the World, Unite!*, 37 SANTA CLARA L. REV. 673 (1997).

Chapter Twelve

Remedies

I. Introduction

Remedies are a mechanism intended to place the parties to a legal dispute into the appropriate positions, legal and economic. That is, in the patent context, patent remedies are intended to place a patentee who has experienced infringement into a position that he or she would have been in absent the infringement. (As noted below, one aspect of remedies—the preliminary injunction—attempts to forecast the outcome of the litigation and respond accordingly.) Typically, patent remedies are determined at the end of a patent suit—after issues of validity and infringement have been decided. Again, note that a preliminary injunction is very often among the very first issues presented in a patent litigation.

There are two broad themes to understand about patent remedies. The first is their importance. By law, patents provide a right to exclude others from the marketplace. Thus, their operation can be enormously powerful, establishing the winners and losers, the pricing and players, for entire industries. A patent remedy can determine whether a product is sold, whether a company continues to exist, and the structure of competition. Because of this power, patent remedies have significant effects, not the least of which are their effects on parties outside the litigation, and the public. Patent remedies, then, are by their very nature thoroughly intertwined with the public interest.

The second important challenge in patent remedies is the difficulty in implementing them properly. The basic problem is evident in the core mission of a patent remedy: to place the patentee in the position that he or she would have been in absent infringement. On the surface, this question may appear straightforward; some money changes hands, perhaps, and a prohibition on further infringement is issued. In reality, however, the task is far more complex. By definition, a remedial analysis must delve into the counterfactual: what would have occurred absent the infringement? Add to this the economic complexities of rapidly evolving markets for advanced technologies, and it becomes apparent that no patent remedies question is easy. And as can be expected in the patent law, the doctrine reflects this complexity.

Broadly speaking, there are two forms of patent remedies—injunctive relief, and monetary damages. The difference between thee two is both in their nature—injunctive relief is a court-ordered prohibition on certain future activities, while damages are court-ordered payments in compensation for past infringement—and the type of behavior they address. Injunctions are often described as prospective relief, because they target behavior going forward in time, while damages are retrospective in nature. With this brief overview, then, we begin with injunctive relief.

II. Injunctive Relief

As a matter of patent law doctrine, for decades the topic of injunctive relief received very little attention, and was regarded as a relatively simple and straightforward topic. The general principles for injunctive relief are well-rehearsed. Injunctions are a matter of equity, and are to be granted when a plaintiff demonstrates: (1) an irreparable injury; (2) that legal remedies (such as damages) are inadequate; (3) that the balance of the hardships favor the plaintiff; and (4) that the public interest would not be harmed by an injunction.[644] In the patent context, the courts (especially the Federal Circuit) had developed what is best understood as a logical shortcut on this analysis. Rather than carefully evaluating the four-factor test in every instance, the Federal Circuit had determined that in the patent context, the first three factors will almost always favor a patentee who has successfully demonstrated infringement.[645] Only the fourth factor was of serious recurring concern. Thus, under Federal Circuit principles, an injunction was to be issued absent a showing that the public interest would be harmed.[646] And indeed, through mid–2006, the cases where the court denied post-infringement injunctive relief were rare (though not absent).[647]

644. See, e.g., 35 U.S.C. § 283 (stating that injunctions may issue "in accordance with the principles of equity."); *Amoco Production Co. v. Gambell*, 480 U.S. 531, 542 (1987) (outlining the principles).

645. See, e.g., *H.H. Robertson, Co. v. United Steel Deck, Inc.*, 820 F.2d 384, 390 (Fed.Cir.1987) ("In matters involving patent rights, irreparable harm has been presumed when a clear showing has been made of patent validity and infringement. This presumption derives in part from the finite term of the patent grant, for patent expiration is not suspended during litigation, and the passage of time can work irremediable harm. The opportunity to practice an invention during the notoriously lengthy course of patent litigation may itself tempt infringers. The nature of the patent grant thus weighs against holding that monetary damages will always suffice to make the patentee whole, for the principal value of a patent is its statutory right to exclude.")

646. *Rite–Hite Corp. v. Kelley Co., Inc.*, 56 F.3d 1538, 1547 (Fed.Cir.1995) (noting "protection of public health" as a reason to deny injunctive relief); see also Richardson v. Suzuki Motor Co., 868 F.2d 1226, 1246–47 (Fed.Cir.1989).

647. See, e.g., *Odetics, Inc. v. Storage Tech. Corp.*, 185 F.3d 1259 (Fed.Cir.

In 2006, however, the Supreme Court, in *eBay Inc. v. MercExchange, LLC*, did away with the Federal Circuit's "general rule" doctrine, holding that such an approach "erred in its categorical grant of such relief."[648] Instead, the Court mandated a return to the four-factor approach noted above, though it was careful to provide no further guidance on the issue:

> [W]e take no position on whether permanent injunctive relief should or should not issue in this particular case, or indeed in any number of other disputes arising under the Patent Act. We hold only that the decision whether to grant or deny injunctive relief rests within the equitable discretion of the district courts, and that such discretion must be exercised consistent with traditional principles of equity, in patent disputes no less than in other cases governed by such standards.[649]

Although the *eBay* majority opinion was exceedingly spare in its language, it issued along with two concurring opinions, each with three justices. In one, Justices Roberts, Scalia, and Ginsberg emphasized that a return to traditional principles did not amount to "writing on an entirely clean slate,"[650] and that in these matters, "a page of history is worth a volume of logic."[651] In the other concurring opinion, Justice Kennedy (joined by Justices Breyer and Souter), exhorted courts to use their discretionary power to "determine whether past practice fits the circumstances of the cases before them." (Kennedy's list of issues for district courts to consider reads like a popular press version of policy problems with the modern patent system: the emergence of patent licensing firms, or "patent trolls;" the granting of patents to business methods; and "vagueness and suspect validity" among modern patents.)

The Supreme Court in *eBay* has thus reset the legal framework for injunctive relief: the traditional four-factor equitable test noted above. The Court is also clear that categorical shortcuts are disallowed; courts must evaluate each of the four factors in each case. Note in this regard that each concurring opinion is rather inconsistent with the majority: the Roberts opinion suggests that, because of the historical record, injunctions should almost always issue.

1999) (denying an injunction due to laches); *Schneider (Europe) AG v. SciMed Life Systems, Inc.*, 852 F.Supp. 813 (D.Minn.1994) (denying an injunction due to pubic health concerns).

648. See *eBay Inc. v. MercExchange, LLC*, 527 U.S. ___, 126 S.Ct. 1837 (2006).

649. Id.

650. Id. at 2. (Roberts, J., concurring).

651. Id. (Roberts, J., concurring) (quoting *New York Trust Co. v. Eisner*, 256 U.S. 345, 349 (1921)).

In contrast, the Kennedy opinion suggests that injunctions should be denied where certain public policy problems are implicated. Therefore, because what little guidance the court gave was in the form of nonbinding opinions, both of which are arguably inconsistent with the controlling majority, the impact of *eBay* is difficult to discern. It may be that it will have little real effect—if the Federal Circuit was correct that the four-factor test will favor patentees most of the time,[652] then we should expect injunctions to issue at nearly the same rate as before. On the other hand, if courts take the Kennedy concurrence seriously, and utilize the analysis for injunctive relief as an opportunity to address broader public policy concerns, then the effect will clearly be broader. The only result that seems clear is that the likelihood of an injunction issuing is substantially less predictable *ex ante* than it was prior to *eBay*. And it may be this effect—the introduction of a new component of uncertainty into patent litigation—that is the truly lasting consequence of *eBay*.

The logical twin of the permanent injunction is the preliminary injunction. Preliminary injunctions are especially powerful tools in the patent context, and fraught with potential policy concerns. First, almost by definition, a patentee who seeks a preliminary injunction will be attempting to immediately change the shape of the marketplace—to stop sales of an accused infringer's product would be a paradigmatic example. As an example, in 1999, the online retailer Amazon.com obtained a preliminary injunction that seriously disrupted the pre-holiday sale activities of what was then its primary competitor (Barnesandnoble.com). Second, the timing of the preliminary injunction inquiry—well before a record is developed that could support a full analysis—is problematic. And third, a preliminary injunction analysis will often require great haste on the part of the parties and courts involved—the remedy is intended to operate quickly, albeit temporarily. So for these reasons, preliminary injunctions raise important policy concerns.

On the other hand, preliminary injunctions are crucial to protecting the rights of patentees, at least in some cases. Patent litigation is a long and costly endeavor; allowing an infringer to continue infringing activity during the course of litigation can be the definition of "irreparable harm." In addition, the availability of preliminary injunctive relief encourages parties to settle patent disputes prior to litigation, forces market participants to pay attention to patent claims, and generally supports the incentive-based

652. See *H.H. Robertson, Co. v. United Steel Deck, Inc.*, 820 F.2d 384, 390 (Fed.Cir.1987).

patent system. But note that many of these positive notes could also be considered negative, if preliminary injunctions were granted improperly. On balance, then, the doctrine of preliminary injunctions must navigate a narrow channel: offering a fast, powerful way to protect needful patentees from further harm during litigation without creating substantial market distortions by improvidently granting such relief. And all this, of course, must occur against a backdrop of seriously incomplete information and significant haste.

As a doctrinal matter, the standards for preliminary injunctions track those for injunctive relief more generally. A similar four-factor test applies: (1) a reasonable likelihood of success on the merits; (2) irreparable harm if an injunction is not granted; (3) a balance of the hardships in favor of the patentee; and (4) no harm to the public interest.[653] Again, for reasons similar to those discussed above, the Federal Circuit has at least partially collapsed this analysis: the two important moving parts are factors (1) and (4), with factor (1)—the likelihood of success—overwhelmingly the critical issue.[654] Note, however, that *eBay's* holding that such categorical shortcuts are disallowed in this equitable context is almost certainly applicable to preliminary injunctions as well.[655] Thus, the best reading of the post-*eBay* legal framework would suggest that all four factors are at least formally in play in each case.

Irrespective of whether all issues are in play, the unique issue in the preliminary injunction analysis, of course, is the question of likelihood of success. Because the analysis necessarily comes well before the infringement and validity questions are ready for final resolution, courts are forced to conduct what amounts to a nonbinding mini-trial on the merits. And yet because the grant or denial of a preliminary injunction will set the terms between the parties during the pendency of the litigation (which can be some years), this "nonbinding" analysis is often anything but. Given the timing, the lack of a record upon which to conduct meaningful analysis, and the necessarily vague legal standard ("reasonable likelihood of success"), the evidentiary burdens play an extremely significant role. Recognizing this fact, the Federal Circuit has established a detailed burden-shifting scheme, as follows:

1. First, the patentee must show that "in light of the presumptions and burdens that will inhere at trial," it will likely prove infringement and withstand claims of invalidi-

653. See *Reebok Int'l Ltd. v. J. Baker, Inc.*, 32 F.3d 1552, 1555 (Fed.Cir. 1994).

654. See *Amazon.com, Inc. v. Barnesandnoble.com, Inc.*, 239 F.3d 1343, 1350 (Fed.Cir.2001).

655. See *eBay, supra* note 650 at 5.

ty. Because patents, by law, are presumed valid, the initial burden on the patentee for validity is essentially satisfied at the outset.[656]

2. Next, if the accused infringer can show "substantial questions" concerning either validity or infringement, then no injunction will issue.[657]
3. Finally, even if the accused infringer points to substantial questions, the patentee can bring forward arguments to show that such allegations "lack substantial merit," and thus be awarded the injunction.[658]

The real moving part in many analyses of preliminary injunctive relief concerns what a "substantial question" is, especially one that goes to the alleged invalidity of the patent claims at issue. On this question, the equitable, case-by-case nature of the preliminary injunctive relief analysis defies easy categorizations, although in general, where patentees find relevant prior art or other at least potentially invalidating information, preliminary injunctions typically do not issue.[659]

Injunctive relief—both of the permanent and preliminary variety—are powerful tools. Doctrinally, the Federal Circuit has favored permanent injunctions, while making preliminary injunctions more difficult to obtain—a distinction that reflects the understanding of the relative confidence that can be attached to decision making at the respective points in a patent litigation. After the Supreme Court's *eBay* decision, the course of the doctrine is unsettled, though it seems unlikely that injunctive relief will become more common than it was before *eBay*. Nonetheless, because of its power as the ultimate form of relief that can be granted with respect to a patent, injunctive relief will continue to be a critical component of the modern patent system.

III. Damages

The award of damages in patent suits is established by 35 U.S.C. § 284. As a matter of doctrine, § 284 has been found to establish two categories of damages awards: the first is lost profits,

656. See *Genentech, Inc. v. Novo Nordisk A/S*, 108 F.3d 1361, 1364 (Fed. Cir.1997)

657. See *Amazon.com, supra* note 650 at 1350.

658. See id. at 1351.

659. See *Amazon.com, supra* note 650 at 1359 (Noting that, "In resisting a preliminary injunction ... one need not make out a case of actual invalidity. Vulnerability is the issue at the preliminary injunction stage, while validity is the issue at trial," and refusing to grant a preliminary injunction on the grounds of several pieces of prior art, which, when combined, might make out a claim of invalidity.)

the ordinary measure of harm done to the patentee by the infringer; the second is a reasonable royalty, which the statute sets as a floor on the potential damages award. Note as well that § 284 allows for enhanced damages, which are awarded when the court determines that an infringement was willful.

The difference between lost profits and a reasonable royalty is straightforward. Lost profits attempts to compensate the patentee for monies she would have made absent the infringement. The paradigmatic calculation is the total of lost sales, minus the costs of those sales. A reasonable royalty, on the other hand, imagines an arms-length negotiation between the patentee and the infringer for a license agreement, and uses the assumed royalty rate and data concerning the infringer's sales to determine the damages award. As a general matter, most patentees will recover more damages using a lost profits calculus than with a reasonable royalty: in the royalty context, the patentee will be assumed to be sharing the total profits with the licensee, whereas with lost profits, all profits will inure to the patentee. But as we will see in more detail below, proving lost profits is a difficult business, and in some cases patentees will be simply unable to prove what "would have happened" absent infringement; in these cases a reasonable royalty award is the only possibility.

A. Lost Profits

On the surface, lost profits damages are a relatively straightforward measure of the economic harm suffered by the patentee as a result of infringement.[660] The two key analysis issues, then, are: (1) how to measure the economic harm; and (2) what is meant by the result of the infringement.

1. Measuring Harm: The Panduit Standard

In *Panduit Corp. v. Stahlin Bros. Fibre Works, Inc.,* the Sixth Circuit (in a pre-Federal Circuit patent case) articulated what is generally regarded to be a useful (though not necessarily the only) test for lost profits damages. The factors which the patentee must establish are:

1. Demand for the patented good;
2. Absence of non-infringing substitutes;

660. See *Aro Mfg. Co. v. Convertible Top Replacement Co.*, 377 U.S. 476, 507 (1964) ("The question to be asked in determining damages is: how much had the Patent Holder and Licensee suffered by the infringement. And that question [is] primarily: had the Infringer not infringed, what would the Patentee Holder–Licensee have made?' ").

3. Manufacturing and marketing capacity to meet the demand; and
4. The amount of profit the patentee would have made.[661]

Each of these components, of course, can prove a daunting evidentiary task. Among them, demand for the patented good is the least difficult, as this is proven by significant sales by either the patentee or infringer.[662] The third factor—capacity to meet demand—also has a low threshold. The patentee need only present evidence that it either had adequate facilities or had the capability of expanding its facilities in a matter sufficient to meet the demand that would have occurred absent infringement.[663] And in one sense, the amount of profits is relatively simple to calculate, being simply the lost revenues minus the incremental cost of sales. However, the critical issue with regards to Factor 4 is how to determine the scope of the potential lost sales, an issue to which we now turn.

2. The Scope of Harm: The Rite–Hite Analysis

One important question with respect to accounting for lots profits is the scope of harm that can be attributed to the infringement. For example, in *Rite–Hite Corp. v. Kelley Co., Inc.*, the Federal Circuit addressed a case where the primary aspect of lost sales to the patentee was on a product that was not covered by the infringed patent claims.[664] Instead, the infringer's (infringing) product was a market competitor to the patentees' product; thus, the patentee noted that, absent the infringement, it would have sold more of its product—notwithstanding that the patentee's product was not an embodiment of the patent.[665] The Federal Circuit allowed these lost sales to be counted in a lost profits analysis, holding that any harm "was or should have been reasonably foreseeable," and as a result of the infringement can be credited in the damages calculus.[666]

The *Rite–Hite* rule has been controversial from the outset. The primary criticism is that the rule effectively expands the rights granted by the patent to include not only those products within the scope of the claims, but also to include related but non-infringing

661. *Panduit Corp. v. Stahlin Bros. Fibre Works, Inc.*, 575 F.2d 1152, 1156 (6th Cir.1978). See also *Rite–Hite Corp. v. Kelley Co., Inc.*, 56 F.3d 1538 (Fed.Cir. 1995).

662. See *BIC Leisure Prods. v. Windsurfing Int'l.*, 1 F.3d 1214, 1218 (Fed.Cir.1993).

663. *Bio–Rad Lab. v. Nicolet Instrument Corp.*, 739 F.2d 604, 616 (Fed.Cir. 1984).

664. 56 F.3d 1538 (Fed.Cir.1995).

665. Id. at 1543.

666. Id. at 1546.

products.[667] Critics point out that patents are intended to protect the limited subject matter within the claims, not a market for which the patentee may or may not have entitlement.[668] The rejoinder to this is that the *Rite–Hite* rule is one of damages, not exclusion: that is, granting the patentee a "foreseeable" scope of lost sales is not at all the same as granting the patentee the right to exclude beyond the scope of the patent.[669] In the view of the *Rite–Hite* court, infringement is measured by the scope of the claims; once infringement is found, the damages calculation is intended to fully compensate for any infringements.[670] Thus, if a patentee can prove harm that was the foreseeable result of the infringement of the claims, the patent law should allow those damages so as to enable full compensation.

Although the *Rite–Hite* rule has conceptual appeal, it does raise a number of important questions concerning the scope of the damages calculation. For example, can a patentee be compensated for the loss of profits on sales of products that it chose not to make? That is, can the patentee recover lost profits from (infringing) sales in a market in which it did not participate? The answer appears to be yes; in *King Instruments, Inc. v. Perego,* the Federal Circuit (on the heels of *Rite–Hite*) held that lost profits damages were available even where the patentee did not sell a competing product.[671] The court reasoned that reasonable royalty damages did not fully compensate in this situation—if it would have, then one could expect a patentee to have licensed the patent.[672] Therefore, because there is no requirement in the law to practice the invention, the *King Instruments* court argued that there should be no penalty on remedies either, and lost profits (to the extent they are provable) could apply. A dissent in *King Instruments* argued that, like *Rite–Hite*, the rule was tantamount to allowing patent protection for the patentee's unpatented business interests.[673] In the dissent's view, as

667. See id. at 1556 (Nies, J., dissenting).

668. Id. at 1560 (Nies, J., dissenting).

669. Id. at 1547.

670. Id. at 1547 n.6.

671. *King Instruments Corp. v. Perego*, 65 F.3d 941 (Fed.Cir.1995).

672. Id. at 951 ("In such situations, if lost profits are not available simply because the patent holder does not market a product pursuant to its patent, infringement may actually be profitable. If licensing (rather than excluding) competitors would have proven more rewarding to the patentee, the patentee would have licensed. Instead, the market dictated that exclusion was the best way to recover innovation investments. Limiting the patentee's recovery to a reasonable royalty, however, would give the infringer what the market denied—a license.")

673. Id. at 954 (Nies, J., dissenting) ("A patent grants the patentee a legal right to a protected market only for patented goods. A patent does not grant the patentee a right to a protected market in unpatented goods. A patent entitles the patent owner to the fruits of the inven-

a matter of policy, if the patentee chose not to commercialize its patented invention, then it should forego any entitlement to lost profits (and rely on a reasonable royalty calculation). To do otherwise would be to reward the patentee "the same as, or even more than, if it had made the investment to bring the goods into the market."[674]

The *Rite–Hite* rule also puts pressure on the courts' ability to draw a line at "forseeability," a concept that is not free of ambiguity. Could a patentee receive compensation for harm caused by the loss of employees or business relationships, if such harms were forseeably caused by the infringement? This is unclear; the precise scope of forseeability will necessarily vary from case to case. It may be that only damages related to the sales of products are eligible, though the *King Instruments* case suggests that even this line is not inviolate.

Finally, a brief note on what is described as "the entire market value rule." This rule holds that an accounting for lost profits may include all the profits made on an apparatus containing several features, as long as the patented feature or component can be shown to be the basis for customer demand.[675] This rule has in some cases been extended to allow recovery for lost sales of separate-but-complementary products, as long as the patentee can prove that it could "normally anticipate the sale of unpatented items as well as patented ones."[676]

3. Non–Infringing Substitutes

When calculating lost profits, the *Panduit* test also requires the patentee to demonstrate the absence of non-infringing substitutes to the patented good.[677] The reasoning is simple: if substantial supply of non-infringing substitutes exists, then the patentee's lost profits will be nonexistent. Similarly, the availability of non-infringing substitutes will often establish a "ceiling" on the amount of lost profits that can be claimed by the patentee; such substitutes will limit the market power that the patent provides.[678] Thus, an accurate measure of lost profits damages requires a reconstruction of

tion, not the fruits of the patentee's business generally.")

674. Id. at 960–61 (Nies, J., dissenting).

675. See *TWM Mfg. Co. v. Dura Corp.*, 789 F.2d 895, 901 (Fed.Cir.1986).

676. See *Kaufman Co. v. Lantech, Inc.*, 926 F.2d 1136 (Fed.Cir.1991).

677. *Panduit Corp. v. Stahlin Bros. Fibre Works, Inc.*, 575 F.2d 1152, 1156 (6th Cir.1978).

678. See *Grain Processing Corp. v. American Maize–Products Co.*, 185 F.3d 1341 (Fed.Cir.1999).

the marketplace—one that would have existed absent the infringement.[679] Such a reconstruction cannot only demonstrate the increased sales that would have benefited the patentee, but must also account for acts that the infringer might have reasonably taken (such as entering the market with a non-infringing substitute). Indeed, the courts have held that even goods that were not currently on the market can be counted as non-infringing substitutes in many circumstances.[680] Thus, after cases such as Grain Processing, the analysis of lost profits damages—market reconstruction—has become more sophisticated, more economically accurate, and more complex.[681]

B. Reasonable Royalty Damages

If a patentee cannot prove lost profits, the patentee is entitled to at least a reasonable royalty for the infringing activities.[682] A reasonable royalty is defined in the law as an amount that one would pay as a royalty to make and sell the patented product on the market at a reasonable profit.[683] As noted above, a reasonable royalty will typically yield a lower amount of damages than would a lost profits analysis, but is often easier to prove—since the patentee need only show two things: (1) the amount of infringing sales, and (2) what the reasonable royalty rate should be.[684]

The key area of dispute, then, in a reasonable royalty analysis is the determination of a royalty rate. In theory, the rate should closely track what the patentee and the infringer would have agreed upon prior to the outset of infringement. This legal fiction, however, is difficult to construct—the fact of infringement means that the two parties did not agree on a royalty rate.[685] Because of the intensely fact-driven nature of the analysis, rates will vary widely depending on the circumstances. Note as well that many of the market reconstruction considerations noted above—in particular the availability of non-infringing substitutes—will play a role in determining the royalty rate as well.

679. Id. at 1350.

680. See *Slimfold Manufacturing Co. v. Kinkead Industries, Inc.*, 932 F.2d 1453, 1458 (Fed.Cir.1991) (allowing prior unsold technology to be a non-infringing substitute); *Grain Processing*, 185 F.3d at 1353.

681. See, e.g., John Schlicher, *Measuring Patent Damages by the Market Value of Inventions—The Grain Processing, Rite–Hite, and Aro Rules*, 82 J. Pat. & Trademark Off. Soc'y 503, 503 (2000).

682. See 35 U.S.C. § 284.

683. See *Goodyear Tire & Rubber Co. v. Overman Cushion Tire Co.*, 95 F.2d 978, 984 (6th Cir.1937).

684. See *Panduit Corp.*, 575 F.2d 1152.

685. See *Fromson v. Western Litho Plate & Supply Co.*, 853 F.2d 1568, 1575–76 (Fed.Cir.1988).

In analyzing a reasonable royalty, courts have taken pains to ensure that the royalty rate is at least as high as that the parties would have agreed to, and may in many cases be higher. The reasoning behind this approach is to ensure that the damages for patent infringement have a punitive element to them. If not—if the royalty rate was identical to that which the parties would have agreed to prior to infringement—then the infringer would, in theory, be indifferent as between licensing or infringing the patent. (In reality of course, the infringer would have had good incentives to avoid the costs and uncertainties of litigation, not to mention the possibility of treble damages stemming from willful infringement.) However, the courts have not approved a specific punitive "kicker" to the royalty rate calculation.[686]

The courts have approved a number of techniques to establish the royalty rate. For example:

- Calculations based on the cost savings associated with use of the patented invention versus substitutes;[687]
- Calculations based on practices in the relevant industry;[688]
- Calculations based on the infringer's (pre-infringement) expectation of profits;[689] and
- Calculations based on royalty rates that were determined after a patent had been found valid and infringed.[690]

Given the range of permissible techniques, and the fact that the discretion of the district court controls, the calculation of a reasonable royalty will vary considerably.

IV. Enhanced Damages, Willfulness, and Attorneys' Fees

Finally, a brief note on enhanced damages. Section 284 notes that "the court may increase the damages up to three times the amount found or assessed." The courts have interpreted that power to refer to cases of "willful" infringement, where the infringer is found to have "deliberately disregarded the patent or flagrantly disregarded the patent laws and had no reasonable basis for believing it had the right to do as it did."[691] If willful infringement is

686. *Mahurkar v. C.R. Bard*, 79 F.3d 1572, 1580 (Fed.Cir.1996).

687. *Hanson v. Alpine Valley Ski Area, Inc.*, 718 F.2d 1075 (Fed.Cir.1983).

688. *Stickle v. Heublein, Inc.*, 716 F.2d 1550 (Fed.Cir.1983).

689. *TWM Mfg. v. Dura Corp.*, 789 F.2d 895 (Fed.Cir.1986).

690. *Studiengesellschaft Kohle, mbH v. Dart Indus.*, 862 F.2d 1564, 1570–71 (Fed.Cir.1988).

691. *Stickle v. Heublein, Inc.*, 716 F.2d 1550, 1556 (Fed.Cir.1983).

found, the district court has discretion to award increased damages, to a limit of three-times the calculated damages.

Whether an infringer's conduct is willful depends on a number of factors, especially including whether the infringer had actual notice of the patent prior to beginning infringement, and whether reasonable steps were taken after notice. (Note that patent owners are required to mark their patented products—or otherwise notify infringers—in order to receive damages for infringement.[692]) Given the possibility of treble damages, prudent companies will typically request an opinion from counsel regarding the validity and/or infringement of a troubling patent prior to beginning infringement. In general, the existence of a well-reasoned opinion of non-infringement and/or invalidity by a competent patent counsel will preclude a later finding of willfulness.[693] However, a poorly drafted or conclusory opinion of counsel that (in the view of the court) merely recites arguments rather than analysis will not suffice.[694] Until recently, when no opinion of counsel was provided, fact finders were instructed to draw a negative inference—i.e., that no opinion of counsel was sought, or that the opinion went against the infringer's interests.[695] This has since been reversed by the Federal Circuit in the *Knorr–Bremse* case; the current law is that when attorney-client privilege is invoked, no adverse inference can be drawn.[696]

The *Knorr–Bremse* court, citing *Underwater Devices*, stated that actual notice of another's patent right triggers an affirmative duty of due care. But in a unanimous en banc decision, the Federal Circuit eliminated the duty of care, as well as the duty to obtain opinion of counsel.[697] Moreover, in *Seagate*, the Federal Circuit stated "proof of willful infringement permitting enhanced damages requires at least a showing of objective recklessness."[698] As such, "to establish willful infringement, a patentee must show by clear and convincing evidence that the infringer acted despite an objectively high likelihood that its actions constituted infringement of a valid patent."[699]

692. 35 U.S.C. § 287.

693. *Rite–Hite Corp. v. Kelley Co.*, 819 F.2d 1120, 1125 (Fed.Cir.1987).

694. *Kori Corp. v. Wilco Marsh Buggies & Draglines*, 761 F.2d 649, 656 (Fed.Cir.1985).

695. *Electro Medical Systems, S.A. v. Cooper Life Sciences, Inc.*, 34 F.3d 1048, 1056 (Fed.Cir.1994).

696. *Knorr–Bremse Systeme Fuer Nutzfahrzeuge GmbH v. Dana Corp.*, 383 F.3d 1337, 1343 (Fed.Cir.2004).

697. *In re Seagate Technology, LLC*, 497 F.3d 1360, 1371 (Fed. Cir. 2007) (en banc) (stating "we abandon the affirmative duty of due care, [and] also reemphasize that there is no affirmative obligation to obtain opinion of counsel").

698. Id.

699. Id.

Seagate and *Knorr–Bremse* make it more difficult for patentees to prove willfulness, and reduce the need for accused infringers to obtain an opinion of counsel relating to the alleged infringement. Thus, it is arguable that less time will be expended on establishing defenses to a willfulness charge, are more time spent on the nature of the alleged infringement.

In addition to enhanced damages due to willfulness, § 285 authorizes courts to award attorney's fees in "exceptional cases."[700] Willfulness of the sort noted above can support a finding of an exceptional case, as can litigation in bad faith, inequitable conduct by the patentee, or other misbehavior on the part of the losing party.[701] Note that attorneys' fees are awarded to the prevailing party, not just a patentee who proves infringement.[702]

700. 35 U.S.C. § 285.

701. *Rohm & Haas Co. v. Crystal Chemical Co.*, 736 F.2d 688, 691 (Fed. Cir.1984).

702. 35 U.S.C. § 285.

*

TABLE OF CASES

References are to Pages.

INDEX

References are to Pages.

†